THE PORTRAIT PHOTOGRAPHER'S MANUAL

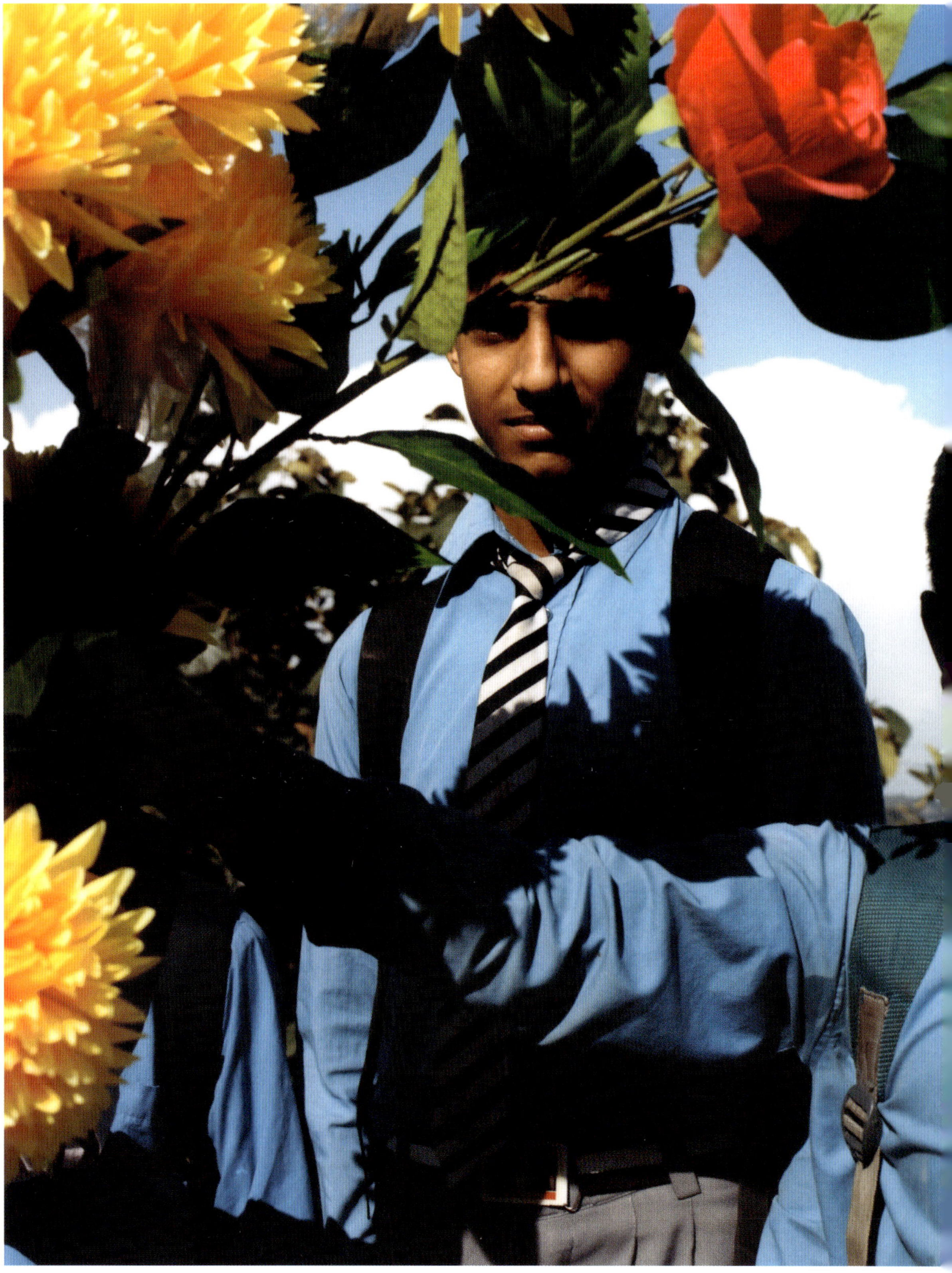

THE PORTRAIT PHOTOGRAPHER'S MANUAL

CIAN OBA-SMITH & MAX FERGUSON

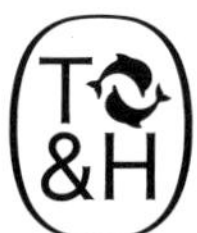

Any copy of this book issued by the publisher as
a paperback is sold subject to the condition that
it shall not by way of trade or otherwise be lent,
resold, hired out or otherwise circulated without
the publisher's prior consent in any form of binding
or cover other than that in which it is published
and without a similar condition including these
words being imposed on a subsequent purchaser.

First published in the United Kingdom in 2023 by
Thames & Hudson Ltd, 181A High Holborn,
London WC1V 7QX

First published in the United States of America in 2023
by Thames & Hudson Inc., 500 Fifth Avenue, New York,
New York 10110

© 2023 Quarto Publishing plc

British Library Cataloguing-in-Publication Data
A catalogue record for this book is available from
the British Library

Library of Congress Cataloging-in-Publication data
available upon request.

ISBN: 978-0-500-29713-1

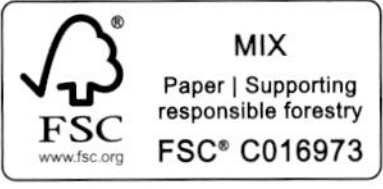

Conceived, designed, and produced by the Bright Press,
an imprint of the Quarto Group
1 Triptych Place
London
SE1 9SH
T (0)20 7700 6700
www.quarto.com

Publisher James Evans
Editorial Director Isheeta Mustafi
Managing Editor Jacqui Sayers
Editor Emily Angus
Project Editor Ruth Patrick
Art Director James Lawrence
Senior Designer Emily Nazer
Design Michael Whitehead

Printed and bound in China

Be the first to know about our new releases,
exclusive content and author events by visiting
thamesandhudson.com
thamesandhudsonusa.com
thamesandhudson.com.au

Image on page 2: © Tom Johnson

Dedication
For Ms Miller, who helped us fall in love with
photography. Our first teacher, without her early
guidance, this book would not have happened.

Contents

Meet the Authors

Here you will discover more about us – we are long-term collaborators, friends and industry professionals.

As this book has been coauthored, we thought it best that we introduce ourselves before getting into anything else. You will find that the authorial voice jumps between us a little in this book. Sometimes it will be obvious which of us has written something, but at other times less so. Although we wrote the book together, we have our own views on some points. Our journeys to becoming authors of a book on photography have been intertwined. We first met at university where we discovered we had gone to the same college and were inspired to take the subject further by the same photography teacher. Shout out to Miss Miller! Although our careers have diverged, with one of us making his own personal projects alongside a career as a commercial and editorial photographer and the other working as a photo editor and educator as well as making his own work, we have worked together many times. This book is the latest in a series of collaborations between us.

Cian

I am an Irish-Nigerian photographer who was born and raised in London. My personal work is centred around documentary and portrait photography. Alongside this, I earn a living from editorial and commercial photography. I also spend time guest lecturing at universities and art institutions around the United Kingdom. My work focuses on communities and subcultures around the world. I am particularly interested in approaching subjects that are often misrepresented, with a view to showcasing them in a different light. The relationship between human experience and environment is at the core of my projects. As my work has developed, I have become more and more interested in the link between photography and history, how an image ages, and also how photography can be used as both a record of a moment in time and a tool to educate future generations. My commissioned work can be found in a variety of places online and in print, including the *Financial Times Weekend Magazine*, *The Guardian*, the *British Journal of Photography*, *TIME* magazine, *The Fader*, *Le Monde*, *Port Magazine*, *Dazed & Confused* and *The New Yorker*, among others.

Max

I am a photographer, writer, photo editor and educator. That might seem like quite a lot of occupations, but they all feed into each other. As a photo editor, I commission some of the most exciting names in photography or collaborate with them on long-term bodies of work. I was the photo director of *Port Magazine* for five years where I worked on shoots with huge celebrities as well as for fashion editorials, still life and many

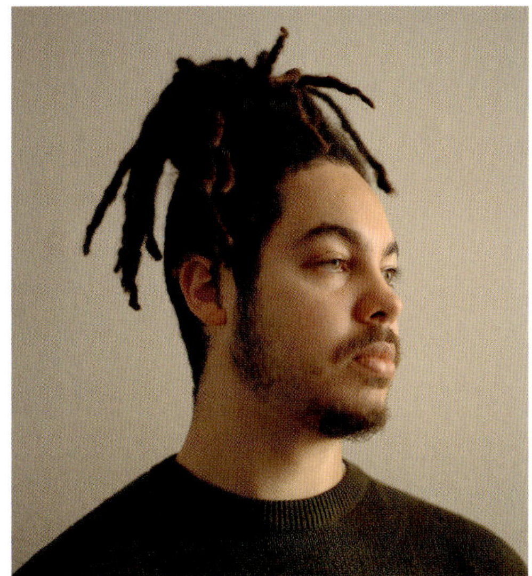

Cian Oba-Smith

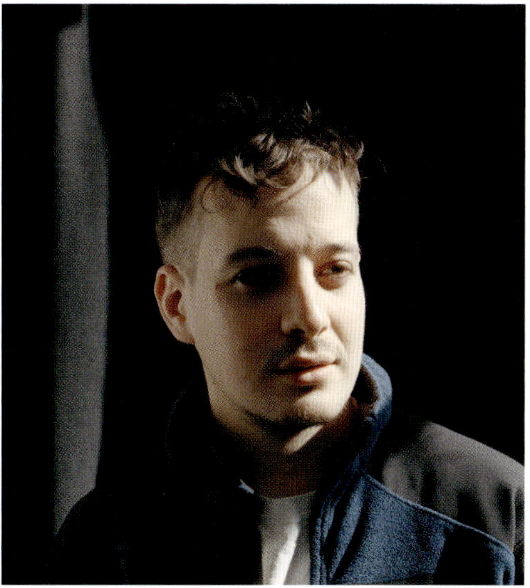

Max Ferguson

other areas. Now I'm at *Granta*, a literary magazine that publishes photographers' personal projects. I also spent several years at the *Financial Times Weekend Magazine* working with some of the best editorial photographers and journalists in the world. We commissioned stories on everything, from food to global politics. Whatever the story, I love thinking of new ways of portraying key issues with photography, and magazines can be a really creative place for that. As an educator, as well as getting students thinking about photography critically for the first time, I really love helping them to nurture and transform their ideas into photographic projects. This also gives me a constant stream of big photographers to work with in the future. I try and keep these professional activities in balance with being a photographer myself too. I recently studied for an MA in photography and, as a result of that, published my first book of photographs, *Whistling for Owls*.

We hope you enjoy reading this book as much as we have enjoyed writing it. Thinking about photography is one of our greatest pleasures – hopefully, some of you can share this journey with us.

About this book

In this book, you will find chapters that break down portrait photography into some of the areas we find most interesting. Running through the chapters are photographer profiles and a series of projects that we hope will excite and educate you. This is not a technical instruction manual, although we cover some technical aspects too, but rather a toolkit to get you thinking critically about taking portraits. By researching, practising and making mistakes there are no limits to how far you can push yourself. We spent a long time considering and discussing which photographers to profile in the book. We had a hard time narrowing these down to just twenty. Some are big names, others are at an earlier stage of their careers, but all of them use portraiture in exciting and different ways. Use their stories to get excited – as we have – and to inspire you into making your own photographs. The projects will help you to develop your photographic skills, both practical and theoretical, as you embark on your photography journey and perhaps your career. Several times throughout the book we talk about the industry, drawing on our experiences to decode the language and hierarchies of the photography world. Approach the book in a way that works for you, taking in what interests you and disregarding what doesn't.

Introduction

What is Portrait Photography?

It is estimated that trillions of photographs are taken every year. And that number continues to grow. But while it is clear that photography is becoming more and more popular, how do you distinguish your images from the trillions of others out there? The simplest way to make your photographs stand out from the crowd is to use good-quality equipment. Over ninety percent of the photographs taken are made using a smartphone. Although these are getting better every year, the control you have using a camera on which you can change the ISO, shutter speed and aperture will raise your photography to new levels. Don't worry if some of these terms are unfamiliar, as they are explained in more detail in the Glossary (see page 188). Crucially, however, what will distinguish you as a photographer from people who just take photographs is how you think about photographs, how you read photographs, and how you understand the limitations of an image.

Let's look at what a photographic portrait actually is, as the first question this book needs to answer is the simplest one. One definition of a photographic portrait is that it is an intentional image of a person made using a camera. There will, of course, be times when this definition does not fit, but it seems the best for most situations. In his *New York Times* column, Teju Cole, who is perhaps the photographic thinker of this generation, breaks down the process in the following way: 'A photographic portrait records a human encounter. The photographer's intent and the sitter's agreement, and vice versa, are made visible.' Cole then goes further and shows how we, the viewer, can be included in the relationship too: 'The portrait also contains the tacit hope that a third party,

the viewer, will be able to register the traces of that previous encounter.'

The purpose of a photographic portrait can vary greatly. It might, for example, be taken by a machine and used to verify your identity in a passport as you cross international borders. It might be used to recall a moment later on, perhaps a family dinner or the birth of a child. It may also be to show the world that someone existed. You might even be photographing yourself as an act of protest. So, there are countless examples of when photographs of people might be used.

Let's take the cover of *Port Magazine,* shown on the opposite page from when I was their photo director, as an example of a photographic portrait. The cover features the actor Caleb Landry Jones, who was photographed by Rahim Fortune at his parents' farm in Texas. We can infer several things from the image alone and a few more from cultural signifiers. In fact, learning to read images can help you understand what these might be. You will be dealing in the murky world of signs (semiotics) here, however, so there are no concrete answers. Your reading might be different to mine, which is fine. Mine would be that the image, which is in black and white, shows Jones smoking and looking away from the camera. His long hair is untidy and he's wearing an open shirt with a white T-shirt underneath. Seeing a cigarette on the cover of a magazine is highly unusual nowadays. All of these factors lead me to interpret the portrait as being designed to give the actor a rebellious image. He is wearing clothes by the luxury fashion house Yves Saint Laurent, which

▶ *Port Magazine* Issue 28 – Caleb Landry Jones shot by Rahim Fortune and commissioned by Max.

PORT

10th Anniversary Issue

FEATURING
Akala
Malachi Kirby
Caleb Landry Jones
Matt Smith
Katherine Waterston

GUEST EDITORS
Michael Shannon
Great people in film

Linsey Young
Female creatives and their artist mothers

Formafantasma
Inspiring people through ecology

NEW WRITING FROM
Jack Underwood
David Keenan
Matthew Turner
Bhanu Kapil

ALSO
Takashi Miike
Ramin Bahrani
Alexandra Daisy Ginsberg
Kwame Kwei-Armah OBE
Max Vadukul
Alexis Harding

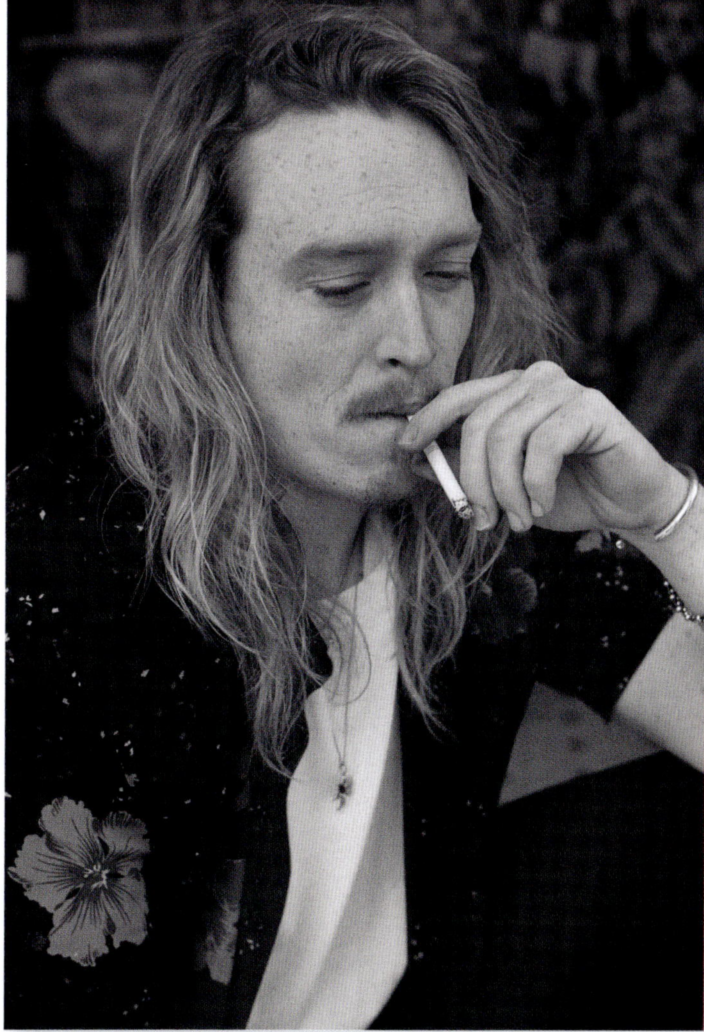

£8

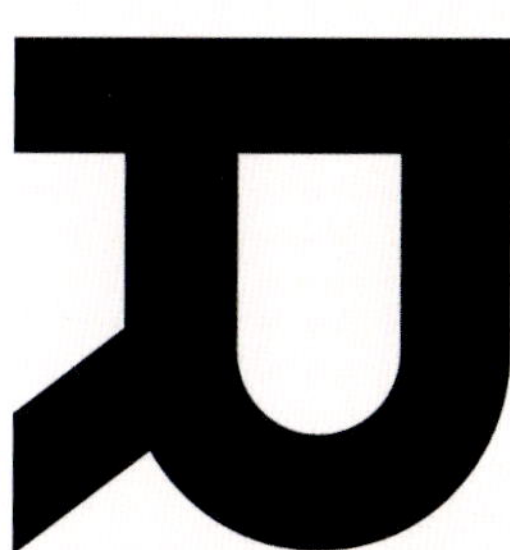

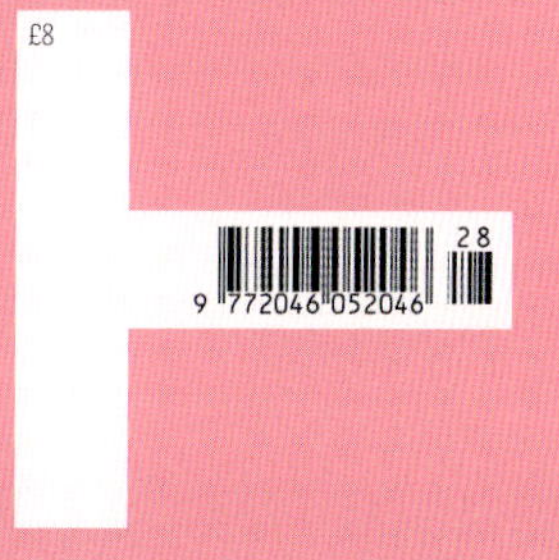

9 772046 052046   28

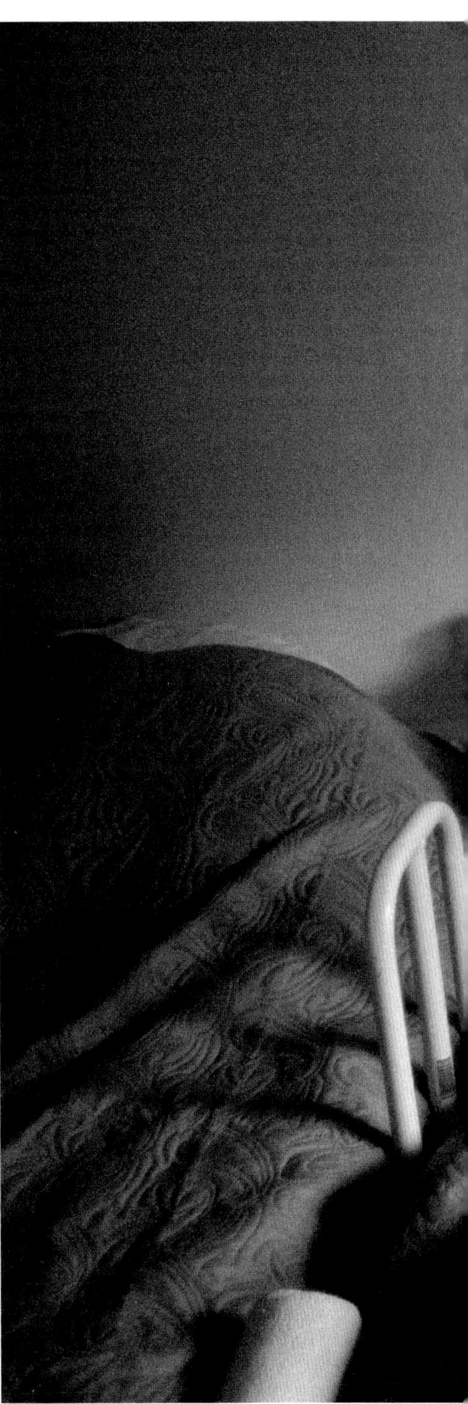

isn't particularly rebellious, so there are a few ideas being examined here.

In the remainder of this introduction, we will look at some of the basics of portrait photography. Starting with the main tools you will use – cameras – we then work through when you might use black and white or colour; help you think about how to choose your subjects; and touch on the ethics of portrait photography. Reading this section first will prepare you for the profiles and projects you will find in the rest of the book. Most importantly, remember to have fun with photography – it might be something you spend the rest of your life doing. **MF**

Cameras

Equipment, although important, will not turn a bad photographer into a good one, or vice versa. Good photographers can make good pictures with any camera. Some of the best advice I received early in my journey as a photographer was to find a camera you are comfortable with and to learn how it works inside out. Once the technical side of making pictures becomes second nature, you can then focus on the deeper aspects of the medium; by this I mean the use of visual language to communicate your ideas and learning how to do this naturally in an intuitive way.

That being said, to be able to find the camera that works best for you, it's important to have a general understanding of the different types available as well as their history, so I will try my best to provide a brief overview here. Cameras have come a long way since the invention of photography in 1826 by Nicéphore Niépce (1765–1833) and the first photograph to feature a person, which was taken in 1838 by Louis

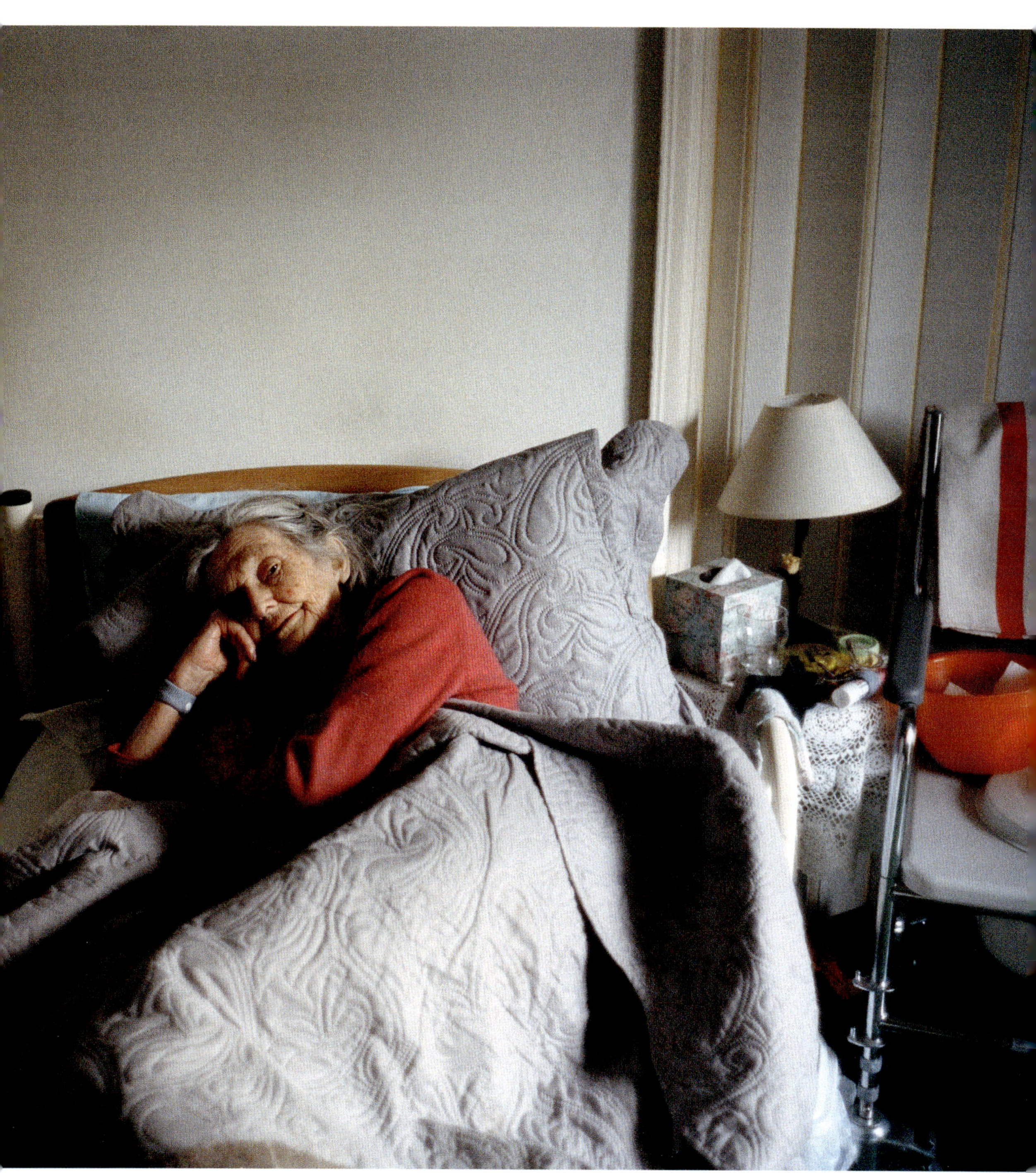

Daguerre (see page 45). The daguerreotype was the first publicly available photographic process; it used a sheet of copper plated with silver, which was then made light sensitive with chemicals and kept in a light-tight box. When the photographer was ready to take the picture, the copper sheet was inserted into the camera and exposed to light, after which it was heated and then treated with various chemical processes to make the image permanent. The process was complicated, with exposure times varying from three to fifteen minutes. Technological advancements brought the times down to around one minute, but that is a very long time to sit still to have your photograph taken! Thankfully, cameras have advanced a lot since then and this way of working is only used for artistic purposes rather than out of necessity.

Today, there is a plethora of cameras on the market, making it impossible to look in detail at each one, so instead I will outline the main types you're likely to come across on your journey in photography.

SLRS, DLSRS AND MIRRORLESS CAMERAS

The most common types of camera you'll encounter as a professional are single-lens reflex (SLR) film cameras and digital mirrorless cameras. SLRs have a mirror system that allows the photographer to look through the viewfinder and see through the lens. When the shutter is pressed the mirror flips up, exposing the digital image sensor or photographic film to light, so recording the image. Mirrorless cameras use a digital viewfinder to mimic an SLR's viewfinder system – you get a live view of what the lens sees in a much smaller package with silent shooting because of the omission of the mirror system. Personally, for digital photography, I prefer the mirrorless system. I like to have a more compact

system and the lower battery life compared to a digital single-lens reflex (DSLR) doesn't bother me. Both types of camera have their advantages and disadvantages. For example, mirrorless cameras are lighter, but slightly more fragile. DSLRs suffer from camera shake at slower shutter speeds, whereas mirrorless cameras do not have the same issue because there is no mirror system. Generally, I see mirrorless becoming the most commonly used camera in the future as the technology improves. Sony have been developing mirrorless-camera technology for longer than anyone else. In my opinion, they lead the pack, although Canon, Nikon, Panasonic, Fujifilm, Olympus and Leica all offer excellent mirrorless digital cameras.

The two most popular brands for DSLRs are Canon and Nikon, who both make good cameras with the choice being a matter of preference. If you are looking for a 35mm SLR, then there's a huge number of good-quality film cameras out there, but I think the main four brands are Canon, Nikon, Pentax and Olympus. I learned how to shoot 35mm film using a Pentax K1000, which is a great camera for a beginner because of its easy-to-read light meter system. A few other good beginner 35mm SLR cameras are the Nikon FM2, Canon AE-1, Olympus OM-2 and the Pentax ME Super, among many others.

RANGEFINDERS

The film equivalent of digital mirrorless systems is the rangefinder. Although it is not exactly the same because the viewfinder does not show you exactly what the lens sees, I think it would be fair to describe it as the parent of mirrorless photography. Leica make the best 35mm rangefinders and arguably one of the most famous cameras in the world, due to the incredible quality of

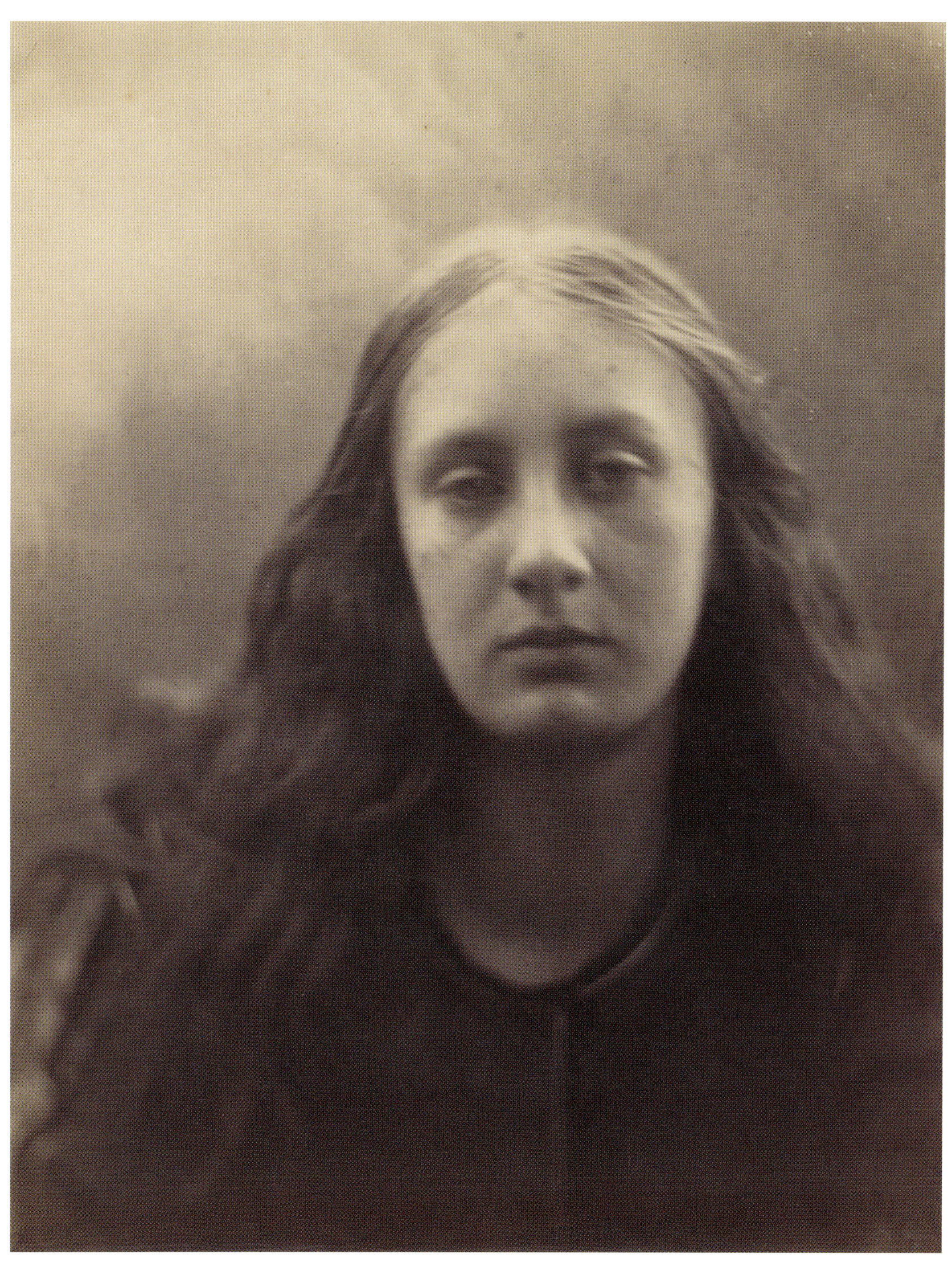

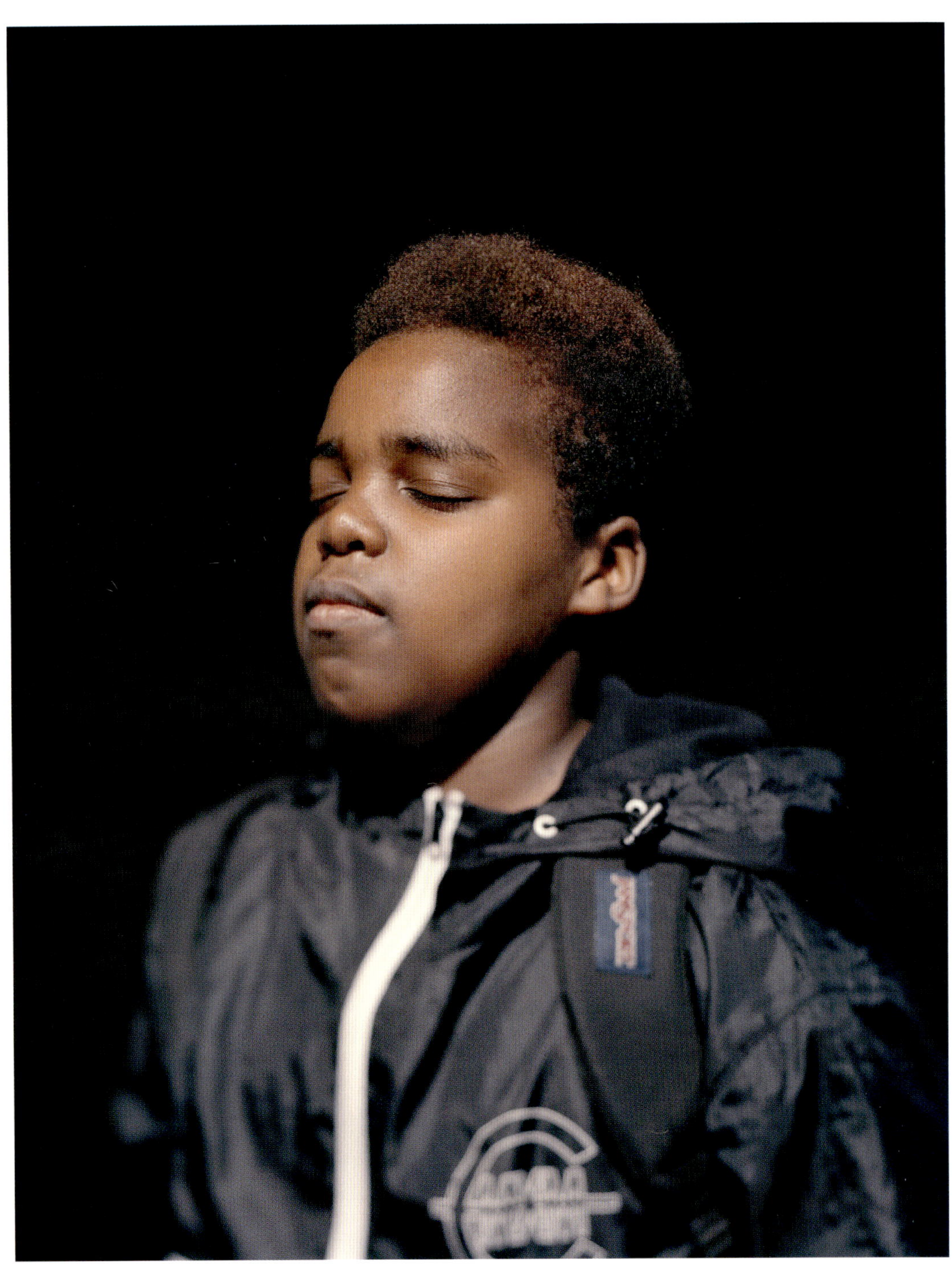

the lenses and the beautifully classic design of their cameras. There are many other excellent rangefinders, but the Contax G2 also deserves an honourable mention for its advanced features, including electronic autofocus and the fact that you can use it to shoot manually as well as using automatic exposures.

MEDIUM-FORMAT CAMERAS

Medium-format cameras exist in both the digital and film categories. The term is used to describe cameras that record images on a sensor or film larger than 35mm, but smaller than 4 × 5 inches. The advantage of this type of camera is that a larger negative or image sensor produces a more detailed image with greater resolution. But this often comes at the cost of increased weight and size. The most popular digital medium-format cameras are made by Phase One, Fujifilm, Hasselblad and Leica. All of these cameras provide incredible resolution but at a hefty price tag. If you're interested in medium-format film cameras, the best are made by Hasselblad, Pentax and Mamiya. They all have high-quality lenses and are well designed. They used to be a relatively affordable option if you wanted to dip your toe in the world of medium-format cameras, but with the growing popularity of film photography the cameras have increased significantly in price.

LARGE-FORMAT CAMERAS

Large-format cameras are the child of the daguerreotype and probably the closest form of original photography used today. Large format denotes all cameras that are larger than medium format. The most commonly used formats are 5 × 4 and 10 × 8, which refer to the size of the negative in inches. Large format is advantageous because it produces very large negatives – a 5 × 4-inch

negative contains around fifteen times the amount of information than a 35mm negative, which means you get incredible resolution. Large format also offers a better degree of control due to the movements you can make with the camera such as rise/fall and tilt/shift. Rise/fall allows you to adjust the area that is captured in an image – for instance, if you are photographing a building, you can raise the front of the camera where the lens is to give the impression that you are shooting from a much higher point, which allows you to capture the whole building in the image without distortion. Tilt/shift allows you to control the plane of focus, which means you can throw more of the image out of focus. Tilt controls movements forward and backward, throwing as much or as little out of focus as you want from top to bottom. Shift controls movement horizontally, throwing the image out of focus from side to side – this can be used to get both eyes in focus if the subject is not looking straight onto camera. The portrait opposite is a good example of this. Here, I used tilt to throw most of the image out of focus, leaving just the eye and some of the hair sharp. The downside is that the image on the ground glass (viewfinder) is upside down and back to front, which can be confusing. This format is also very expensive to use, which, although a drawback, can make you more considered in your approach, so it does come with some benefits.

SMARTPHONES AND PORTRAIT PHOTOGRAPHY

There is an expression in photographic circles that says: 'The best camera is the one you have with you.' Although this is true to a certain extent, it would be better phrased along the lines of: 'It's better to have any camera than none at all.' The camera most people carry around with them is a smartphone. Although these can take decent photographs and are helpful for reference images, I advise photographers to avoid using them for portraits. The 'portrait mode' included with many phones attempts to mimic 'bokeh' (the blur seen in the out-of-focus parts of a picture), but, in my opinion, this looks too computer generated and the subject can seem as if they have been cut out and placed on a background. Instead, always carry a 'proper' camera with you – the point at which I improved most quickly was when I began to take my 35mm camera with me everywhere. It keeps you thinking about photographs and this in turn helps you to improve naturally.

Film versus Digital

The debate among photographers over the merits of film and digital cameras is one that continues to rage on, and I don't see this being resolved any time soon. I learned how to take pictures using black-and-white film, processing and printing my pictures in a dark-room, so it was my first love affair with photography and one that has continued to this day. I make all of my project work on film, so it's definitely my favourite way of working, but I also use digital cameras for specific jobs.

There are certain tasks that digital cameras do better than film cameras. For example, I've had a few jobs working on film sets doing unit stills (pictures for promotional purposes as well as behind the scenes) and the lighting is often very dim because video cameras don't need as much light. In these circumstances, digital is much more effective, since modern cameras tend to perform better in lower light levels. Mirrorless cameras also have silent shooting, which means you can shoot images during takes – something you cannot do with film cameras without using a blimp (a camera housing that muffles sound).

Digital cameras also provide you with more flexibility, as you are able to switch ISO at the press of a button, whereas with film you have to shoot at the same speed until the roll is finished. Digital cameras can have more upfront costs, but once you have bought your equipment, they are not too expensive to run. In contrast, with film photography, you have to keep up with the ever-increasing costs of film and processing.

You're probably now asking yourself why photographers bother to shoot with film? Apart from the aesthetic qualities, such as grain, unique out-of-the-box colours and a less 'flat'-looking image, which for me are good enough reasons alone, the process of making the image is the main advantage. Film makes you take your time and really think about the image you are going to create. It's a slower way of working and because of the limitations on the number of images per roll or sheet of film, it forces you to work in a measured way. The larger the format, the slower the process, and the more you have to compose your image and consider the final outcome. When I shoot on digital, I tend to get trigger happy – I shoot more than I need to and end up spending ages going through all the photos to try and edit down to the final selection.

With film you do the majority of the work before the image is taken, whereas with digital most of this takes place afterwards. Once scanned, film requires little retouching or editing. With digital, I find that I need to spend a lot more time in post-production to get an image that is less glossy and 'digital looking'.

▶ Cian Oba-Smith. Jorie, Isle of Dogs, London, 2020.

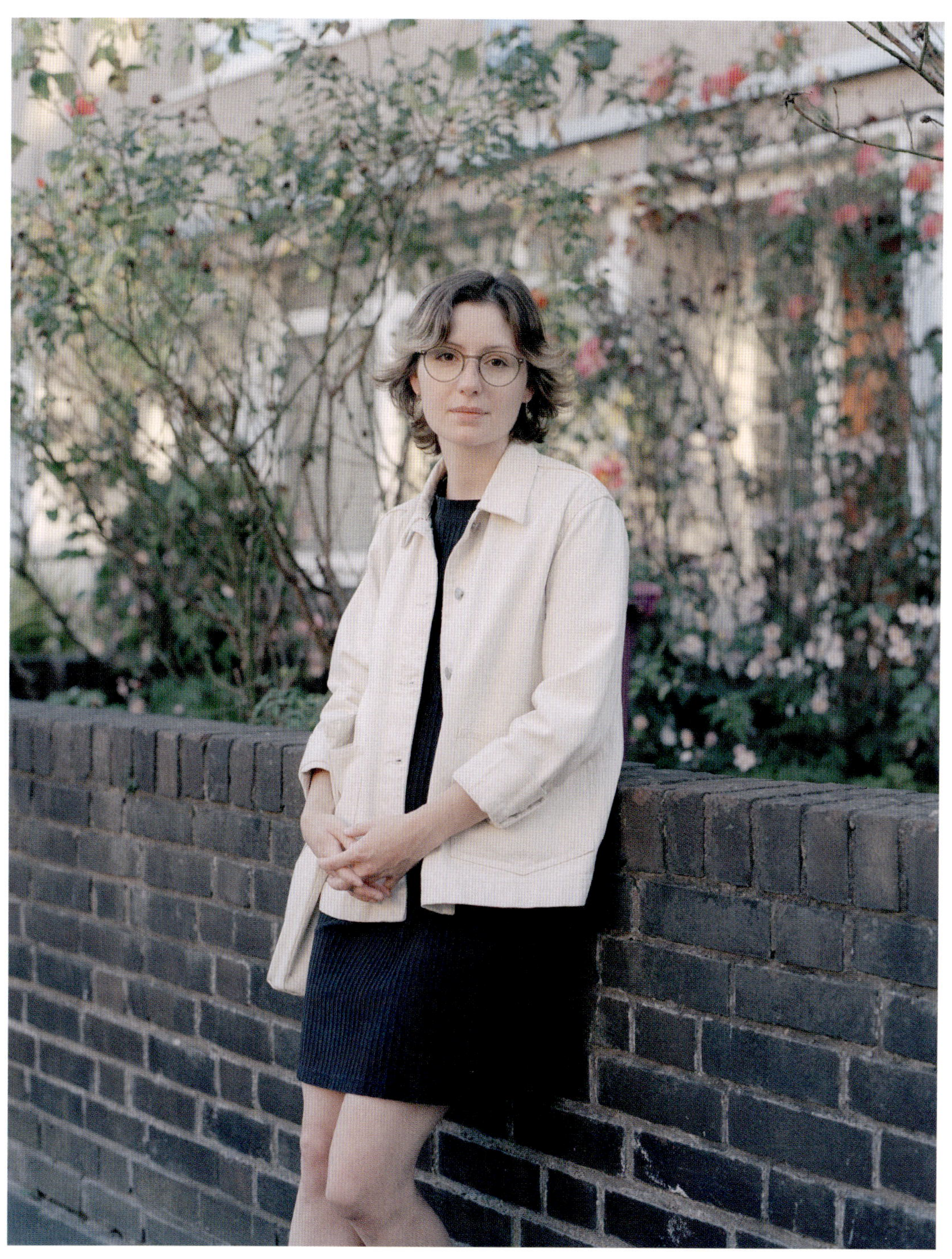

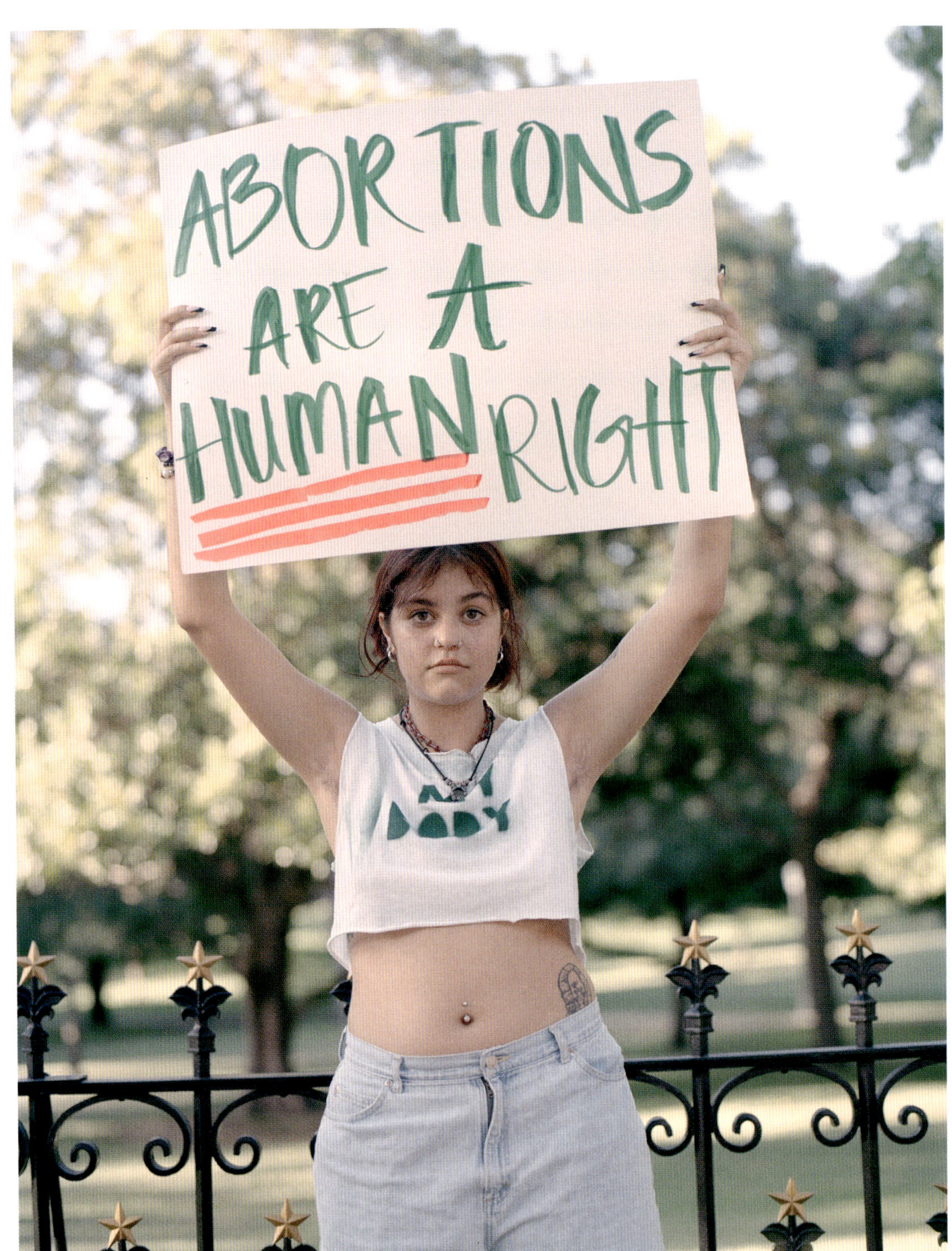
ABORTIONS ARE A HUMAN RIGHT

Lenses

The lens you choose is much more important than the camera body to which it is attached. A great lens on an average camera will still take great pictures, whereas a bad lens on an amazing camera will take bad pictures. This is because the lens is what essentially views and captures light on the film or image sensor, while the function of the camera's body is to record what the lens sees. Individual lenses have their own qualities, but the similarities lie in the focal lengths.

In general, you should avoid wide-angle lenses, especially for closeup portraits, unless this is for stylistic purposes. This is because they tend to distort facial features, resulting in a large nose and small ears – not a good look! A 35mm lens can be used for environmental portraits or closer portraits; it is a good all-rounder, but it's on the wider side. Alternatively, you could use either a 50mm, which works for full lengths and closeups, or an 85mm, which is more portrait-specific and works particularly well for head and shoulder shots. Bear in mind here, however, that you may sometimes run into issues when trying to fit the whole person in the frame.

For a good versatile lens that works for most types of photography, the majority of photographers will opt for a 35mm or a 50mm. It basically comes down to personal preference – and the easiest way to establish what works for you is to try out different lenses and figure out the lens that best fits your style of shooting.

Colour versus Black and White

Photographers have been arguing about whether colour or black-and-white photography is 'better'

since colour photography was invented. Originally, when colour film was made available to the public in the 1930s, it wasn't seen as an artistic subgenre by most photographers. Rather it was the medium that people used to document their day-to-day life and that advertisers relied on to sell products. According to American photographer William Eggleston, Henri Cartier-Bresson (1908–2004), one of the most famous photographers of the 20th century, once said to him at a party: 'William, colour is bullshit.' It wasn't until decades later that it started to gain any sort of recognition as a legitimate art form.

Thankfully, we now regard both as legitimate forms of art, although colour photography has overtaken black and white as the most dominant form of photography, both in mainstream society and in the art world. Having said that, the art world still produces a huge number of photographic projects in black and white, and I would say that the amount of colour work being made is only a majority by a slim margin. Throughout this book, you will find that this is reflected in the photographers we have selected, as we felt it was important to curate a group of photographic artists who are representative of both historical and contemporary portrait photography.

Colour and black-and-white photographs are both read very differently over time. In general, black-and-white images are perceived as being timeless, whereas colour images can feel more nostalgic as they age. In my opinion, this is because the additional information that colour photography can provide creates another layer of nostalgia and makes it easier to see the differences between today's world and the past.

Some Technical Tips

Below is some technical advice and tips for working successfully with both digital and film cameras:

DIGITAL AND FILM PHOTOGRAPHY

• Shoot manually if your camera has that feature (other modes are for lazy photographers). This keeps your approach to creating pictures intentional, makes you conscious of your overall approach, and allows you to retain more control over your final image.

• In general, it is better to underexpose digital images and overexpose film.

• Format your blank memory cards if you're shooting digital – this is the equivalent of loading a fresh roll of film. 'Blank' cards still retain information in the same way that hard drives do. If you delete all of the pictures on a memory card, it still holds information, but formatting them will delete it. As long as you have backed up the images, you should format them every time you put in a 'blank' card.

• Keep film in the fridge and, if you're not using it for a while, put it in the freezer to keep it fresh! Make sure you take the film out in advance to allow it to return to room temperature before using it.

• A higher ISO equals more grain or digital noise, so keep your ISO at 800 or below for digital, unless your camera is designed for low light. With film, you can shoot at any speed for artistic purposes, but you will lose detail in the image as your ISO goes up.

• Slide film is less forgiving than print film. With print film, you can be off an exposure by a stop or two and still get a good negative.

• With digital cameras, always shoot in RAW mode. RAW + JPG is useful for flicking through and selecting images after shooting, but RAW is essential because the file retains all the information. It's like having a digital version of a negative.

• A wider aperture (f/2.8, for instance) creates a shallower depth of field, meaning you get more bokeh behind the subject. This affects how the image is read, so choose your aperture wisely.

OTHER EQUIPMENT

• Use a cable release and a tripod with medium- and large-format cameras to avoid camera shake on slower shutter speeds. If you have a mirrorless camera, use the electronic shutter mode for shooting at slower speeds.

• Background rolls can be useful if you want to isolate your subject from their surroundings. A simple paper roll and some gaffer tape can create a studio outside (see page 96).

• Reflectors can be helpful for many types of portraiture, particularly editorial and fashion. They're used to fill in the shadows. Just tilt them back and forth and watch your subject to see when they catch the light. White reflectors are the most subtle, silver ones are more pronounced, while gold ones are similar to silver but with more warmth.

• A light meter helps you to get the correct exposure and is useful for studio work and shooting with film cameras. Some phone apps are surprisingly good, but invest in a 'proper' meter when you can – the Sekonic L-308 is easy to use and a reliable one to start with.

STORING AND CATALOGUING

• Develop a system for storing your negatives, and start doing this from the beginning of your career – you'll

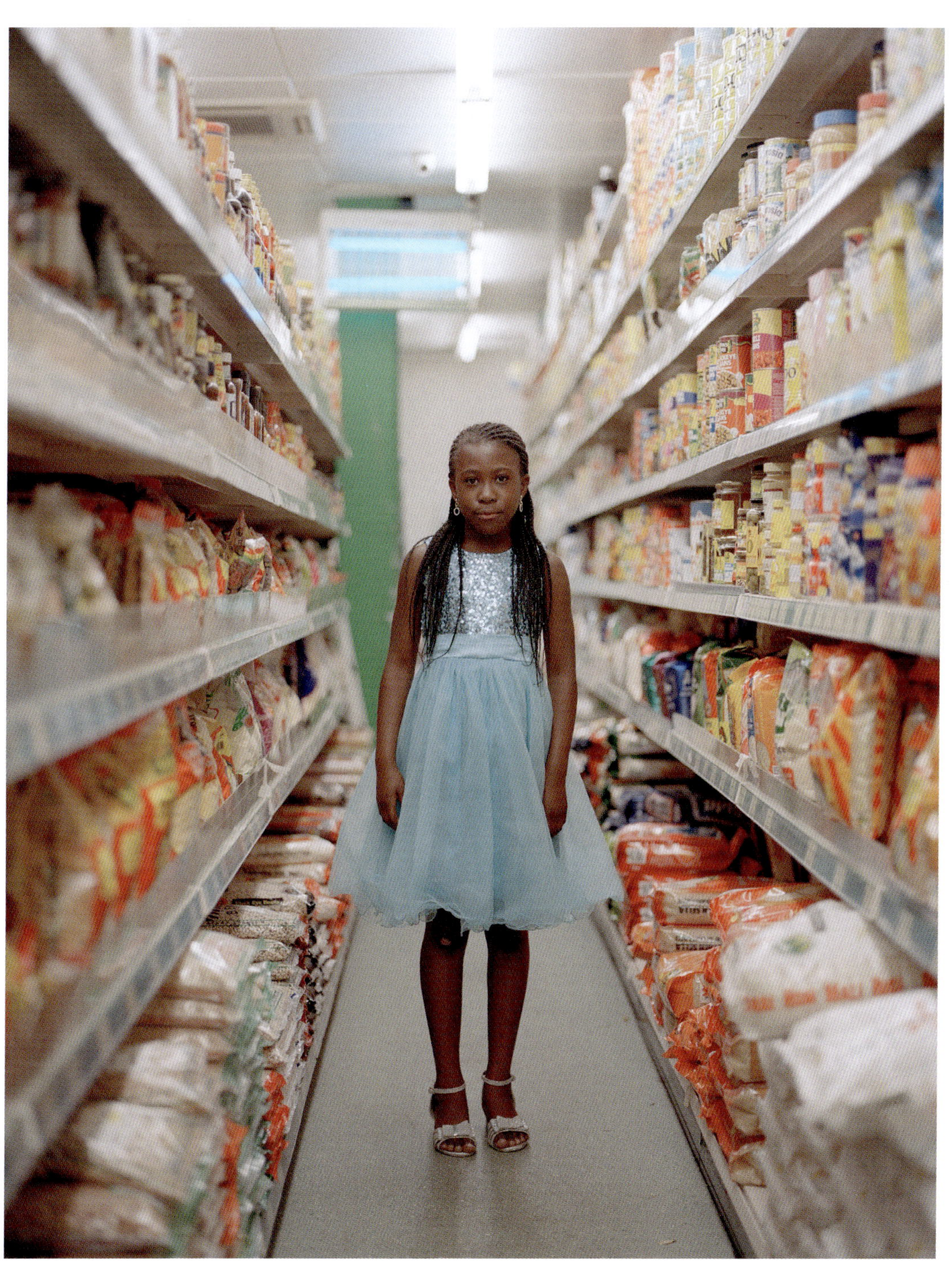

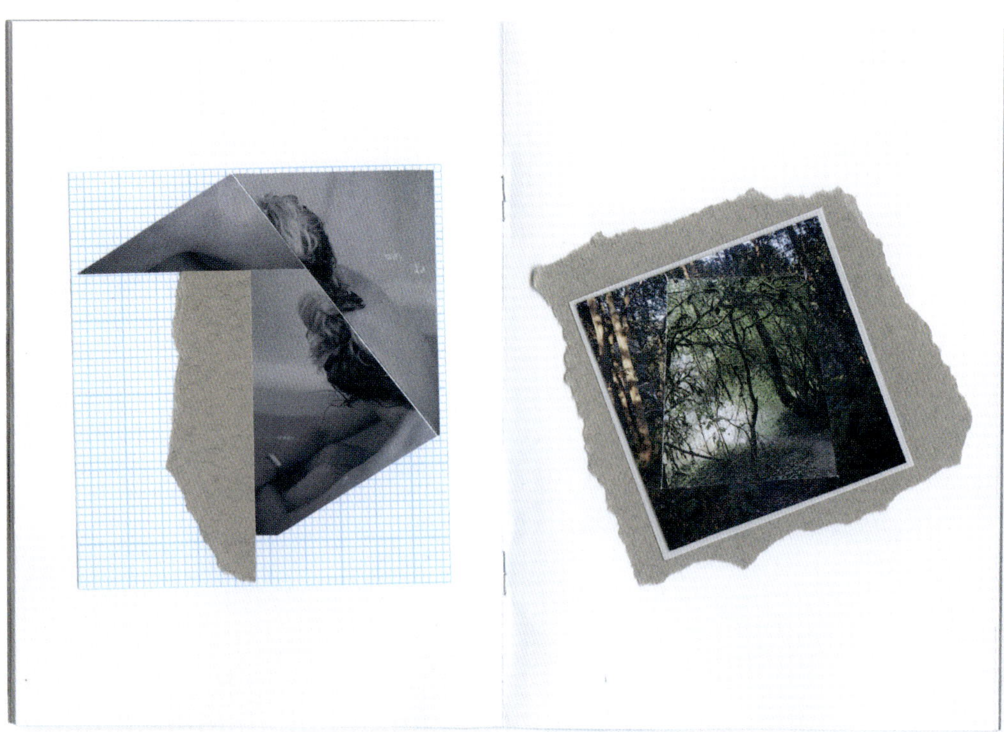

thank yourself later! I keep my negatives in labelled boxes and then use a Word document to list which box corresponds to what work. When I'm looking for something specific, I search my document and look in the corresponding box.

• Develop a workflow early on to catalogue your digital files. I organize mine into three sections: personal, work and projects. I catalogue personal images based on the year they were taken, with subcategories for each month. I categorize work images based on the client and then the individual shoot. Projects are placed in individual subfolders. **COS**

Research

Research is a key part of the workflow of all photographers. The portraits you take do not exist in a vacuum. They are contextualized by thousands of years of art history, critical thinking and culture.

Scan of a spread of experimentations with collage from one of Max's sketchbooks.

Understanding how your work fits into these worlds can help you to create work without fear of copying or plagiarizing. Whether you are researching a personal project or creating mood boards for clients, it is important to know what you are referencing and why. Research can take several forms – for some people, it is researching the work of other photographers; for others, it is reading around the subject. The portrait photographer Laura Pannack once told me that she gets most of her inspiration from taking screenshots of films she is watching. As with many areas of this book, it is about discovering the research process that works best for you. Research allows you to make pictures that are informed by what has come before you. This makes it less likely that you will make similar work to that of other photographers.

Let us look closely at a specific example. Imagine you want to work on a project consisting of portraits of a local community group; an ethical allotment that grows food to donate to the local community. There are several types of research that you could do here. We can split these into primary and secondary research. The primary research will involve speaking to the people at the allotment and building relationships with them. You could even take some preliminary photographs. The secondary research is going to be everything you do around the project. For example, you could find other photographers who have made similar work. Chris Hoare's *Growing Spaces* (2021) springs to mind here, but it doesn't need to be people making work about allotments. Some of the references might be visual to help you build an idea of how you want the photographs to look. Even key decisions, such as whether to shoot in colour or black and white, could be made in the research phase. You might want to watch movies about communities or read articles, essays, poetry or fiction. The possibilities are endless.

It's vital that you record your research in some way so you can return to it for reference later. The most common method for recording research is a sketchbook. Sometimes this might be a place for your visual references or a place to get creative when you're not taking pictures – as is the case with the collages made out of some old images shown opposite. Normally, I work between two sketchbooks simultaneously. I use one sketchbook for my visual ideas. I usually make these books by hand by sewing some folded pages together. I print out small photographs and stick them in. I then write notes around them. The other sketchbook is a small hardback notebook with lined pages. I use this to write down ideas about projects or text I might include. This is the one I carry with me everywhere. If for some reason I don't have it with me, I will use the note section on my phone. While I was doing my second degree in photography, I started making lots of research journals in InDesign and found that having a digital space to record my progress was really useful. Sketchbooks and notebooks are also great for writing down people's details when you take their portraits. Whatever method you use, just make sure you keep track of your thoughts and research somewhere.

Choosing a Subject

How you choose who to photograph will become a key part of your photographic practice. How you then decide to photograph them can change the meaning of your photographs significantly. Someone you have stopped in the street is not going to be photographed in the same way as a professional model, for example. Broadly speaking, you can divide people into two main categories when selecting subjects: choosing them serendipitously or casting them. There are, of course, spaces between these approaches and you can work within these, if you wish. Here we break down the specifics of what these different approaches involve.

First, let's consider serendipity. This is how Cian often works. He puts himself into a situation where there will be people to photograph and then he will stop people and ask them if he can take their portraits. I suspect that most of the photographers whose work can be categorized as documentary photography work like this.

Many photographers, especially those who work in fashion and are used to featuring models in their work, like to cast people for their personal projects. Campbell Addy is a wonderful photographer who shoots both fashion and personal projects. He also used to run a casting agency, which he relied on to find models for his photographs. Casting does not only involve professional models; it can also be anyone who you preselect for your photographs. Often, photographers will use their social media platforms to find suitable people. If you are going to photograph a group who have an online community, you might also reach out to them first on social media, so you are not going into a situation cold.

Street casting is somewhere between the serendipity and casting approaches. Again, this term originates from the fashion world, where models are selected for fashion shoots from a local area by the stylist or photographer. They are then dressed by the stylist before the photographer makes portraits of them. This is a fairly common practice for fashion magazines. Some photographers will also find people on the street, take their details and then photograph them at a later date. This is often how casting agencies find new 'talent' as well.

If you are making a project that is about a group of people, you will need to be honest about how you are planning to represent them. Conversations around how they want to be portrayed might be useful too. If you were photographing, let's say, people who game online, you might want to reach out online to find them. It's unlikely that stopping people in the street will be successful for this. If, however, you are making a project about people who live on the same road as you, then it is probably better to speak to them directly. This is an extreme example, but it is advisable not to recruit models online and pretend they are the residents of your street, unless, of course, you are commenting on the truthfulness of the image.

Intention

This brings us to one of the key considerations we've had while writing this book: that one of the things you can do immediately as a new photographer to push yourself further is to be intentional in how you take photographs. This might mean different things to different people, but here we are suggesting that you photograph carefully and with purpose. This is a mindset that may take many years to achieve, but the beginnings of it can come quickly. Note that there are not countless versions of the portraits you see in this book sitting on Cian's hard drive. He might work through a series of crops or poses, but he is intentional with every image. This is not something that comes easily and it will take practice, but try and build intentionality into your workflow from the start. If you have chosen to photograph someone who you think will work well in a portrait, this is the first stage of intent. But try and think on the spot about several things at once. Why have you stopped this person and how do they fit into your work? Can you quickly manipulate the surroundings to make a more interesting photograph? Try and visualize the crop you want to make and how the background or lighting will look before you press the shutter.

Shooting on film is by no means essential for any photographer, but it does help when you are learning to bring intentionality to your work. You are limited by how many shots you can take and each shot also has a cost to it. If you take hundreds of photographs of each subject, you might get lucky and have some

▶ Cian Oba-Smith. Ciarra and Shatique,
Syracuse, New York, USA, 2019.

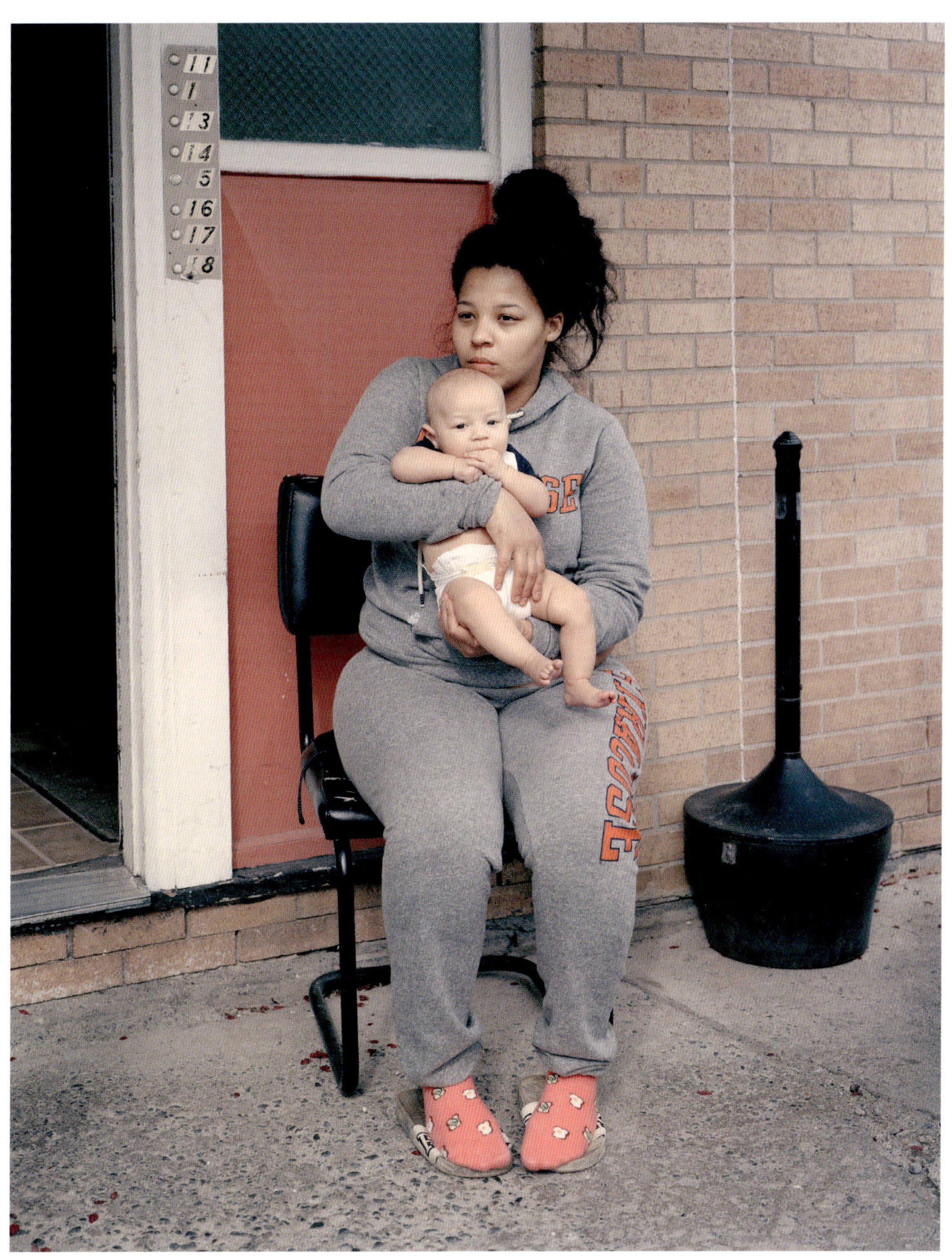

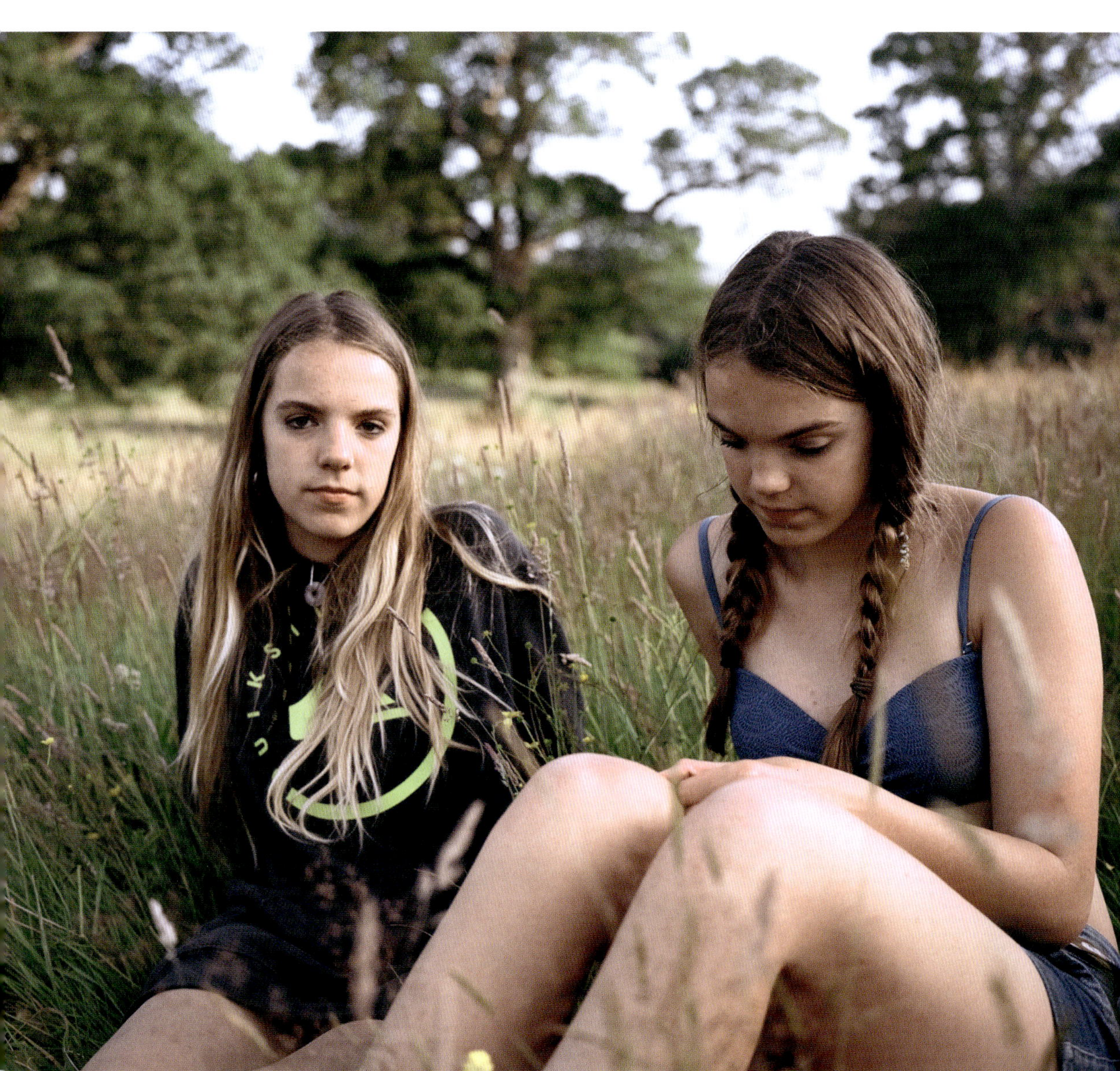

good ones. But it is better just to take one or two and be confident that you will get what you want. Cian is a great example of a photographer who works like this. **MF**

Planning

This is one of those areas that is not often discussed by photographers, but I think it is really important. People often talk about planning in the sense of researching and reading around a subject, but they often overlook planning out the execution of the shoot itself, whether that is a one-day portrait or going away from home for a month to work on a project. I learned to plan more thoroughly when I was an assistant photographer and it's become something that I do almost every time I work on a project.

As we discussed earlier, the initial planning stages come from the selection and research of your chosen subject matter. Once this stage has been completed, I generally move onto the main planning phase. Every photographer approaches how they plan a shoot differently and this is something that can vary slightly depending on the project or portrait you're focusing on.

When making projects, I regularly use 'Google My Maps'. In the past, before the advent of the smartphone, photographers might plot pins on a map to mark out where they would be photographing. Although this is still useful, I find it easier to have a custom digital map that I can grab for reference at any time. Being able to drop pins on points of interest or locations that you are planning to photograph and having the ability to draw boundaries is really helpful in certain

◀ Sian Davey. *The Twins*,
from the series 'Martha', 2018.

circumstances. For instance, when I was making my series on redlining in Syracuse, New York, I used Google Maps to redraw the original redlining map on a custom map and then explored the original communities to investigate the long-term effects of redlining on the African-American community.

When working on a commissioned project, my approach is similar if I am photographing multiple subjects, but I tend to do less logistical planning in general. A lot of photographers who enjoy a more extensive visual plan might use tools such as Pinterest or folders on Instagram to save images that they find inspirational and to create a broad visual of the look they want to capture when they're on the job.

I still like to keep an element of spontaneity in how I approach image making, however. For me, the planning stage is just to set some parameters to prevent me overlooking something important. Once these parameters are in place, I still allow photographs to find me. In fact, a lot of my project work featuring communities arises from wandering around and stumbling across people or places to photograph. When I am making a portrait of an individual, I try to retain that same spontaneity. Always bear in mind that portrait photography is a conversation and it's important to maintain a collaborative dialogue with the person you're photographing.

Creating

The process of creating work is difficult to examine because it is so different for every photographer. But overall, it is important to be true to who you are when making portraits. Don't try too hard to conform to what you think you should be doing; just trust your instincts and allow your eye to guide you – your personality will likely shine through in your images.

There are a few fundamentals that you should be observing when creating your photographic work. Throughout the book, for example, we discuss how you should tackle making portraits in a broad sense, including the stages you follow in the moment, such as approaching subjects, lighting, framing and interacting with your subject. We also look at what comes afterwards when you edit, sequence and share your work. In general, you will come across a wide range of photographers who take different approaches to the art of portrait photography, both in terms of subject matter and visual style. **COS**

Showcasing Photographs

As your confidence in making portraits grows and your skills improve, the places in which your photographs appear may change too. At first, you might just be making photographs to show to family, post on social media, or help with a friend's business. These are all fantastic reasons to take pictures, but the time may come when you are asked to be part of an exhibition or to publish a book.

So many photographs only exist on our screens – why not take the plunge and start printing them out? Also, once photographs are printed out and in physical form, they often become more interesting, tactile and complex. Even printing photographs on a cheap printer at home can be useful when you are trying to select your best photograph, for example. Books and exhibitions are still regarded as the most prestigious physical outputs for many photographers. DIY zine-making can be traced back to radical anti-racist Black publishing in 1980s London and is a great way to start getting your work published. It was using these skills that I initially began publishing pictures before I set up my own imprint, Oval Press, through which I now publish 'proper' photobooks. The skills we hope to demystify when it comes to choosing what to shoot, sequencing images and editing photographs will all stand you in good stead when you begin producing your own books, zines and other publications. Marc Vallée is a photographer and zine maker who works heavily in portrait photography, creating bodies of work around his subjects. He almost always self-publishes his work in zines, making a couple of hundred of each. His books and zines are now held in collections in Tate Britain and New York's Museum of Modern Art (MoMA), for example. Cheap online printing services or a home printer and needle and thread may be the start of your photo-publishing career.

Beyond DIY zine making, which will always have its limitations, it is also possible to publish proper photobooks on your own. Even established photographers, such as Stephen Gill with Nobody Books and Bryan Schutmaat with Trespasser, chose to set up their own publishing companies rather than working with existing publishers. By self-publishing, they retain complete control over the books they make and also reap the profits (if there are any).

Photobook publishers often ask photographers for up to £20,000 to fund the publishing of their work. Some publishers will fund books from some photographers themselves and charge other photographers to make a book with them. If you search on Kickstarter for previously funded photography titles, you will find

▶ Cian Oba-Smith. Zakia, Syracuse, New York, USA, 2019.

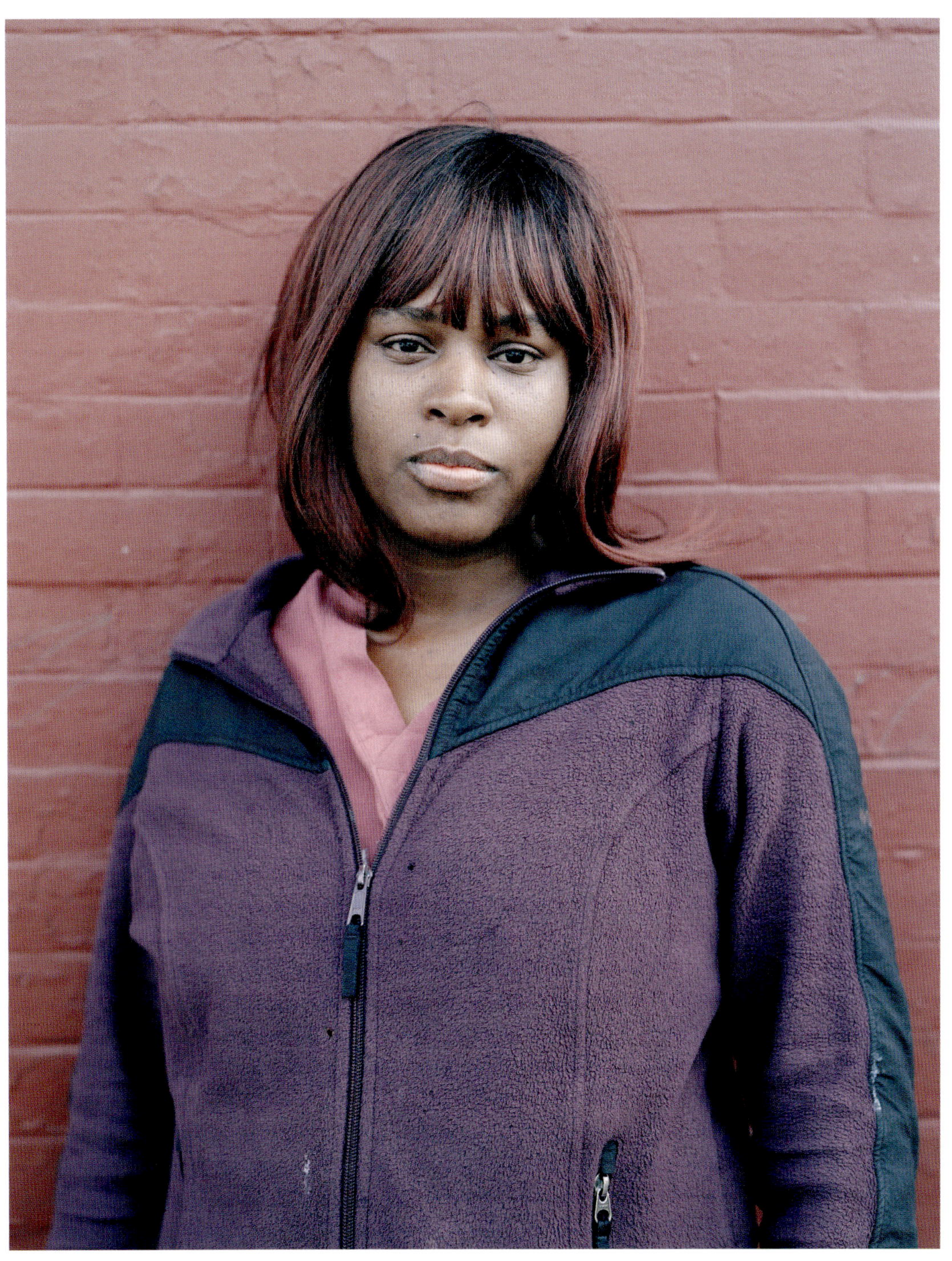

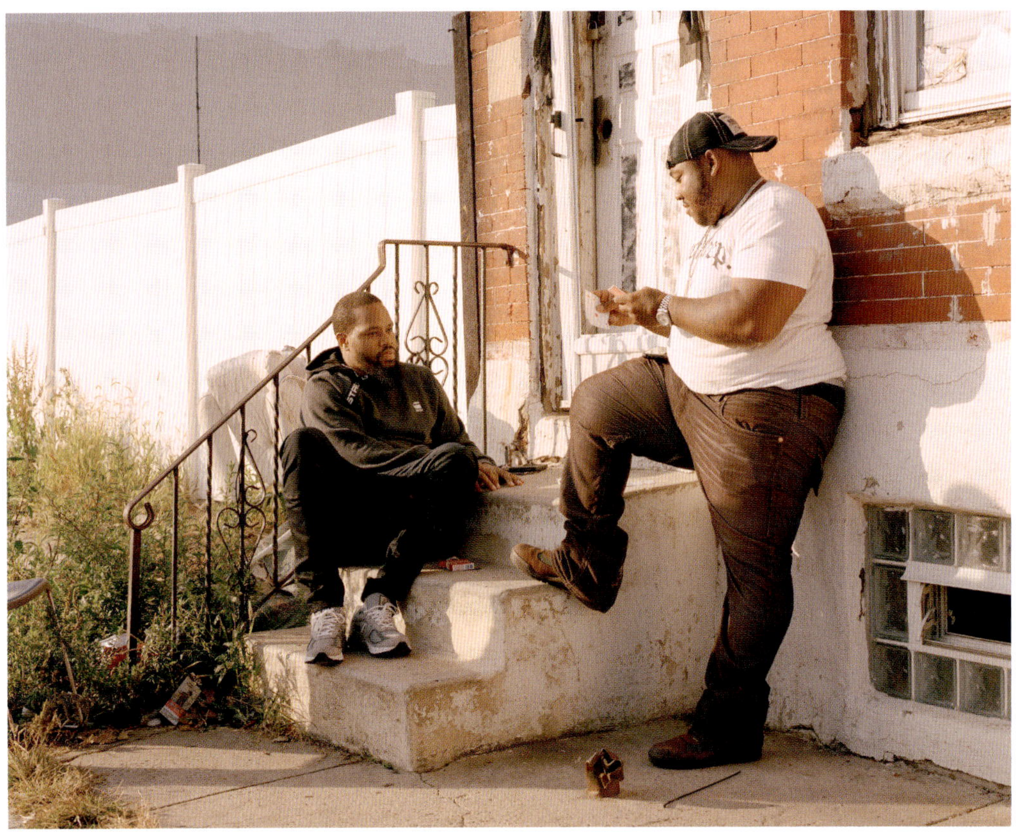

some self-published titles, but you'll also find several from photographers who are crowd-sourcing their investment to work with well-known photography publishers. How much of that investment is returned to the photographer will vary depending on the publisher and how well a book sells. This alone shows that traditional photobook publishing is not always a good route to publishing your work. What do publishers offer? The three main benefits of working with an established publisher are access to design skills, distribution and press. It is worth noting here that, although these can be regarded as real benefits, they are all things you can either do yourself or bring in other people to help with. Indeed, you can work directly with a designer/editor, distributor or publicist. The world of publishing has never been more accessible.

Exhibitions can be harder to organize yourself than zines and photobooks, especially in major cities such as London where events spaces are incredibly expensive, but there are always solutions if you think outside the box. At the prestigious French photography festival Rencontres d'Arles, where most exhibitions are in beautiful old buildings or fancy new gallery spaces, I once saw an exhibition that used missing-cat-style posters pinned to trees. Many cafés and bars also offer free wall space to artists. I've been thinking for a long time that the postal service (apart from during the 1990's mail art movement) has been wildly underused by artists for sharing their work. Coming together with other photographer friends can make the exhibition experience easier and cheaper. Many photographers form collectives that not only help them connect with the local community, but also allows them to exhibit in spaces they couldn't secure alone.

There are also countless photography competitions that offer exhibitions, features or cash prizes to the winners. Some of these are good and funded properly by external sponsors, with judges drawn from the industry. Others, however, are expensive to enter, funded by the submissions and exist to create profits. It can be difficult to work out which competitions are good and bad, so think carefully before you enter. If they're free, you don't have too much to worry about, but with many costing around £20–30 per entry, they can become an expensive way of getting your work out there. **MF**

Community

We live in interesting times within the photography community, but also in a broader sense throughout society. Social media and the Internet in general have allowed us to create connections with like-minded people globally without necessarily knowing them in real life. Instagram in particular has changed the meaning of the word 'community'. At the time of writing, the way the app is designed encourages users to stumble across other photographers, and this creates a natural network of like-minded artists. Social media has also definitely had a huge impact on the resurgence in the popularity of film photography. When I first started taking pictures, film was quite niche. Over time, film photography has grown in popularity to the point where my non-photographer friends also shoot with film; a situation that has been hugely accelerated by the Internet and social media.

Instagram has always been the social media platform most geared towards photographers because it is historically based around the concept of sharing images (see page 64). Twitter tends to be a good place for discussions around photography because it was originally a text-based platform. TikTok sits in an interesting space – I regard it as a platform on which people can show the process by which they make their images, as well as the results of that process.

As much as the Internet is great for connecting with other photographers, both internationally and at home, the best way to make connections with others is the same as that in which photographs are meant to be seen: physically and in real life. Some connections can be made digitally, but nothing beats seeing those people in real life. I am connected with people in countries all over the world through Instagram, but a lot of those people I'm proud to be able to call friends in real life too. I've also built a community of people outside social media through 'traditional' methods, which I'll discuss next.

Before the advent of social media and the Internet, the photography community was much smaller. I grew up when the Internet was becoming more prevalent and social media increasingly popular, so I missed the time when it didn't exist at all. However, I have spoken to and worked with photographers who have been in the industry for a lot longer than me and they remember those earlier times. What worked back then still works now. Meeting people physically at events is a great way to build a community of photographers around you who you can call friends, but who will also be able to give you feedback on your work.

I built up a network of people in a number of ways, both at university and after I graduated. If you're studying at university or planning on studying there, then a great way to build a network is to socialize with people on your course, as well as on other art courses such as graphic design, filmmaking and fashion. When I was studying, I collaborated with other people on those courses and this meant that on leaving university I had a broad network across different industries. This led to commissions through friends and personal connections for the first few years, while I was trying to get on my feet and establish myself professionally.

The other approach I took at university that I have found especially helpful since graduating was making sure I attended as many lectures as possible. I would also always ask for feedback from the people who came in to speak, and this led to so many opportunities when I graduated. For example, I got my first commission for a newspaper through a picture editor who came in to speak at my university. I also connected with Zed Nelson, the photographer who I assisted for three years when I moved back to London.

All of this is achievable without studying for a degree. In fact, there are lots of private views and lectures in London that are open invite. I suggest you follow any galleries you are interested in and sign up to their mailing lists. This is where you'll typically receive information on speaking events as well as private views. Photographers and picture editors will also promote private views and guest lectures on their personal pages. Turn on post notifications for people you're particularly interested in connecting with. That way, you won't miss any events they are part of.

A couple of great organizations that provide networking opportunities are Create Jobs and The Dots. They promote talks on their websites, some of which are in person, as well as other events that are online, so you can participate regardless of where you are based. It is so important to get feedback from people who you respect, either for their own photographs or for their taste in photography. Asking these people to look at your projects and pictures with a fresh pair of eyes is crucial to improving as a photographer and learning to be self-critical.

Having said this, you should also try to get feedback from people outside of the world of photography. Photographers in general tend to end up creating work for the photography industry, instead of for the public, so it is useful to get the opinion of 'normal' people such as your friends and family – people who don't necessarily have a background in the arts or photography. That way, you will get a much broader perspective on your work and are more likely to avoid producing work that is excessively pretentious and less accessible to non-photographers. **COS**

Portraits within Society

Beyond the 'intentional' portraits we all make, how do photographs of people, which are a key part of modern culture, play into our daily lives? Perhaps the most obvious way is through selfies, which we discuss at length later in the book (see page 78). But with apps like BeReal building compulsory selfies into their social networks, it doesn't seem to be a trend that is going to disappear any time soon. We are also bombarded with

▶ Cian Oba-Smith. Mark mourning at the Queen's funeral, London, 2022.

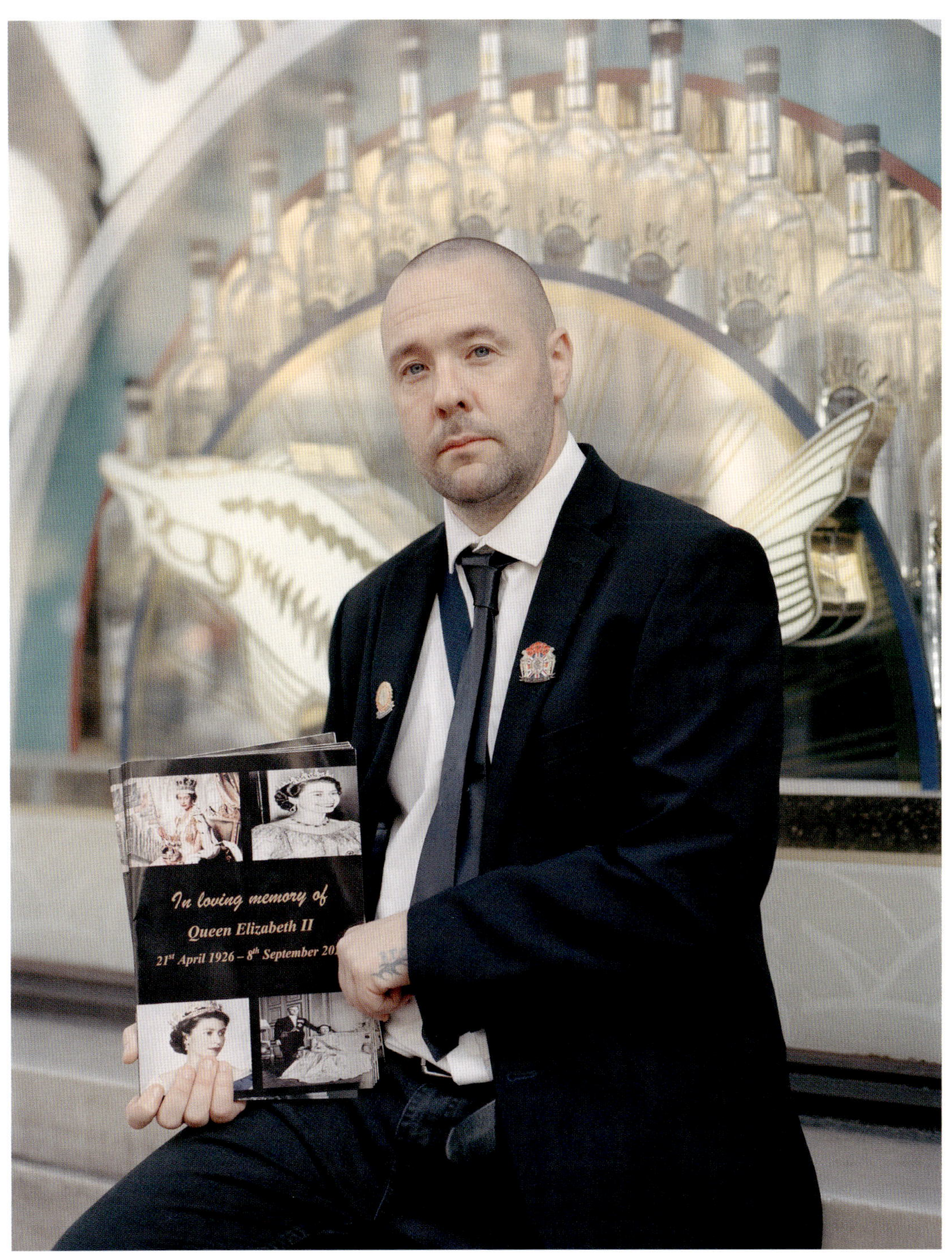
In loving memory of
Queen Elizabeth II
21st April 1926 – 8th September 20

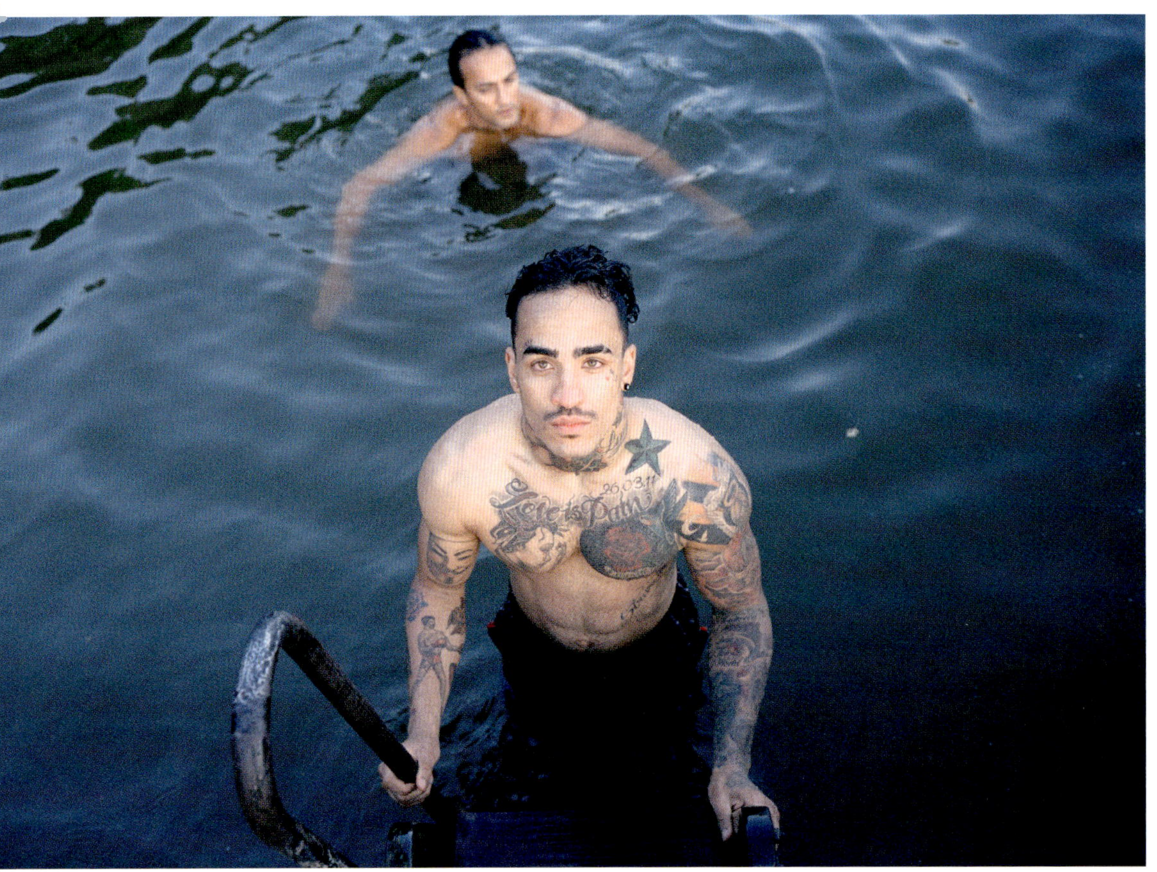

photographs through advertising. We may see dozens, if not hundreds, of these images a day, and they frame how we think about portraits in ways that are hard to quantify. From the normalization of unrealistic beauty standards to the sexualization of women for a (presumably) male gaze, the photograph plays a vital role in how we as a society come to view the people within it.

Questions of Ethics

Ethics in portrait photography are a set of rules, individual to each photographer, that govern how we take photographs. Ethics in photojournalism, nature photography and war photography, for example, are based around strict rules regarding truthful reporting, impartiality and not manipulating photographs. In fine art photography, these rules may not be the same. You can play with the truth to question things, and manipulating pictures is fine, but it can become confusing in documentary photography, as many photographers hover somewhere between fine art and photojournalism. Making work about real people is always going to raise ethical questions. This is why it is important to establish your own set of ethical guidelines in your work. Understand why you think these guidelines are right and be ready to discuss them with people if you are challenged. Perhaps you will decide only to photograph someone if you have asked, and received, their permission. Perhaps you will only go into communities with whom you have already formed a relationship. Maybe you strive not to show pictures that are unkind. Whatever you decide, come back to your choices often, read about photographic theory (see page 37), speak to people who make similar work to you, and ask your subjects how they feel about the work you are making. Ethics should not prohibit the photographs you take, but rather an understanding of the ethical concerns of photography should increase your knowledge and thinking, making you a better photographer.

Ethics and portrait photography are intimately linked with, among other things, power and truth. Their relationship with the latter is the most frequently discussed, so we will start with that. The majority of photographs could be described as being both truthful and deceptive. A portrait of a person sitting on a chair surely occurred as we see it. But the chair may have been swapped for a different chair or the person dressed in different clothes. The image is perhaps intended to sell the clothes or the chair. There may be hundreds of people on chairs sitting around the camera who we cannot see. Clearly, photographs are unreliable at showing us what actually happened, yet we use them as evidence, both casually and in courts and police stations.

In perhaps the most seminal book on the medium, *On Photography* (1977), Susan Sontag argued that 'To photograph people is to violate them, by seeing them as they never see themselves, by having knowledge of them that they can never have; it turns people into objects that can be symbolically possessed.' I think that this thinking is still pertinent to how portraits of people are made now. It's not that you should not take someone's portrait, but more that you should understand the power dynamic involved when you do. Sometimes the power deficit is wide, but sometimes, through collaboration, conversation or time, the gap can be much smaller. Who you photograph is also important. A man photographing a naked woman is unlikely to be working within the same power dynamic as a female photographer making a portrait of a naked man. Hundreds of years of the male gaze in art, culture and life are weighted onto the photograph as soon as it is made. Photographic portraits do not exist in a vacuum.

Alice Zoo, a writer and photographer, interviewed Vanessa Winship for the first instalment of her long-form newsletter *Interloper*, which is, in effect, an essay titled 'In Defence of Portraits'. In the essay, Zoo comments on the fact that Winship, a photographer who is known for her portraits, chose to omit people from her last book. They talk about being reluctant to include people in the book within a framework of discussion on representation and ethics. It's a wonderful piece of writing that covers some of the issues discussed here in more depth. It can be found easily via a quick Internet search for Alice Zoo.

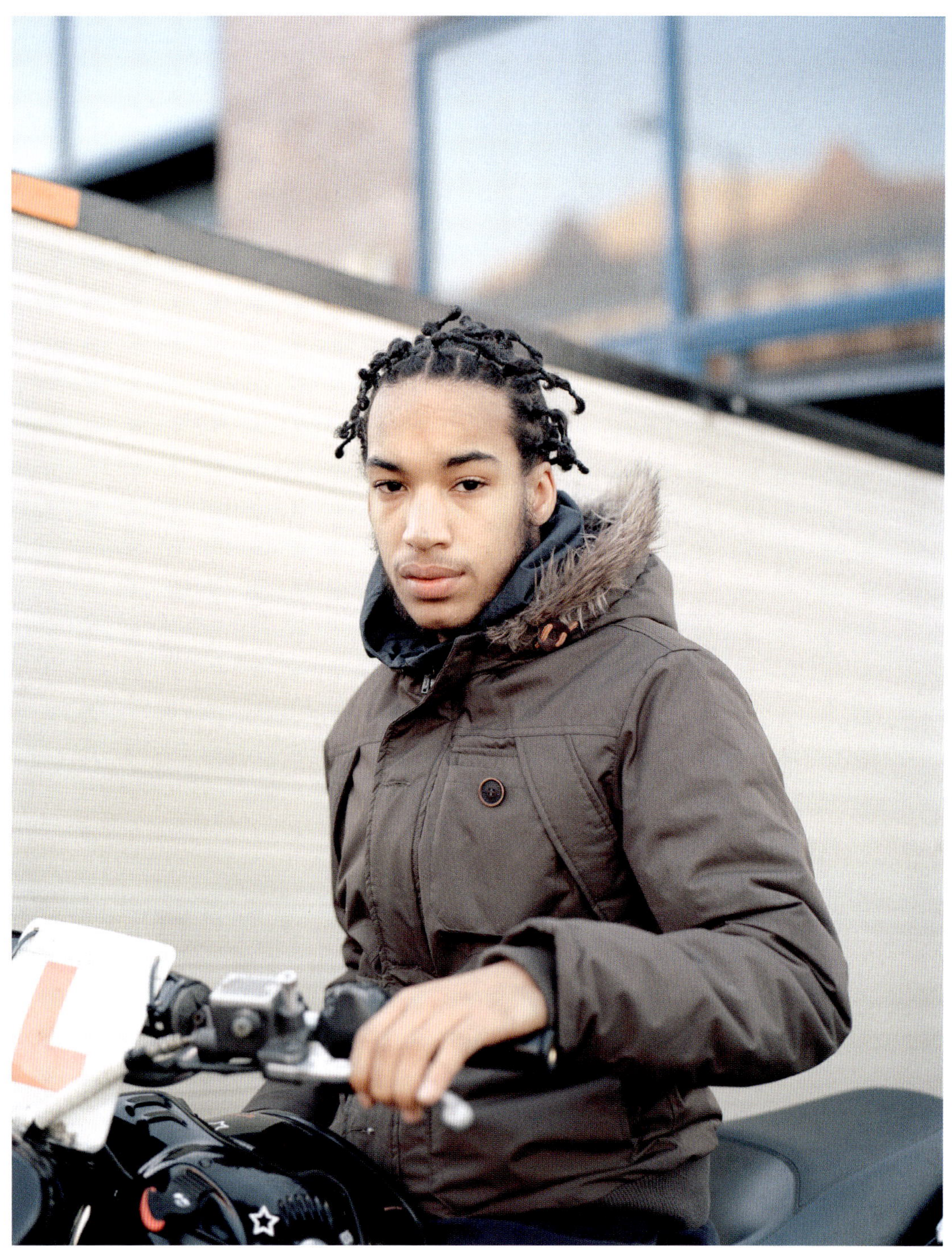

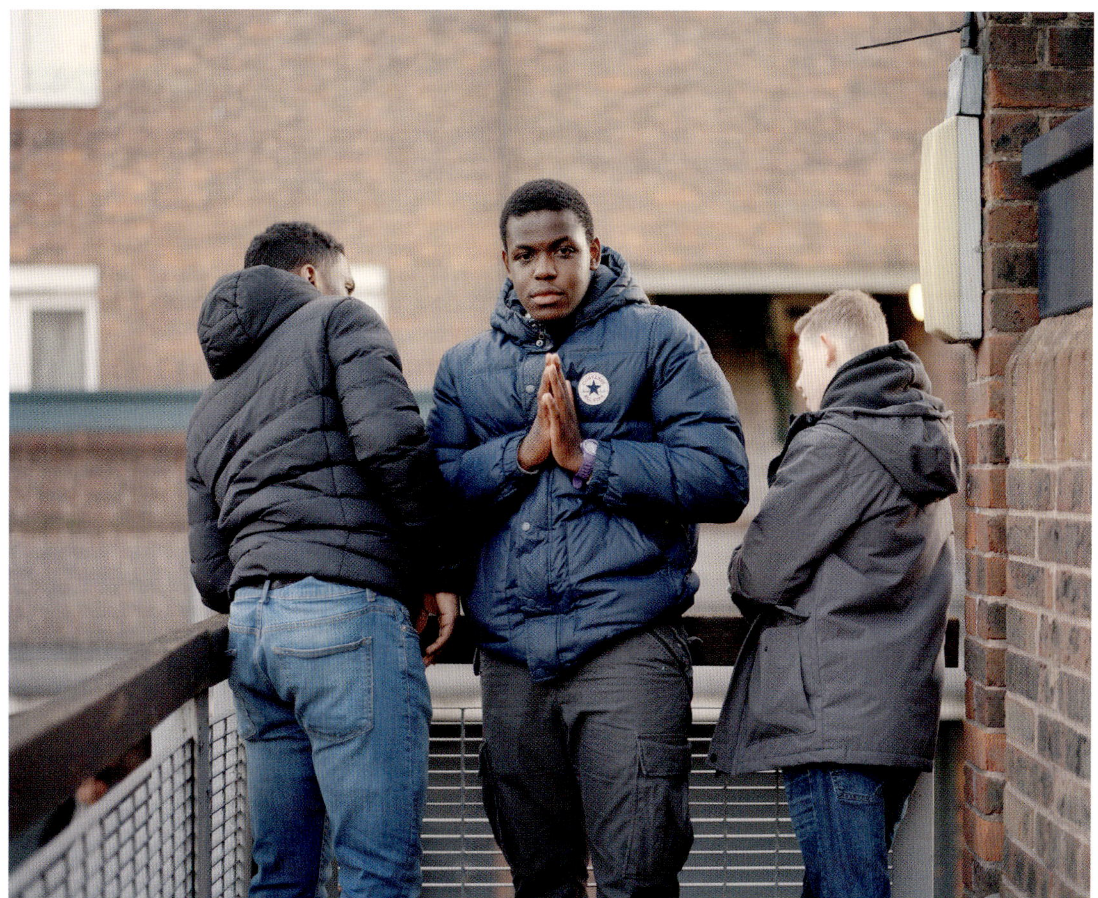

Photographic Theory

Neither Cian nor I would claim to be theorists on portrait photography. Our knowledge and understanding comes mostly from real-world experience, studying or discussions at exhibitions, on shoots or even in the pub. But we do both read about photographic theory.

For those who want to understand as much as possible about photography, there is great pleasure to be had from delving deeply into photographic theory and criticism. The names mentioned here, as well as the photographers we feature, should form the beginning of your own research. The theorists Roland Barthes (1915–1980), John Berger (1926–2017) and Susan

Sontag (1933–2004) are all big names that you will see time and time again. Sontag's *Regarding the Pain of Others* (2003), for example, is a takedown of the frameworks of documentary photography. It questions the photographer's privilege and photography's gaze on the pain of those who are less privileged. Barthes' *Camera Lucida* introduces two terms for how photographs affect us, which you may see used in art writing: 'studium' is the understanding of what the photograph is about (that is, its context); 'punctum' is the subjective effect of a photograph on the viewer. Both have the ability to move the viewer to intense emotions. Berger, my favourite of the three, partly because I find his writing much easier to understand, wrote about how art and photography fit into the wider world. His seminal book *Ways of Seeing* (1972) was turned into a BBC TV series. It may seem a little dated, but you can watch the episodes on YouTube.

All three of these theorists have passed away, so who is speaking now? Luckily, there is a new generation of writers, thinkers and critics taking on photography and how we understand it. In *The Civil Contract of Photography* (2012), Ariella Azoulay argues that photography cannot be separated from catastrophic world events such as colonialism – it's a critique of photography, her home country Israel and the West. Cultural historian Mark Sealy also discusses photography's relationship with colonial power and methods that need to be unlearned. Tina Campt and Saidiya Hartman are incredible writers and thinkers on photography who you may wish to investigate further.

Much of this theory is extremely dense. After two photography degrees and more than a decade thinking about photography, I still struggle to read most of it. But don't be put off all theory because of the inaccessibility of some texts. Some you will find easier and some harder. I first got into theory through John Tagg's *The Burden of Representation* (1988), partly since it was the first book on theory I managed to finish reading. Teju Cole's writing on photography is also very accessible and easy to understand. Until 2019 he wrote a column for *The New York Times* called 'On Photography', which you can still access on their website. It is a wonderful place to start for anyone who wants to think about photography more critically. **MF**

▶ Cian Oba-Smith. Abdullahi, from the series 'Andover & Six Acres', London, 2015.

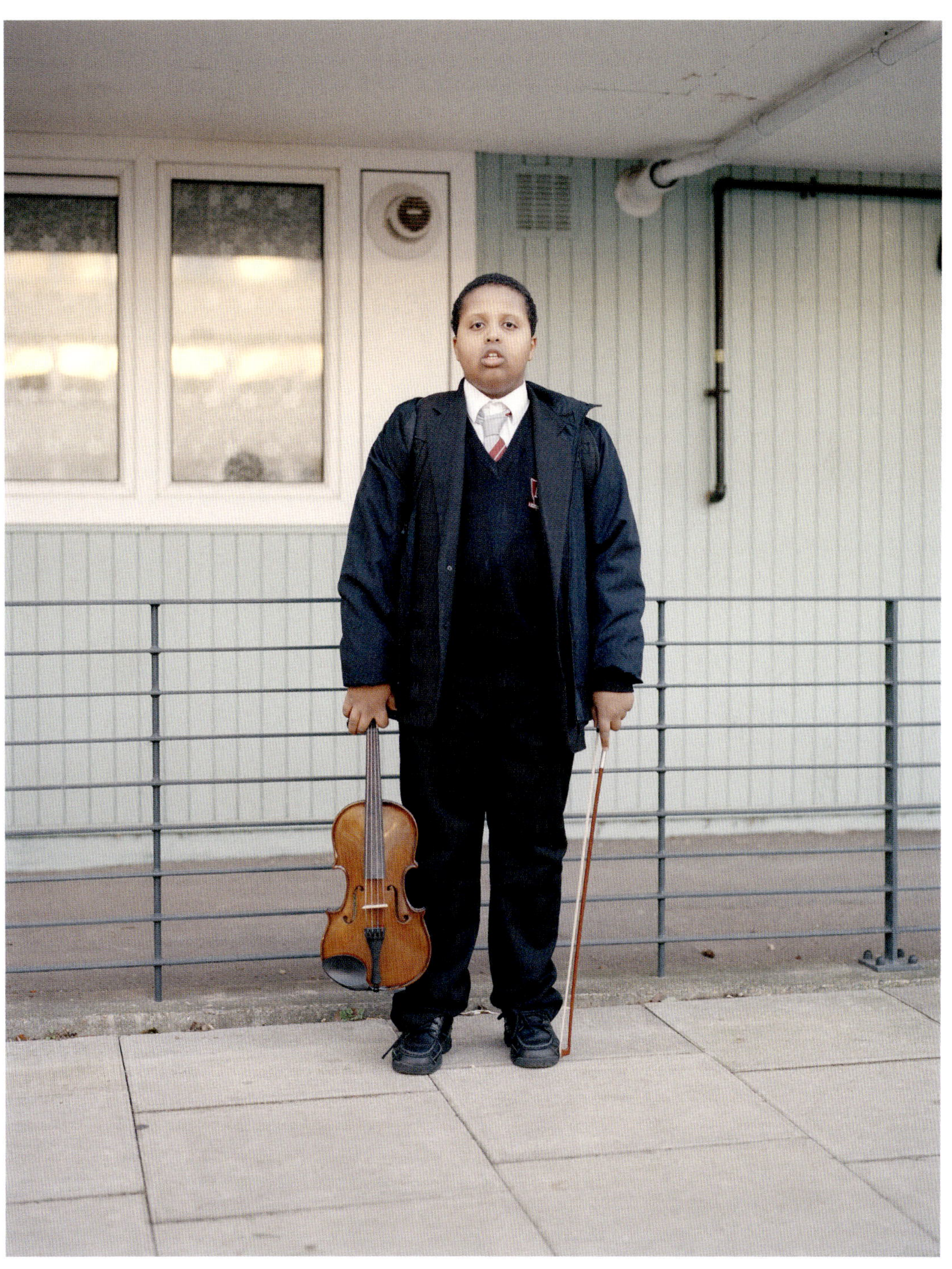

CHAPTER 1

Introduction to Portraiture

Portrait photography and the history of painting are, of course, linked, but photography has become so much more intertwined with every part of our lives than painting ever did.

Projects

While writing this book, we thought a great deal about what, if anything, separates the theory of portrait photography from wider conversations about photography in general. Part of this separation comes from the histories of painting, sculpture and other artistic media such as carving, etching, printmaking and drawing that existed many hundreds of years before the camera was invented. Perhaps, therefore, it's not reductive to break down photography into different subcategories. After all, portrait photography itself can be further categorized according to the titles of the remaining chapters in this book. Portraits also have a place in almost any category of photography, whether this is documentary, fashion, editorial or the recording of political conflict. Clearly, the boundaries are messy. So, here we have not tried to disentangle the many strands of photography, but, hopefully, we have succeeded in showing you how portraits can weave among them.

Consider Paul Delaroche's painting *The Execution of Lady Jane Grey* (1833). You can see this huge oil painting at The National Gallery in London. It depicts the execution of Lady Jane Grey (1537–1554), who was beheaded at the age of seventeen, after just nine days on the throne. This painting is the most detailed depiction we have of the execution, but it was painted almost three centuries after the event and the young queen is wearing contemporary Victorian clothes. This is a highly romanticized portrayal and it's interesting that Delaroche was evidently not attempting to create a realistic visual account. Immediately, we can appreciate that a painter's ability to create anything from history, memory or imagination puts him at odds with the photographer, who begins with the whole world and must reduce everything to the contents of their viewfinder. A portrait taken by a camera is almost certainly of someone who sat, alive, in front of the photographer. We can be confident that what we are seeing really happened.

Contemporary photographers such as Hannah Starkey (see page 60) enjoy working within the space between truth and fiction. It is this power that makes photographing people both exciting and dangerous. And power can be a dangerous thing. Indeed, there is a famous quote by 19th-century American politician Robert G. Ingersoll (often wrongly attributed to Abraham Lincoln) that 'Most people can bear adversity. But if you wish to know what a man really is, give him power.' This idea that power can corrupt is useful when considering the world of photography and ethics. Quite simply, to photograph someone is to hold a position of power over them. If you photograph a sibling or your partner, the disparity may be smaller than if you photograph someone who cannot refuse you. So, think carefully about why you are making portraits of people and whether they wish to be photographed. Are you both gaining something from the experience? Asking permission can be intimidating, but it is a wonderful practice that allows you to work more ethically.

The link between ethics and portrait photography is always worth thinking about, discussing and interrogating, especially as many photographers have been accused of working unethically and some even illegally. In fact, photographers such as Terry Richardson have rightfully been removed from their positions of power after multiple allegations of sexual misconduct and exploitation. Richardson's photographs from the years when he was one of the world's most successful and powerful photographers make for difficult viewing. Many of them are sexually explicit images of him with young models and this raises uncomfortable questions about the fashion and photography industries that kept giving him (and others) the biggest jobs. Richardson is an extreme example, however, and we hope that the photographers who feature in this book demonstrate how to work considerately and compassionately with the subjects of portraiture.

This chapter aims to explain some of the basic ideas behind portrait photography, while exciting you and encouraging you to think of the many possibilities you have for telling stories, making pictures and developing your photographic practice. In the essay 'The White Bird', the photography and art critic John Berger asserts: 'That we find a crystal or a poppy beautiful means that we are less alone, that we are more deeply inserted into existence than the course of a single life would lead us to believe…'. If that could be said of a poppy, perhaps it's fair to say that we like photographs of people because they make us feel more connected. **MF**

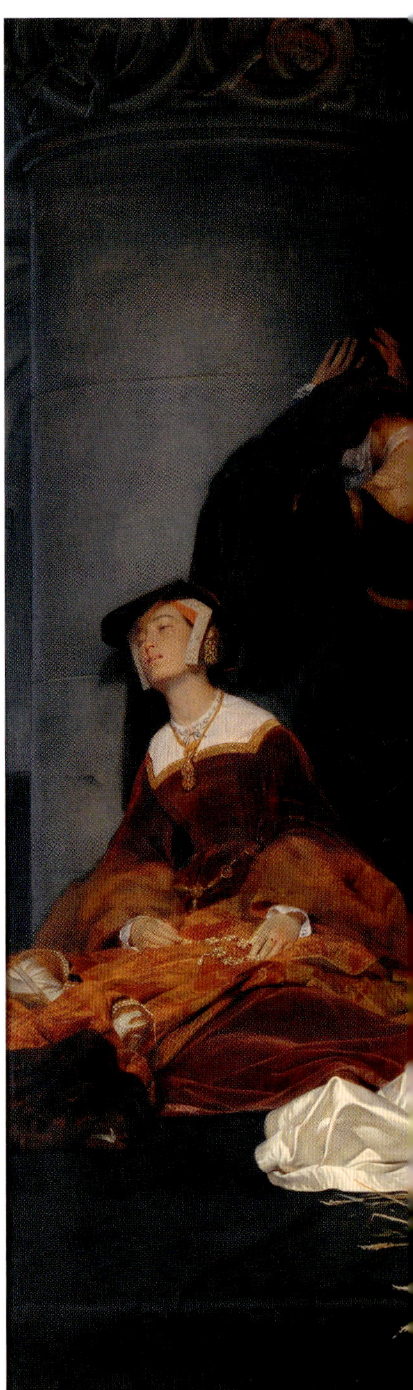

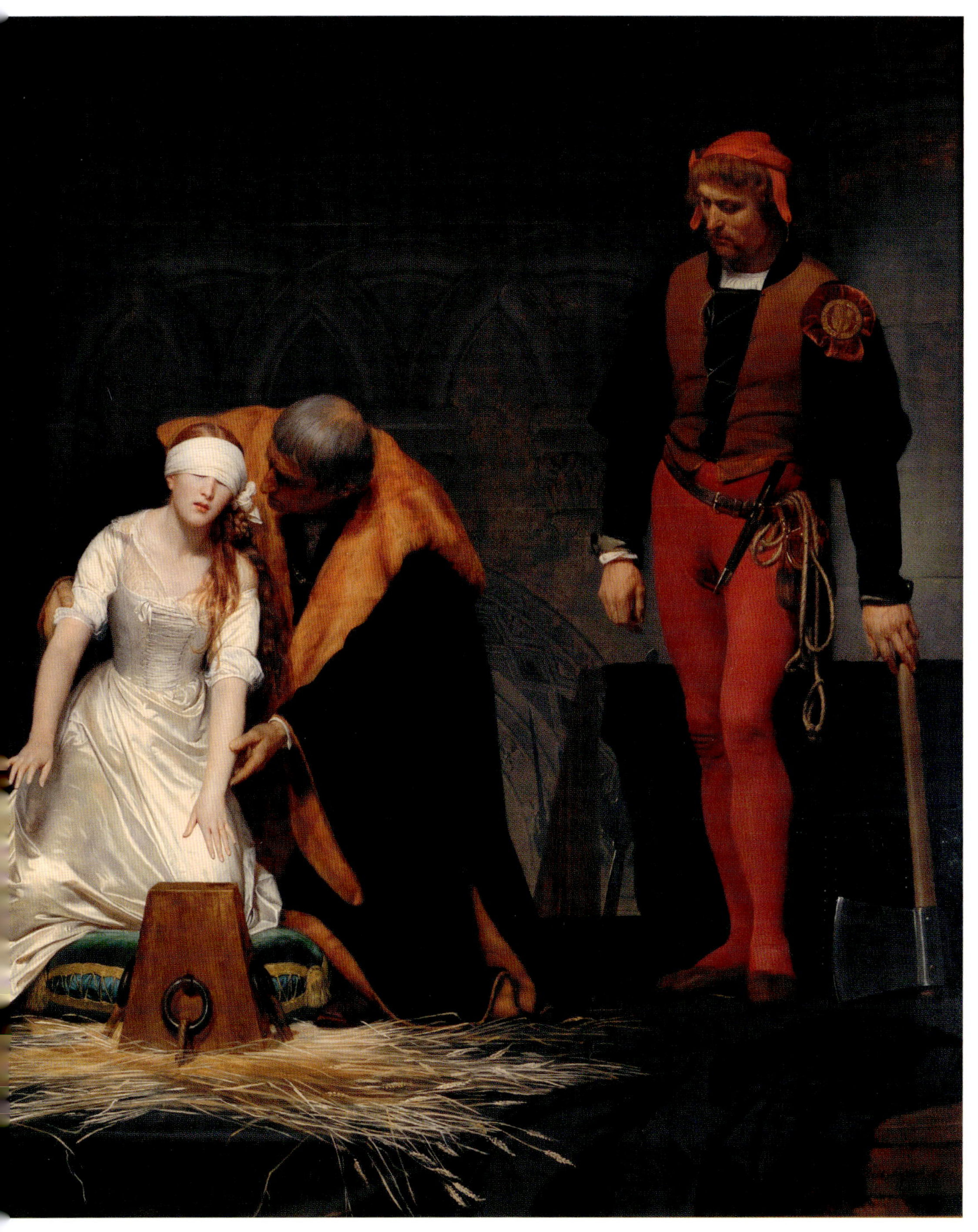

A Brief History of Portraiture

Developments in photographic technology over the years have pushed photographers both creatively and technically and continued to make image creation more accessible.

Key stages in the development of photographic techniques include the invention of the daguerreotype (1939), the Kodak Box Brownie (1900), Kodachrome film (1935), digital cameras (1990) and mobile phone cameras (2000). But it is the mobile phone that has been pivotal in making photography accessible to so many and, indeed, it's estimated over seven billion people now have access to a smartphone worldwide. Photography has gone from being a pastime of wealthy elites to a global mass media. Writing a history of photographic portraits in so few words is going to lead to some glaring omissions, but a key moment to note is the Farm Security Administration's (FSA) programme of photography, which was initiated as part of Roosevelt's New Deal and impacted our understanding of photography greatly (see page 130). There are other things to discover if you would like to find out more, but please be aware that, as with most histories, this is a complex subject with established narratives dominated by White American and European photographers.

When cameras were first invented in the 19th century, they required such lengthy exposure times that no one could possibly sit still long enough to have their portrait taken, which meant the photograph predated photographic portraits by some years. The earliest photograph thought to include people is one by Louis Daguerre, using his new method of fixing images (the daguerreotype), of the Boulevard du Temple in Paris from 1838 (see opposite). It appears to depict an empty street but, in fact, the traffic was moving too quickly for the camera's slow shutter speed. The only people who were standing still enough are the two figures in the bottom left of the frame – one of them is cleaning the other's shoes. Only a year later, in 1839, developments in photographic chemistry allowed people to

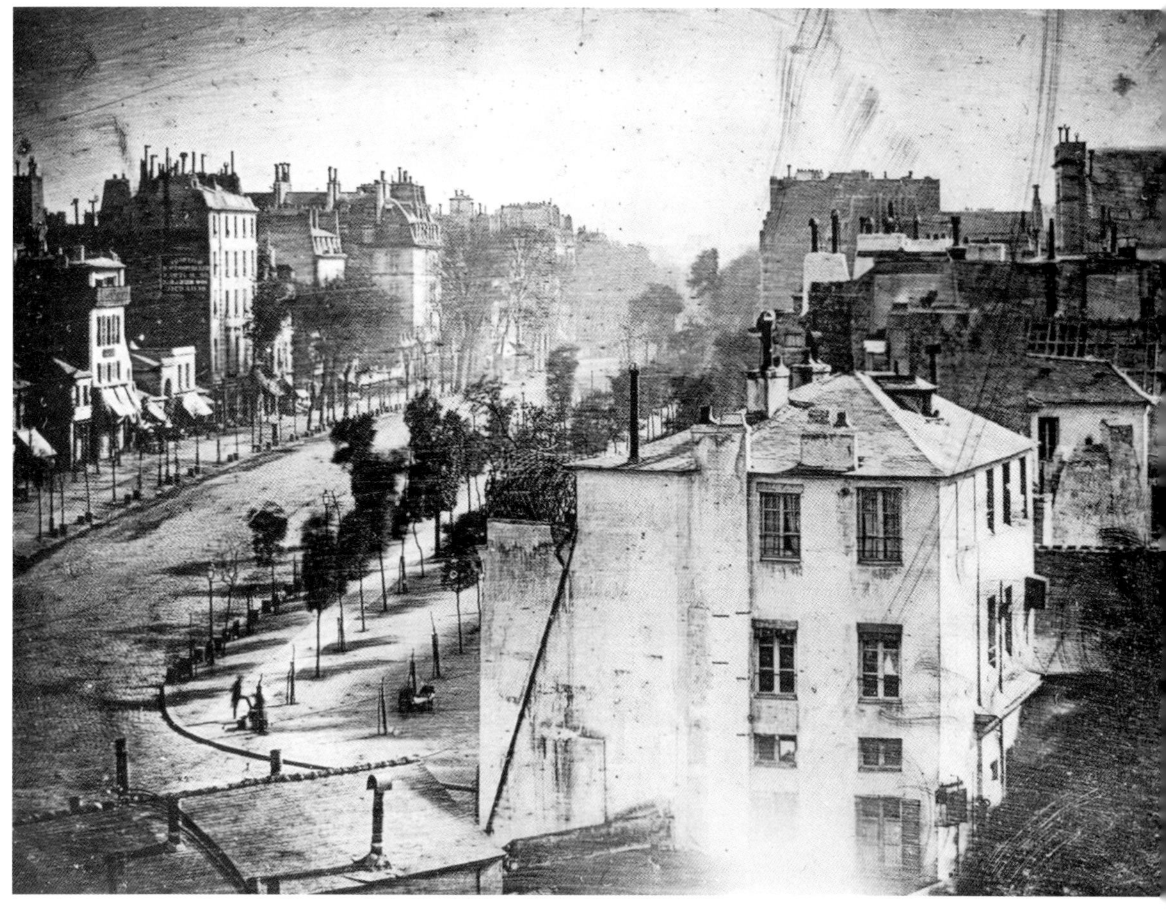

The 'Boulevard du Temple', made by Louis Daguerre in 1838. The two people at the bottom left of the frame (one is shining the other's shoes) are considered to be the first people ever photographed.

take portraits with their cameras. One of the earliest of these is a self-portrait by American photographer Robert Cornelius.

In the late 19th century, photographic portraits were extremely popular and visiting a photographic studio to have a portrait taken was all the rage. And this wasn't only the case in Europe. As early as 1870 the Chinese photographer Lai Afong opened a studio in Hong Kong where he presented some of the most important people of the day with *cartes de visite*, which were small, postcard-sized portrait prints first patented in Paris but soon popular around the world. For several decades this was the main form of portrait photography. In the United States during the American Civil War, *cartes de visite* were widely circulated. The abolitionist and former slave Sojourner Truth (1797–1883) sold *cartes de viste* featuring her portrait to raise funds for her work. The text above her name read: 'I Sell the Shadow to Support the Substance' (see page 46), which is a phrase that could be applied to many uses of photography. These photographic portraits have now become historical records of lives once lived.

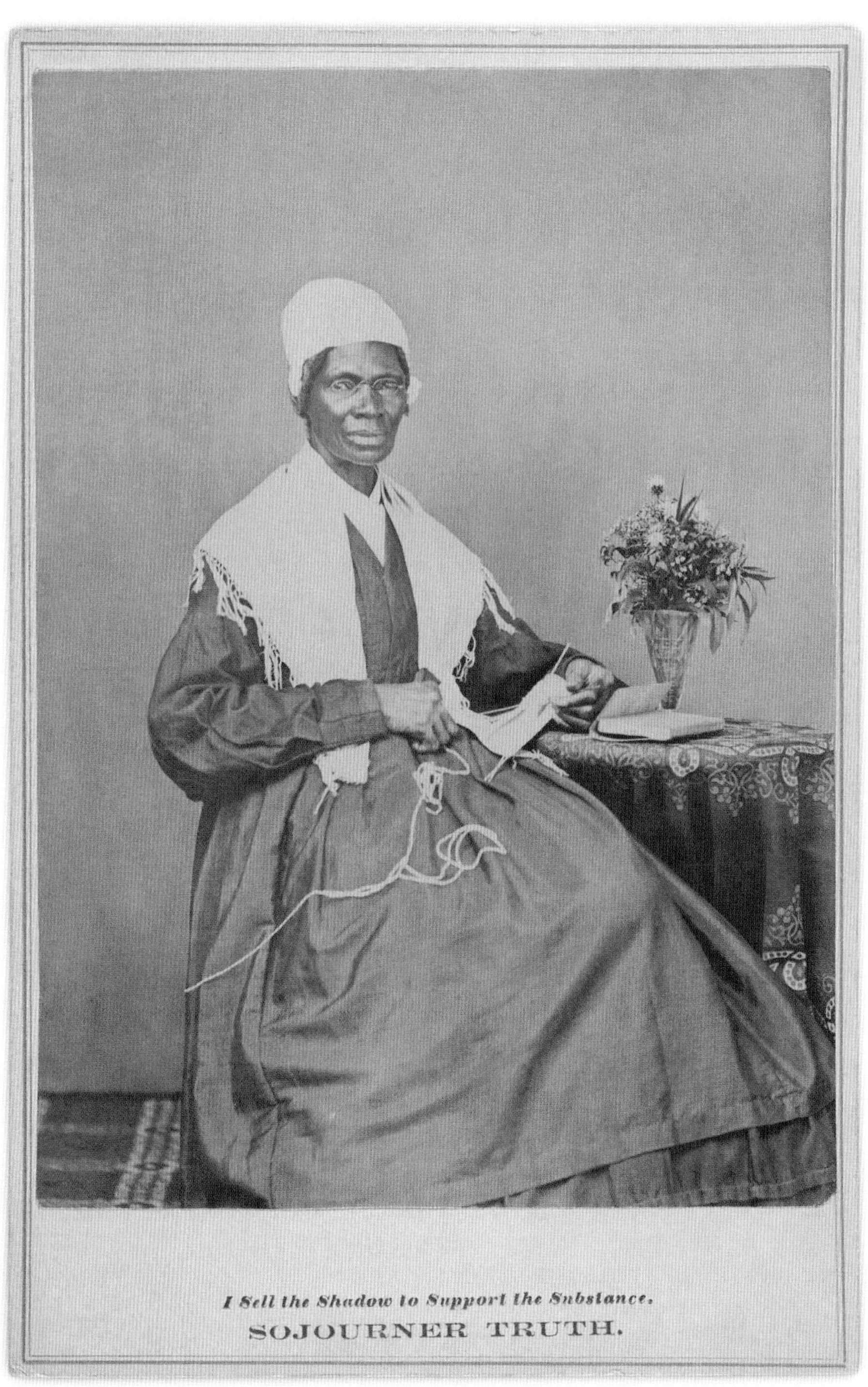
I Sell the Shadow to Support the Substance.
SOJOURNER TRUTH.

In the 1930s, *Life* magazine rebranded to become the first magazine to focus on photography. This marked a turning point in the history of photographic portraiture. Articles needed illustrating with photographs and for the first time portraits were being produced to accompany text in the pages of magazines. This is something that still happens today with editorial photography and forms a major part of the industry. An interview with someone famous, for example, needs a portrait of them to accompany the words. Throughout the following decades, magazines played a pivotal role in how we look at, think about and take portraits. As well as *Life*, other magazines that have influenced this development include *Time*, *Nova*, *Colors* and *The Face* and, more recently, newspaper weekend periodicals such as *M*, *Le Magazine du Monde*, *The New York Times Magazine* and the *FT Weekend Magazine*.

By the 1960s portrait photography had become fully integrated into global fashion, art and culture. Areas began to splinter away to create new styles of photography. West African studio photographers such as Malick Sibidé – who was born in 1936, the same year that *Life* magazine was relaunched – opened a photographic studio in Bamako, in Mali. Here, Sibidé spent decades photographing people, both in his studio and on the city's streets. Around the same time in Bobo-Dioulasso, Burkina Faso, the photographer Sanlé Sory set up his iconic Volta Photo Studio.

With the 1990s and the new millennium came a digital revolution in photography. Digital cameras, sensors and mobile phone cameras became increasingly technologically advanced. With this came Adobe's photo-editing program Photoshop, which allows people to edit, control and change the photographs they take. Photographs have always been faked, but at this time we began to see it happen on an industrial scale. Fashion images in magazines were retouched. Adverts were retouched. These shifts towards unattainable body shapes and lifestyles shifted the power of photographic portraits further towards creating desirable lifestyles and helped fuel capitalism.

From the beginning, photographing people has been used as a tool of power and surveillance. The practice spread around the world via European colonialists. For decades, people were photographed, categorized and dehumanized – with their images used to validate the racist and capitalist control exerted by the United Kingdom, Germany, France, Belgium, Portugal and other countries with predominantly white inhabitants. Photographs from the Belgian King Leopold II's brutal colonization of what is now known as the Democratic Republic of Congo are especially harrowing. They should be looked at with an understanding of what happened and what they represent. Conversely, photographic portraiture has also been used countless times as a tool of resistance – and emancipation. One of the most recognizable photographs of all time is Alberto Korda's portrait of the Marxist revolutionary Che Guevara (1928–1967), which has now become symbolic of anti-capitalism. From mugshots to passport photos, from selfies to surveillance cameras, the relationship between the photographic image and the subject is murky and complex. **MF**

Cian's Journey into Portraiture

Here I talk about my own work and what drew me to photography, along with a bit about my background and who my subjects are. How can you develop your own journey into portraiture?

I started studying photography when I was sixteen and was lucky to have an incredible teacher with a passion for photography who passed that same drive to make pictures on to me. At the time of writing this book, I am thirty years old, so I have been making pictures for a little over fourteen years and working professionally as a photographer for eight years. Initially, I was interested in street photography, but I quickly became fascinated with portraiture. I was drawn to the connections formed by making a portrait of someone and was interested in photography as a way of searching for commonalities between people. After a short period, this area became the focus of my photography.

Most of my personal projects look at communities in some shape or form. I am particularly interested in the link between the environment and the person, how our environments shape us and our relationships with each other. I often focus on marginalized communities – people that have been ignored by the establishment or misrepresented in popular culture – in an attempt to raise awareness and alter perceptions by offering a different perspective. I have made work about various subjects, some of which you can see throughout this book. They include redlining in New York, the Covid-19 pandemic in London (see the portrait on page 51 of a woman wearing a face shield), Black horsemen in Philadelphia (see the portrait of Ike on the opposite page or the portrait of Stevie and Ruffian on page 50), knife violence in London (see the portrait of Rajai, opposite), copycat architecture in China (see page 50) and urban dirt bikers in London, among many others.

The portrait of Rajai (opposite) is from a series I made about the epidemic of knife violence in London and the impact it's having on young people in the city. Being born in London and growing up there, I believe

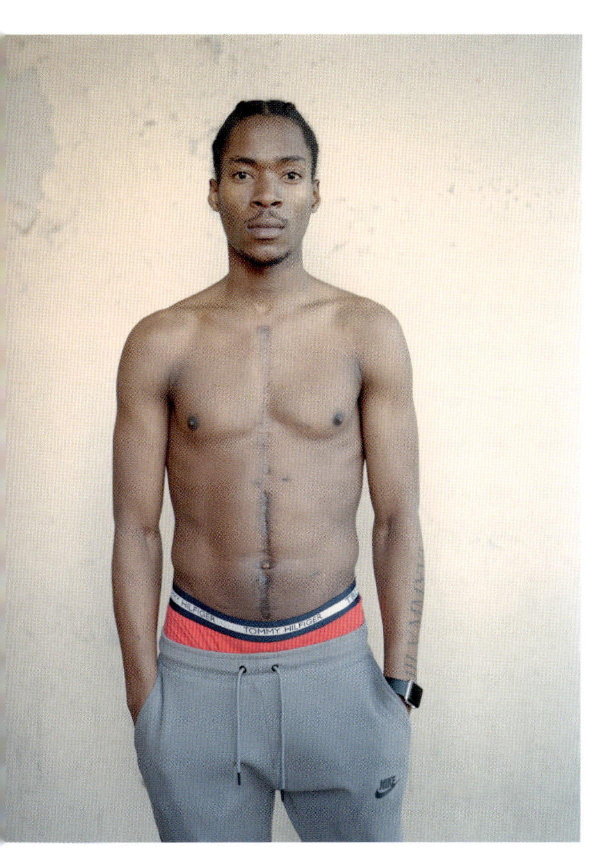

Cian Oba-Smith. Rajai, London, 2020.

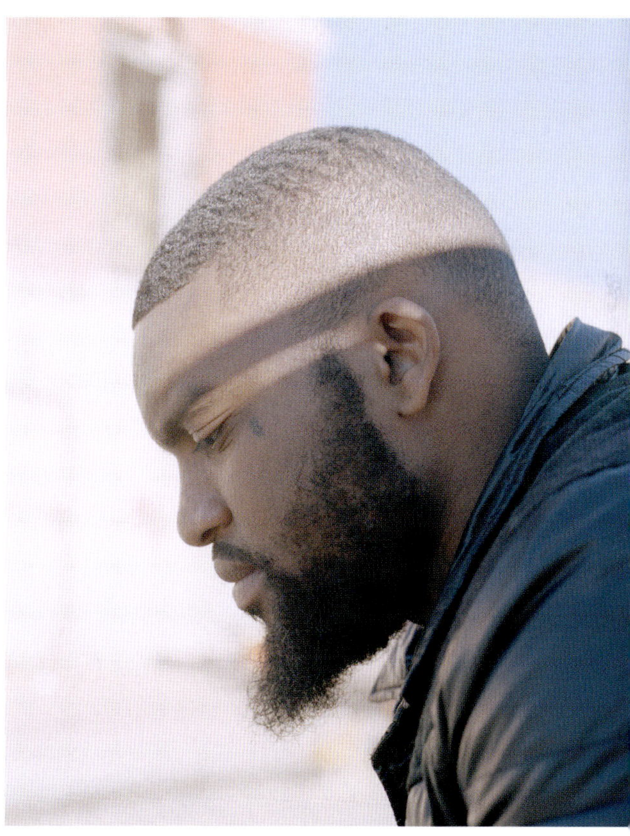

Cian Oba-Smith. Ike outside the stable, Philadelphia, USA. From the series 'Concrete Horsemen', 2016.

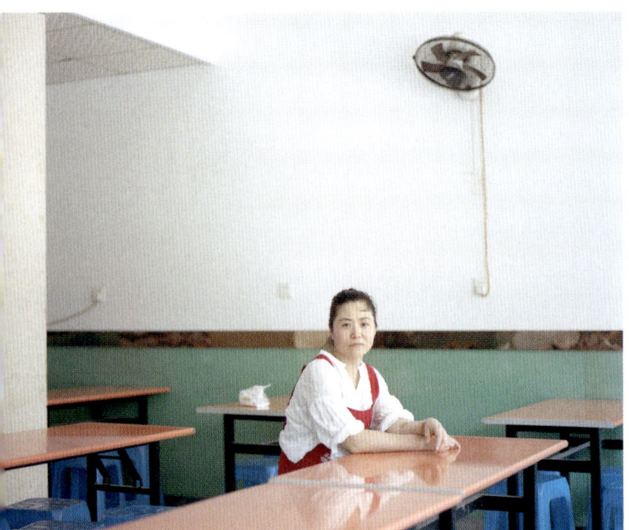

that knife violence is something all young people in the city must navigate. I had friends growing up who were stabbed, or stabbed other people, and had my own encounters with people using knives as a tool for intimidation. The narrative around knife violence is that it's gang violence or gang related, but the reality is that it affects young people in London everywhere. This misconception is what motivated me to make the project.

Rajai's portrait was made on my Toyo 45AII large-format camera. I wanted to show the physical damage as well as the mental scars that going through the trauma of knife violence leave on a person. I feel that Rajai's eyes reveal the story of the mental pain he has experienced, while his body shows the physical scars. Rajai was stabbed multiple times in 2016 and survived after having open heart surgery – if the knife had been an inch closer to his heart, he would have died. **COS**

Conclusion

My approach to photography has been shaped by my life experiences and perspective on the world. What stories do you feel you are able to tell through your own personal experiences? Try to approach photography from a place of passion and understanding. If you connect with the work you're making, there will always be people out there who connect with it too.

▶ Cian Oba-Smith. A woman poses for a portrait in London during the first Covid lockdown. From the series 'A Quiet Prayer', 2020.

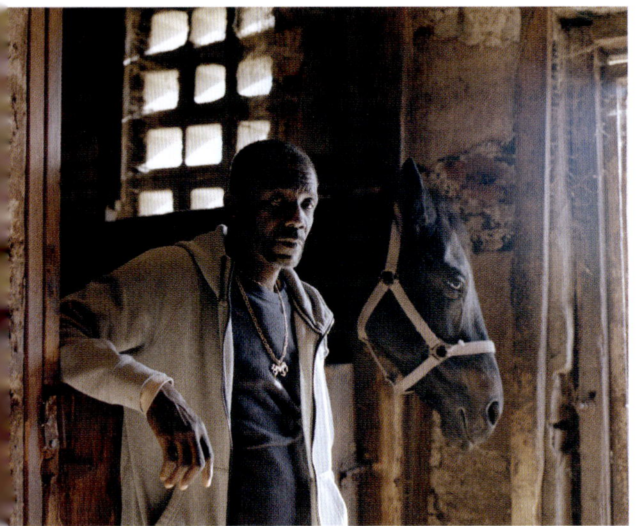

▲ Cian Oba-Smith. Stevie and Ruffian, Philadelphia, USA. From the series 'Concrete Horsemen', 2016.

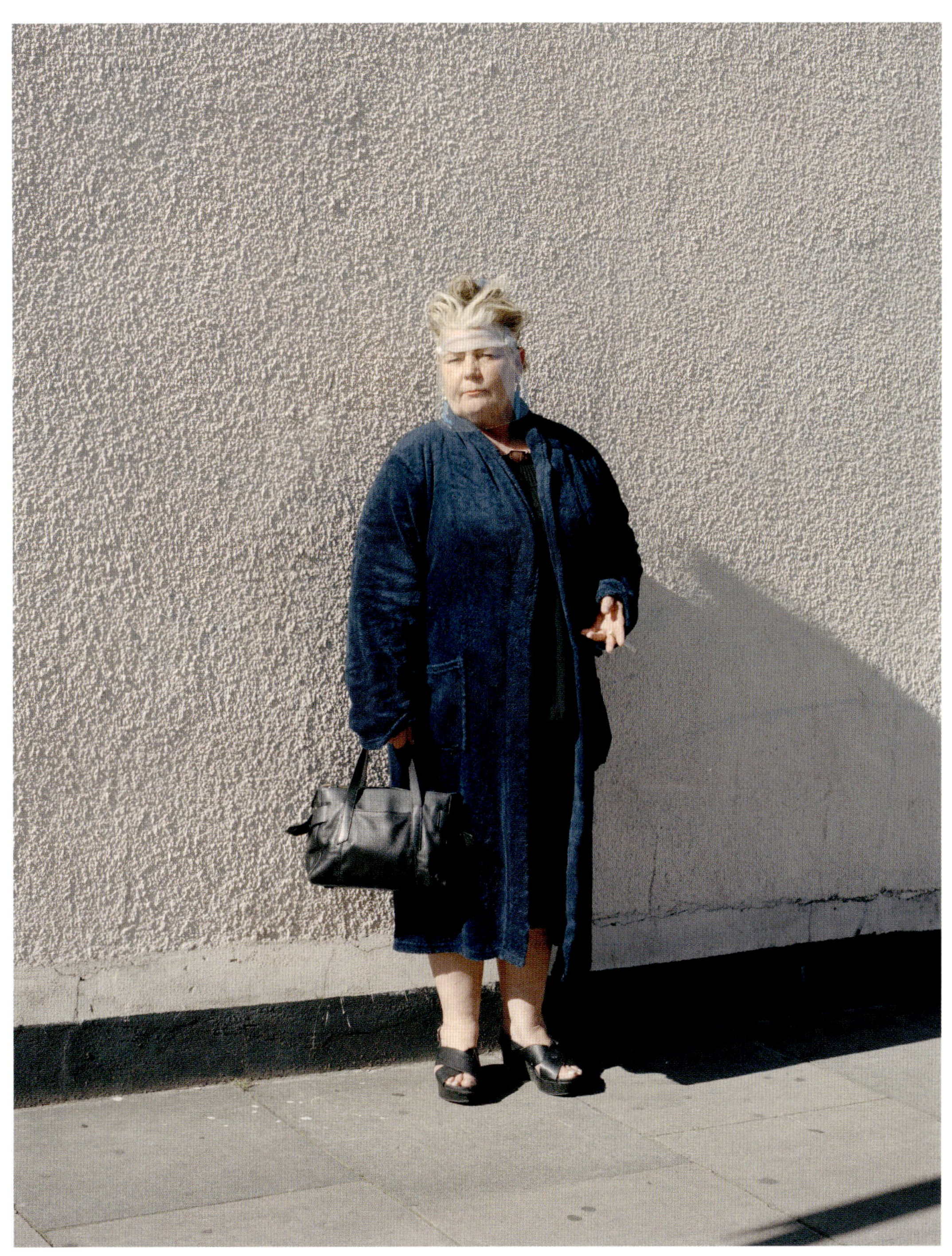

PROJECT 02

Taking Better Portraits

What makes a good portrait? Well, portraiture – and photography in general – is a subjective art form, so this is a difficult question to answer.

To make this question easier to answer, perhaps we should analyze what we normally focus on when reading an image, then from there we may be able to work out the various elements that go into what is typically considered a 'good' portrait. The aim is always to make better portraits and to improve our abilities as a portrait photographer. There are no good or bad portraits, but there are portraits that do not reflect what we set out to create initially.

To pinpoint what makes a good portrait, we need to look at how it is structured or put together. For instance, when creating the portraits featured here of Kaheem from my 'Concrete Horsemen' series (opposite) and Thugrida from my 'Bikelife' series (see page 54), I used the same structured approach. Everyone will have their own views on the different elements that make up a portrait, but I believe it is composed by taking into account the subject, environment, lighting, composition, technical aspects such as exposure, and emotion. Let's look at each of these in turn.

Although all aspects of constructing a portrait are important, your starting point is always the subject matter. This could be something very simple, such as a portrait of your friend hanging out in the park, or it could be something more removed and complex like travelling to another country to document a subculture that is unknown to most people. Regardless of where your subject fits on this spectrum, the first stage of making a portrait is deciding what and who to photograph.

In my opinion, the next stage of the portrait-making process is the environment in which you put your subject. This could be somewhere on location or perhaps a studio environment. Either way, the environment in which you place the subject has a huge impact on how your portrait will be perceived by the viewer. The environment will be dictated to a certain extent by where you're making the work, but there will still be a degree of choice in terms of where you position the subject.

Lighting is an element that is often tied to the environment in which you're photographing, particularly if you're working with natural light. You will sometimes

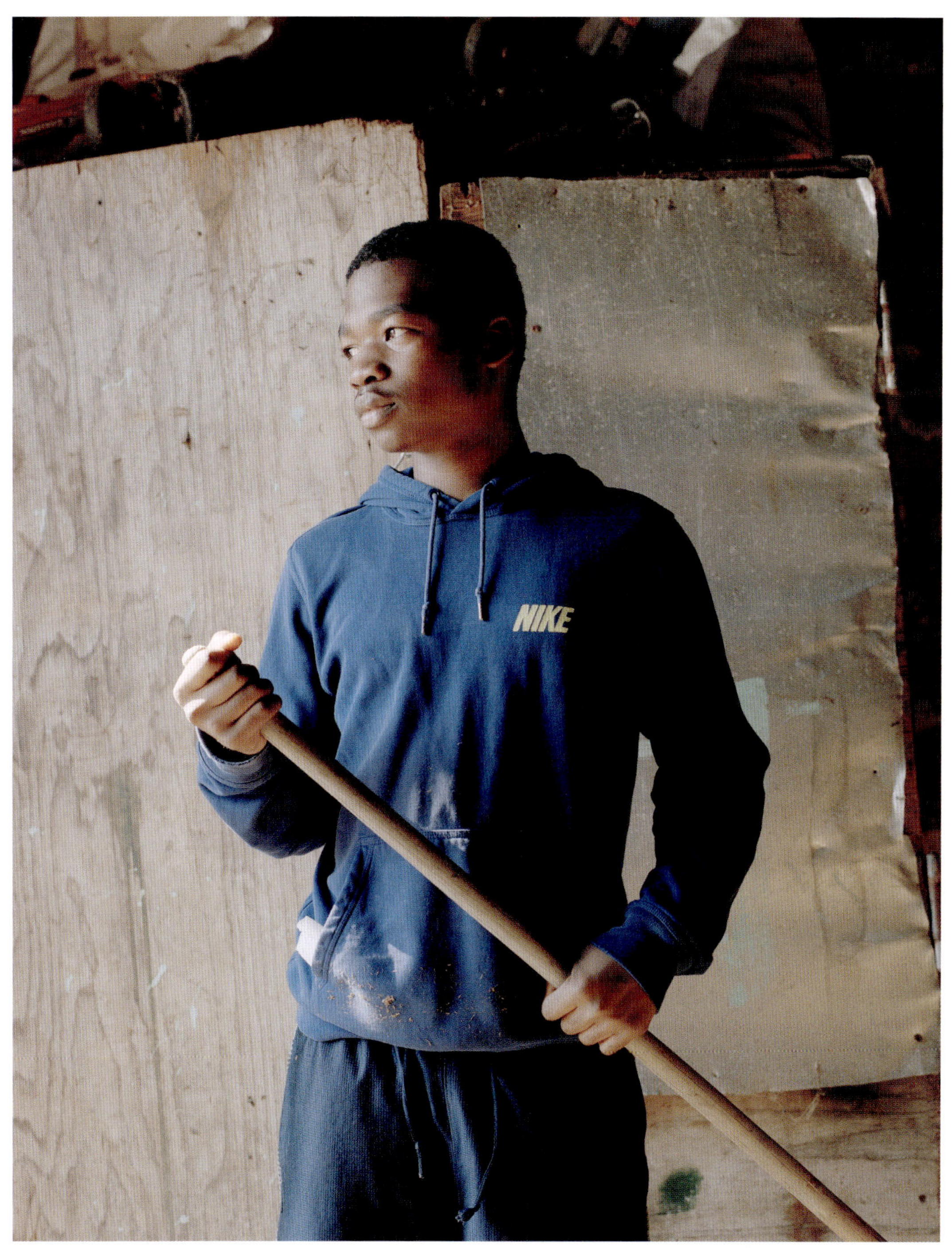

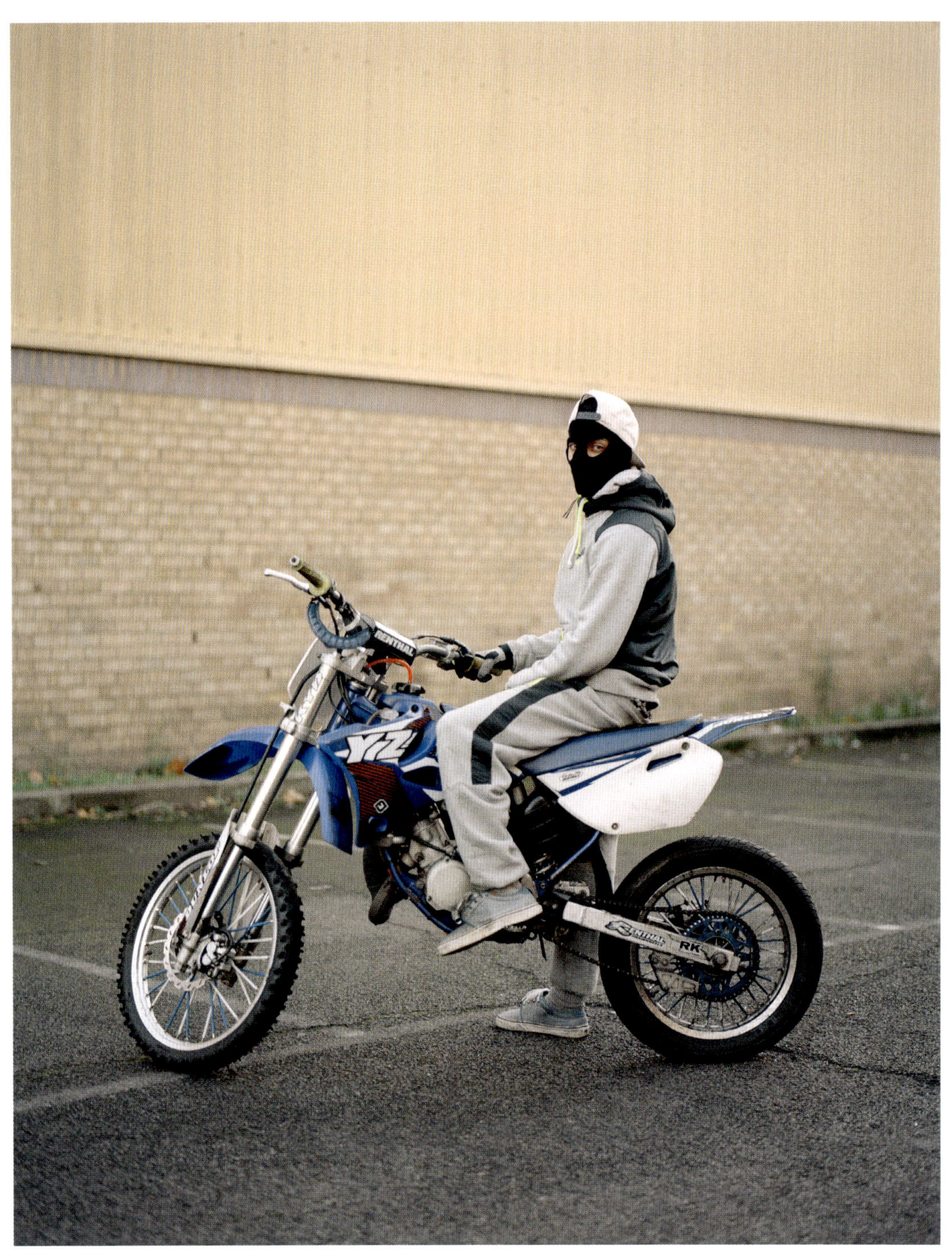

be severely restricted if you're working indoors, which will force you to place your subject in the only area where there is a good light source. Good lighting is one of the best ways to take a portrait from average to interesting.

Once your subject has been placed in the environment you have chosen and you have decided on how you would like to light the portrait, then you will most likely move on to composing your image. What you choose to exclude from the frame is just as important as what you choose to include – this will all have an impact on how your image is read. Be conscious of how much of the person you want to reveal in the frame, as well as what you would like to include in the background.

The final step before you take the picture is to look at the technical aspects. This is the area that most people think carefully about when they're taking a picture. For example, you may want to consider what shutter speed and aperture to set on your camera and how these will affect the image. A slow shutter speed, for example, will create more motion within the image, which is not usually something that a portrait photographer wants, although it does have its uses on certain occasions. The aperture will affect the depth of field, with a wide aperture such as f/2.8 creating a shallow depth of field and more blur behind the subject. In contrast, a small aperture such as f/16 will create a larger depth of field and more of the subject – as well as what is behind the subject – will be in focus.

You are now ready to take the photograph. I see this as the stage when the element of emotion becomes important – this is key when you are taking the picture. At this point, you are capturing the feeling that the subject or subjects are conveying, but also the emotion involved in taking the picture, the gut instinct of when to click the shutter.

Now we have looked at the different elements that make up a portrait, let's turn our attention to where our portraits can be lacking. One way to do this is to examine a collection of portraits that you have made previously. Analyze the images, look at which of the elements you seem to struggle with the most, and then focus on improving in those areas. Much of this will come from experimentation; working out what you find visually appealing and focusing on subjects that you find interesting. Break the rules and establish what you think makes a 'good' portrait, engage in a critical discourse around your images, and you will naturally learn to take better portraits. Although it may sound obvious, making portraits is the key to getting better at portrait photography. As the French photographer Henri Cartier-Bresson (1908–2004) famously said: 'Your first 10,000 photographs are your worst' – and this quote still holds true today. **COS**

Conclusion

As is the case with all types of photography, intentionality is the key to improving how you make portraits. Be conscious of how you are approaching making your portrait in the moment, thinking carefully about the subject matter, environment, lighting, composition, technical aspects and emotion being conveyed. Remember to be self-reflective afterwards, to analyze your pictures and to look for areas of improvement. Above all, try to learn from your mistakes.

Selecting an Image

Selecting your best pictures takes practice. But how do photographers choose which shots to keep?

When we look at a project (or an image) that a photographer has made, we normally only see the final result. But for many photographers there are numerous 'outtakes' that don't make the cut. Selecting the best of the bunch can be one of the hardest parts of making portraits. What makes a good image? And what makes a bad one? Why choose one image over another? The process of the edit (this is what the final selection of photos is called) is a highly personal one for many photographers and has a big impact on how a final project or individual image will be perceived.

Every photographer works in a different way. Some take a minimal number of pictures of one subject. William Eggleston, for example, is known for only taking one picture of anything! Other photographers may take dozens. Personally, I tend to take a minimal number of pictures of each subject – at most, I'll normally shoot one roll of film which, on my medium-format Mamiya RZ67, equates to ten pictures. If I'm working with large-format photography, I'll shoot around two to three sheets at most. This is partly because I make a lot of documentary portraiture and if I'm taking pictures of people who I don't know on the street, it is unfair to ask them to take too much time out of their day. I also think that the portrait I'm looking for normally comes quite quickly and taking lots of images isn't really necessary.

Traditionally, when selecting images, a photographer will work from a contact sheet (a darkroom print of the roll of film). This allows the photographer to see the images alongside each other, so they can make the best possible selection from the photographs they've taken. Regardless of whether you're using film or digital to create your portraits, it is useful to make a habit of this technique.

On the following pages, I've included a contact sheet of a number of portraits that I made with Kareem in Philadelphia, in the United States, for my 2016 project 'Concrete Horsemen'. **COS**

▶ Cian Oba-Smith. Kareem, Philadelphia, USA. From the series 'Concrete Horsemen', 2016.

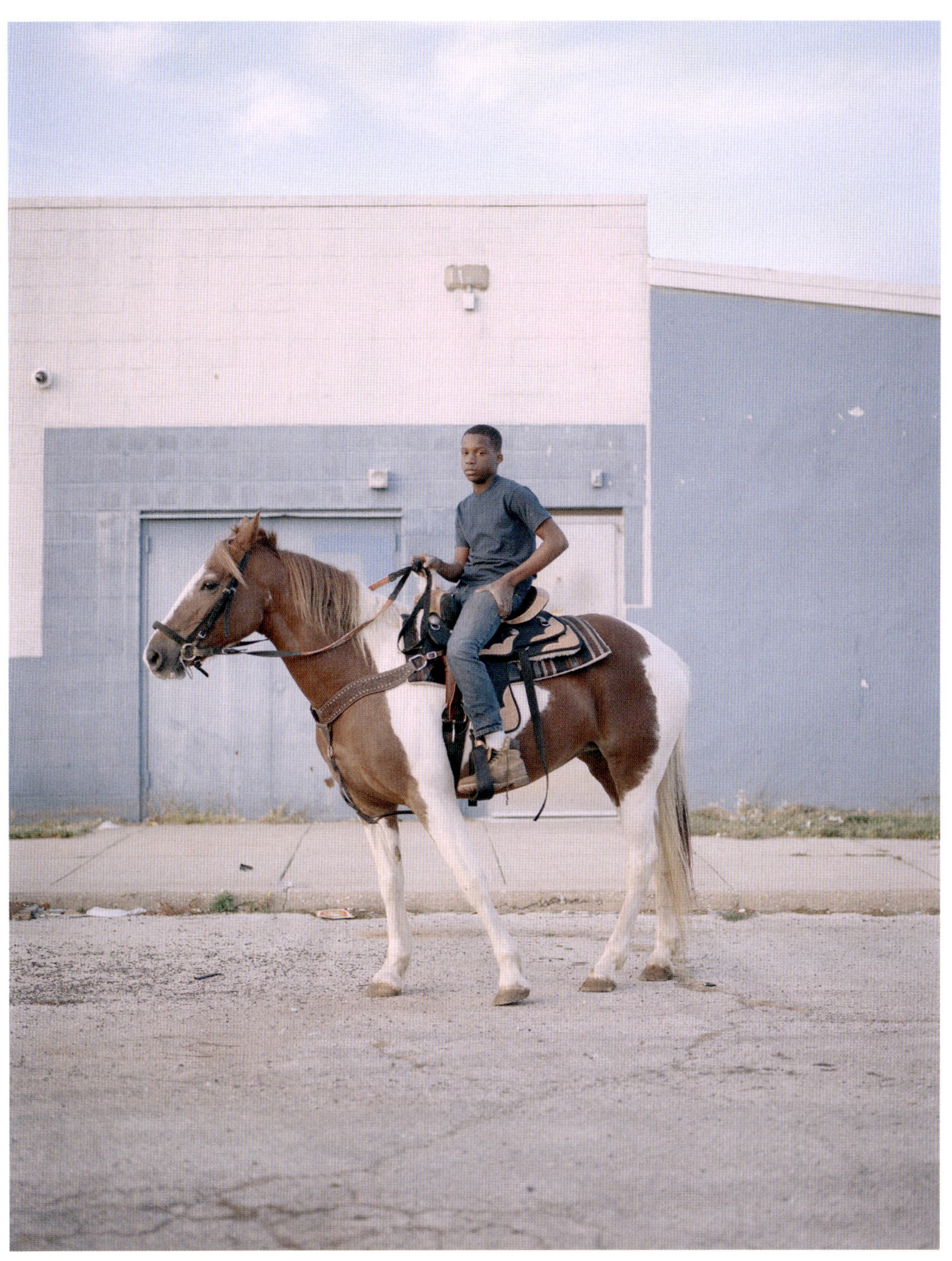

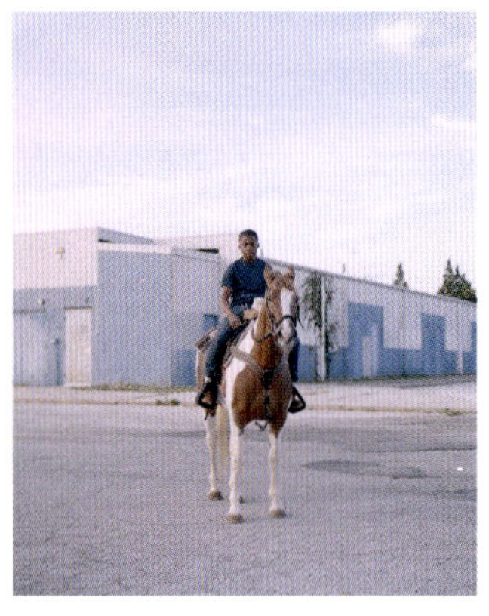 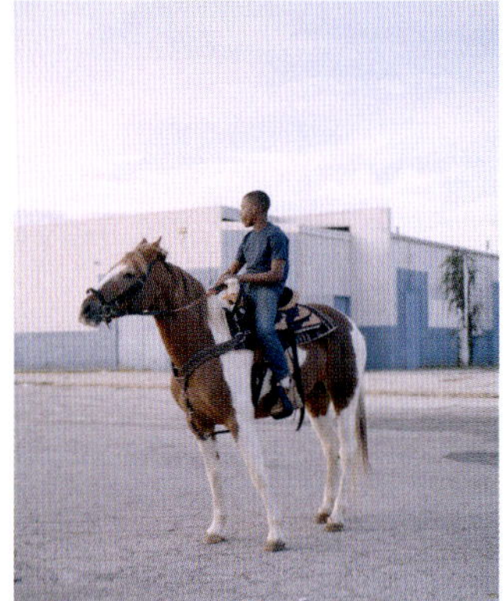 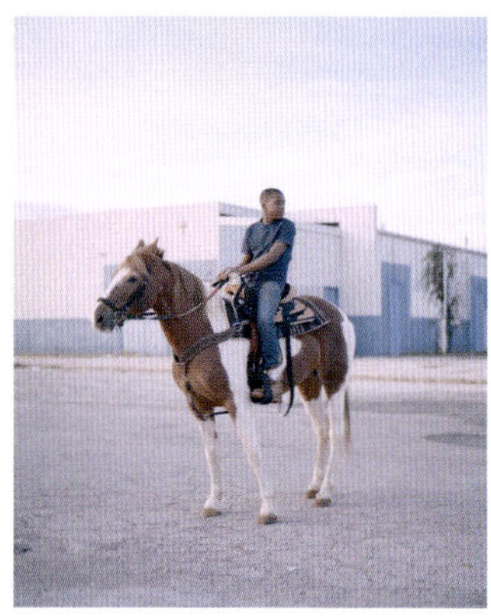

1

This was the weakest image of the group for me. It was the first picture I took of Kareem and, as a result, his facial expression felt performative. There's also too much empty space around Kareem and the horse, which creates a lack of separation between them and gives the impression that the focal point of the portrait is condensed into too small an area of the frame. I also felt that the trees in the right-hand side of the image would distract the viewer's focus from where I wanted it to be drawn to.

2

There were parts of this image I liked, but overall I felt that others in the set were stronger. For example, I preferred the framing in this image to the first one. I moved to the right of Kareem to take this photograph, which removed the distracting treetops from the frame. This also created converging lines from each side of the building, which draws the viewer's eye towards Kareem. In one sense, I liked the fact that Kareem is looking out of the frame, as it makes the viewer question what they are looking at, but in the end I felt that the images in which he is looking into the lens were more engaging.

3

This was the image that I ended up selecting. I chose it for a number of reasons. I preferred the lighting; it's hitting Kareem's face at just the right angle, highlighting the left-hand side and separating him from the background. The background behind Kareem complements the colour of his clothing and isn't distracting in the way it is in some of the other images. To me, his posture feels natural and exhibits strength, which communicates the feeling I was trying convey with this series of images. The angle of Kareem and the horse does a better job of filling the frame here too and highlights the patches on the horse, which mimic the block colours of the background.

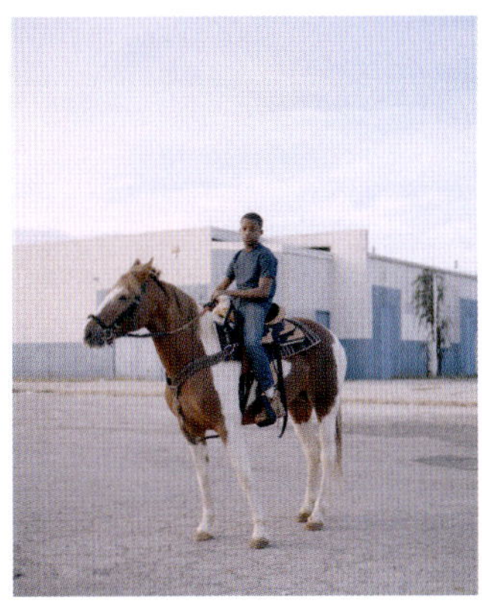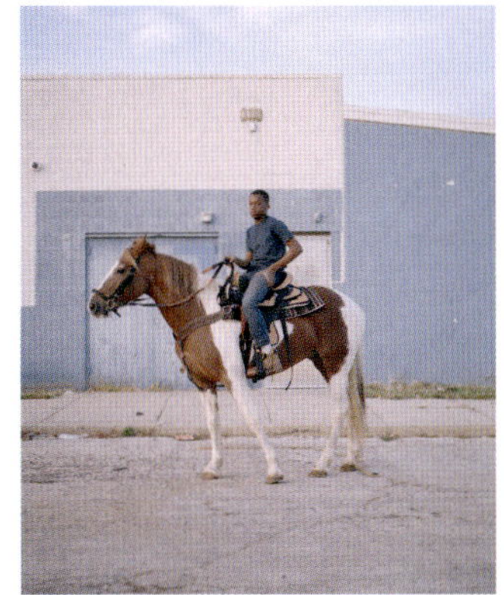

4

Similarly to image 2, I preferred the framing in this image to that of image 1 – there are fewer distractions in the background. However, I felt that Kareem looking out of the frame was distracting and this posture also didn't communicate the strength I was trying to convey with the image. It also feels too candid to me and wasn't in line with the formal nature of the portrait I was trying to make of him.

5

I really struggled to decide between this image and image 3. Of the portraits made at a greater distance from the background, this was the strongest. Like images 2 and 4, the framing is better than in image 1 and there's less in the background to distract from Kareem. This is helpful in making him the focal point. I like the way he's looking straight into the camera, as this helps to draw the viewer in and gives the image a more intense atmosphere. One of the reasons I decided to choose image 3 was because in the image above, the converging lines of the building behind Kareem cut through his head and I found this slightly distracting.

Conclusion

The key to selecting your images is first to work out what you're trying to say with them. What do you want to communicate with the work you're making? How will people read the image and how will the person in the image be perceived? Once you've decided on the message you're trying to send, then look at the visual language. Edit out any images that are technically poor or don't have the atmosphere you want to create. From there, you should be left with a small selection of portraits. Feel the images, always listen to your intuition and go with your gut instinct.

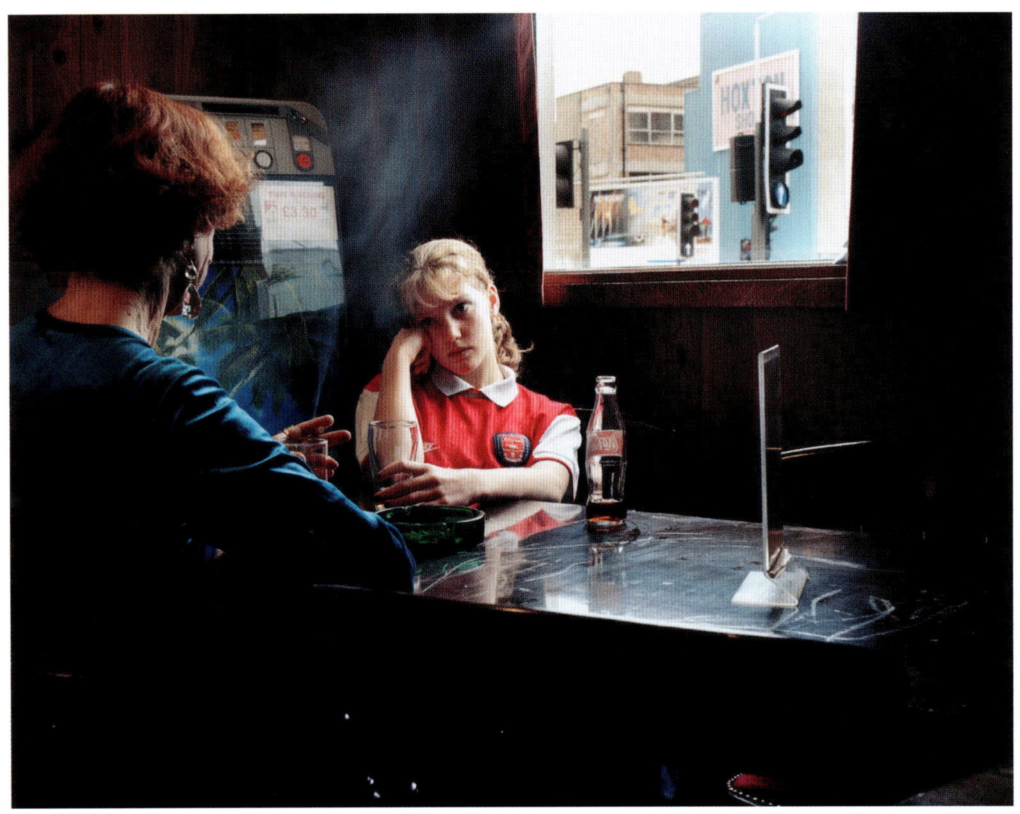

Hannah Starkey

born 1971, Belfast, Northern Ireland.
hannahstarkey.com

Hannah Starkey was one of the first photographers who made me question what I thought I knew. I can remember seeing this image of a young girl leaning back in her chair, drinking a Coke, in an Arsenal football shirt. The woman opposite, who we can't see fully, appears to be older. Perhaps she is the girl's mother. What are the two of them talking about? Small details such as the cigarette the older woman is holding in the same hand as her drink, her earrings and haircut give us some clues, but in truth almost all interpretation of the photograph is left to the viewer. A cigarette vending machine on the left dates the image wonderfully, in a way that perhaps the artist could not have foreseen when she made it in 1998.

The title of the photograph 'Untitled – October 1998' gives nothing away and when Starkey makes

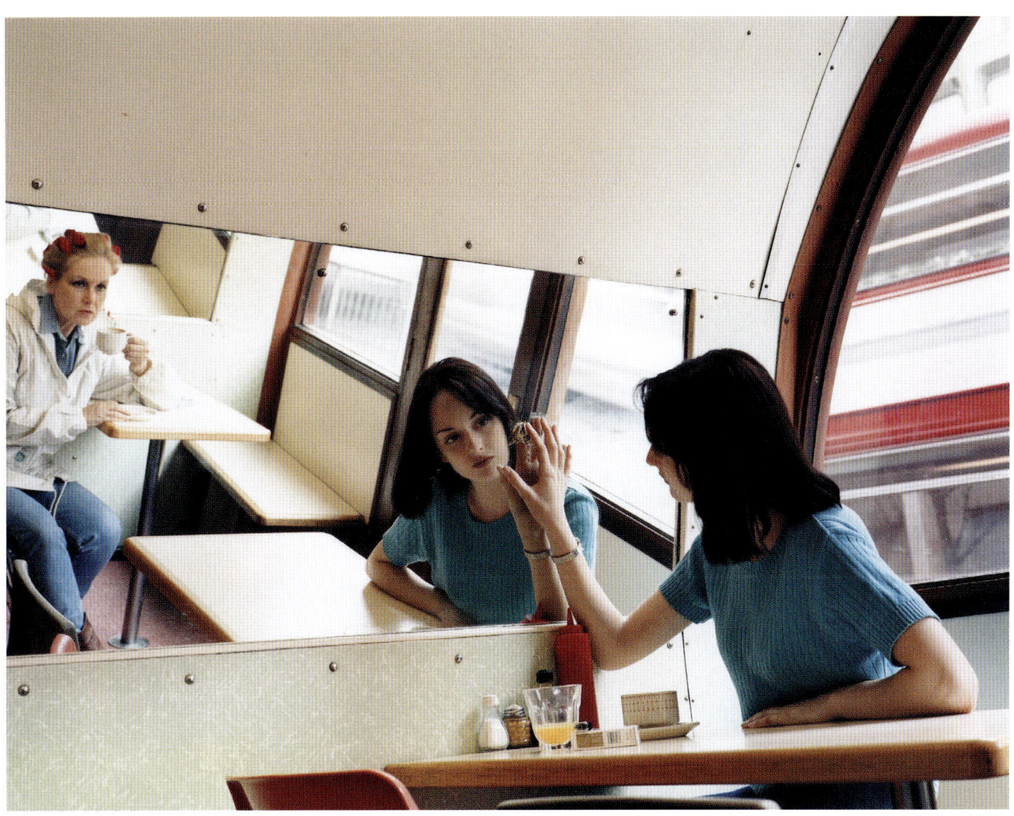

prints of the image, they are big – over a metre wide and a metre tall. There are details to be seen and clues to be deciphered. What I love most about Starkey's photographs are the moods she manages to create. The image set in a pub makes the viewer feel as if they are looking at real life. But we are not. Instead, it is a photograph created by the artist from fiction. In her photography, Starkey builds images around the subjects, using locations in London, as well as lighting and props, to create the staged scenes.

Looking at this image, and several other of Starkey's photographs, you begin to see that she likes to use public interiors as key backdrops in her work. Whereas the first image uses a pub as the setting, the second one is inside a café. There is a pack of cigarettes on the table and half an orange juice. Formica panels bolted to the wall curve away, suggesting we are in an archway – perhaps under one of London's many railway lines. Outside, the blur of a bus blocks our view. Again, we see an interaction between two women, but this time we are viewing it in the long glass mirror. The perspective in the image is a little unsettling. One woman is touching the mirror with her hand, while on the left another woman is watching her – as are we. Does she perhaps represent us, the viewer? This photograph reminds me of Edouard Manet's famous painting *The Bar at the Folies-Bergère*, showing a woman behind a bar at the famous Parisian cabaret music hall. She is reflected in the mirror behind her, while a man in a top hat (who may represent the person looking at the painting) gazes at her. We watch him watching her and are complicit in his gaze. **MF**

Bryan Schutmaat

born 1983, Texas, USA.
bryanschutmaat.co

Bryan Schutmaat usually works slowly on his bodies of work. Some can take several years to complete and he likes to shoot with a large-format analogue camera that further decelerates image making. But this work – the book *Good Goddamn* (2017) – was shot over a few days. It documents the last few days of Kris's life, who is pictured here, before he begins a prison sentence. That information is essential to understanding these haunting and melancholy photographs. It sets the scene for the viewer.

The picture shows Kris lying in some long grass. We're looking down on him. His right hand is holding a can of Coors beer and his left arm is draped across his face – whether in despair or ecstasy, it's hard to tell. The composition is interesting because when we look down on a subject we feel as if we are standing over them – that we are present in the scene, but here he's covering his face. Maybe it's us that's intruding on Kris's last days of freedom. Schutmaat, who is better known for his straight-on portraits – both in colour and black and white – often utilizes a slightly unsettling composition. Sometimes images are blurred, or cropped tightly, as is the case here.

In the photographs featured in this book, which can also be viewed on Schutmaat's website, you can see that the layouts he chooses are simple, clean and classic. Photographs are the same size and always appear alone on a page, either facing a white page or another single image. Each image is as valuable as another. Schutmaat's projects are usually presented as photobooks, which he publishes under his own imprint Trespasser Books. This design approach has become a trademark look for their publications, which have a large format, but do not contain many pages. As well as his own books, which have become cult objects for photobook collectors, Schutmaat also publishes alongside other photographers, enjoying recent collaborations with Donavon Smallwood and Mark Mahaney.

In his most recent body of work, Schutmaat has been picking up and photographing hitchhikers and, in turn, aiding and documenting the transient people passing through the state of Texas, USA, where he lives. **MF**

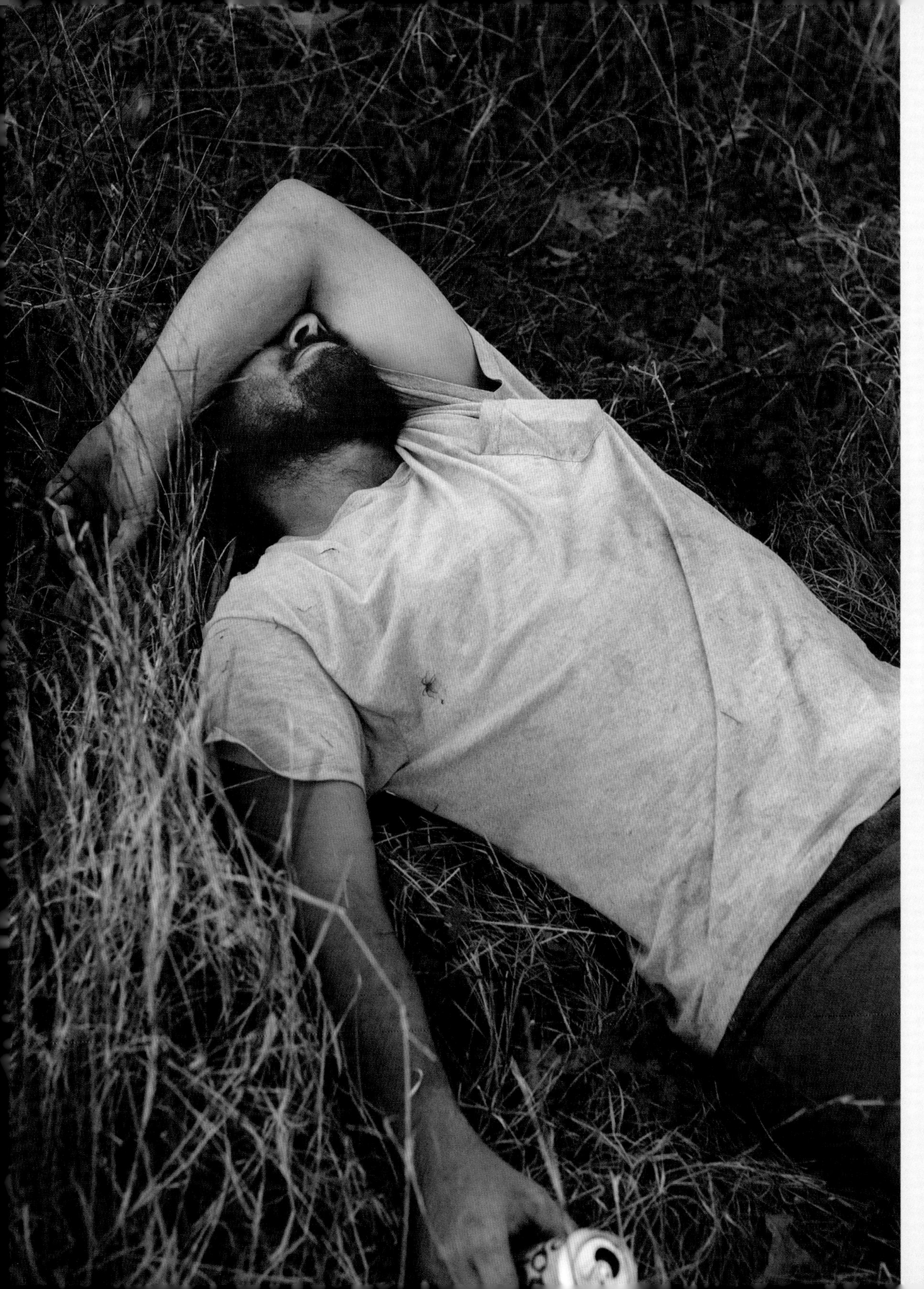

Photography and Social Media

By social media, in this instance, we mean Instagram. Among the major companies, this platform is most widely and easily used by photographers.

Have a look at the photographers featured in the book and see how they use Instagram to share their photographs. Cian's Instagram page is a good place to start – he mixes personal work with magazine commissions (editorial) and advertising work (commercial). Tom Johnson, a successful fashion photographer, uses Instagram in a similar way, although his posts naturally lean towards shoots for fashion magazines. Tom also posts BTS (behind the scenes) content on his stories. Very few of the featured photographers use Instagram to post photographs of their personal lives, but if they do, they usually put them on their stories. If you enjoy posting about your personal life on social media, consider having two profiles – one professional and one personal.

There is also a dedicated community of photographers on Twitter and a new generation of photographers using TikTok to build their careers. Twitter is an interesting platform for discussions around photography, while TikTok allows practitioners to show how they work behind the scenes. Many of the tips and thoughts given here for Instagram are transferable to other platforms such as these. So, whether you're looking to join a community of like-minded photographers, get your first paid commission or simply be inspired, there are some tips to help you navigate the murky world of likes and engagement. One simple approach is to think of your Instagram account as a rotating portfolio, which allows people to see your work. Keeping the number of posts under control using the 'archive' feature is a good idea and you should also make sure your profile looks slick when people find it for the first time. It's a harsh fact, but people may only spend a few seconds looking at your profile before deciding whether to follow you.

While you want your photographs to look great on the app, shooting work just because you think it will look good on Instagram is probably not a great idea. Instead, create the work you love and find a way to make the format work for you. It's about selecting the right photograph, rather than shooting for the algorithm. This can be tricky as your 'best' photograph might not necessarily get the most engagement. If you consider the speed at which you scroll through your own feed, you'll understand how long people will spend considering your photographs. It could be less than a second. Capturing someone's attention is the challenge. Picking images that are of something specific and more focused – such as a portrait of one

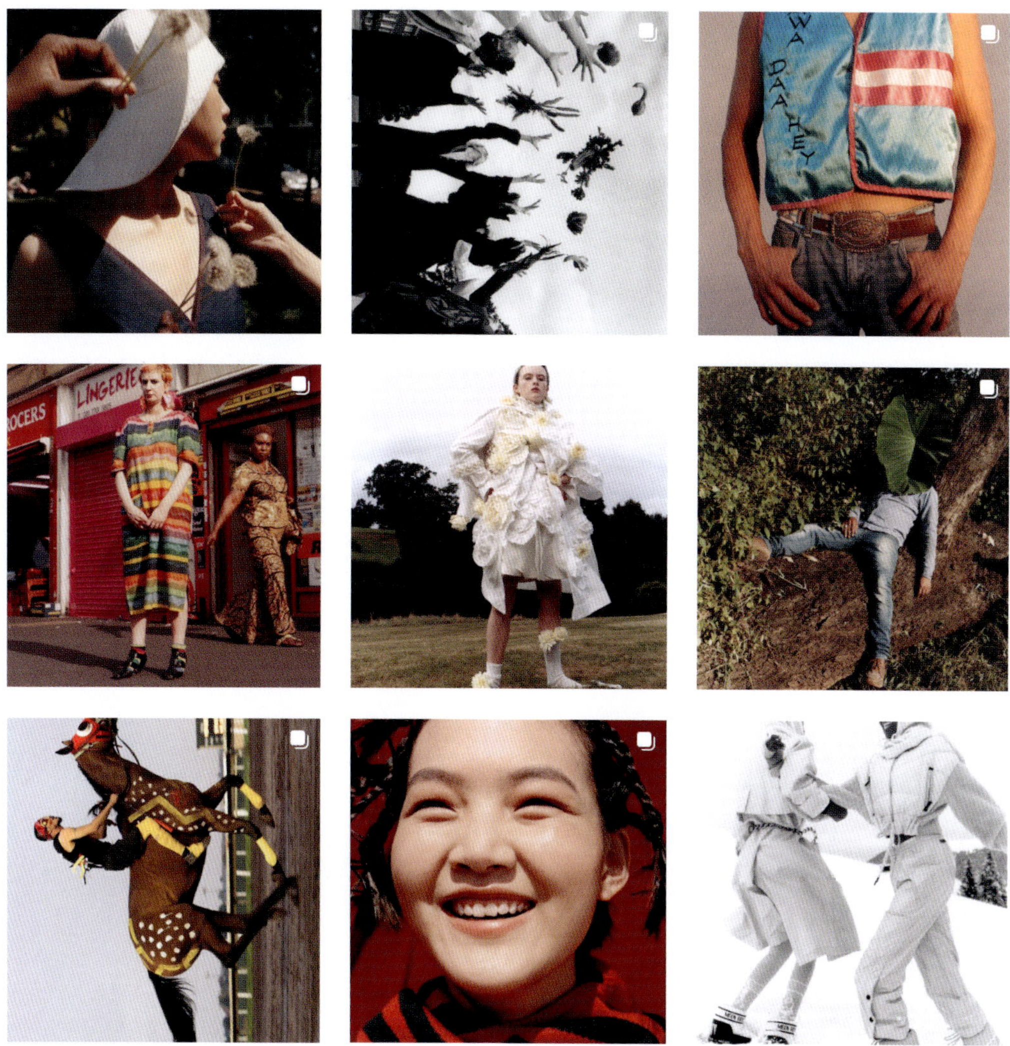

person rather than a crowd of people – usually gets more engagement.

Like everything, planning will make your posts more effective. Decide what you want from your social media and work backwards from there. Do you want to meet new people or get your work seen by people in the photographic industry? Maybe you just enjoy sharing your photographs. You need to post regularly but not all the time – once or twice a week is a good

Images from Tom Johnson's (see page 100) Instagram account. Notice how he posts close crops of portraits and rotates landscape photographs by ninety degrees.

starting point. Spend some time planning posts for the first few weeks, thinking about what they will look like when viewed in peoples' feeds and in a grid on your page. Remember that if you post a portrait or landscape image, it will be cropped to a square when

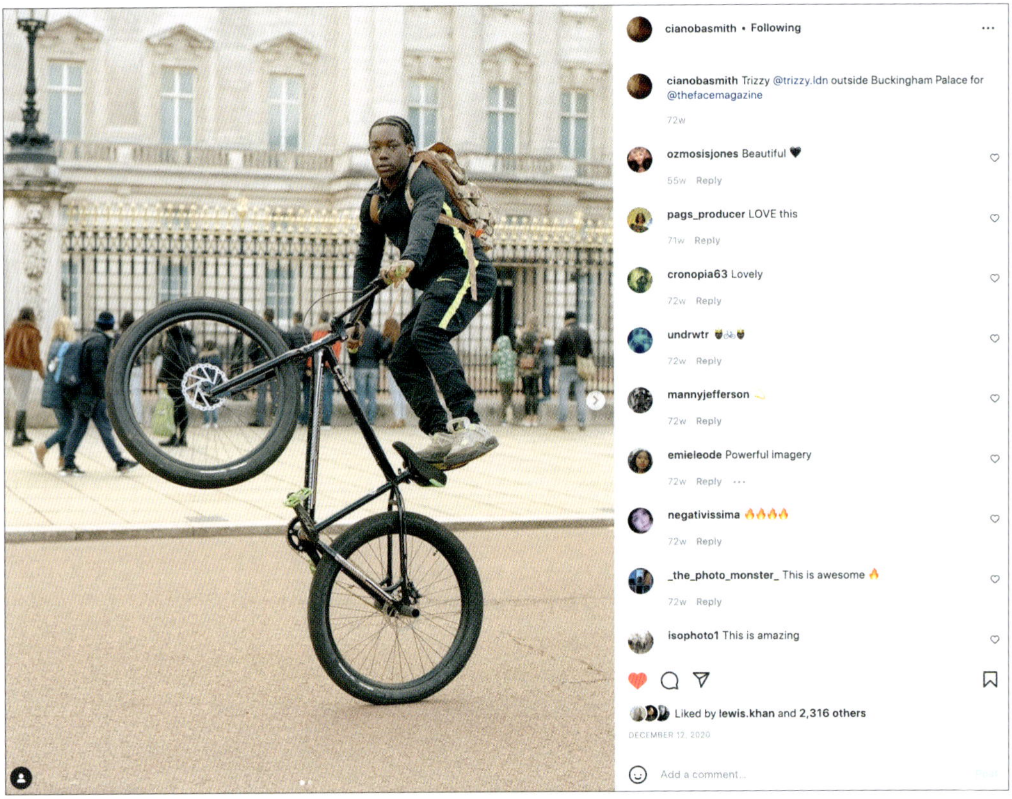

cianobasmith • Following

cianobasmith Trizzy @trizzy.ldn outside Buckingham Palace for @thefacemagazine

72w

ozmosisjones Beautiful 🖤
55w Reply

pags_producer LOVE this
71w Reply

cronopia63 Lovely
72w Reply

undrwtr 👏🚴👏
72w Reply

mannyjefferson 〰
72w Reply

emieleode Powerful imagery
72w Reply ···

negativissima 🔥🔥🔥🔥
72w Reply

_the_photo_monster_ This is awesome 🔥
72w Reply

isophoto1 This is amazing

Liked by lewis.khan and 2,316 others

DECEMBER 12, 2020

Add a comment...

Screenshot from Cian's Instagram account.

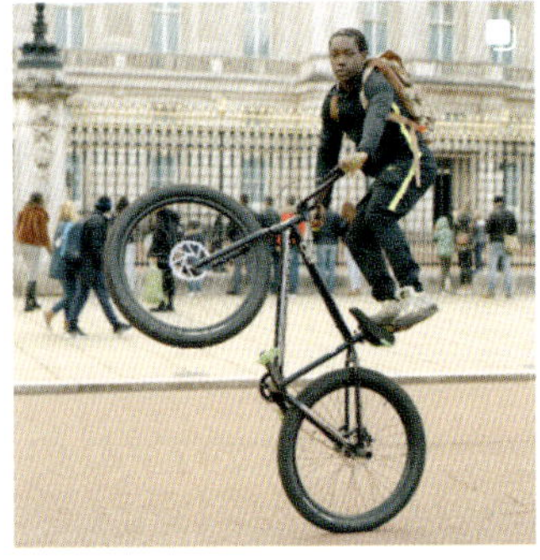
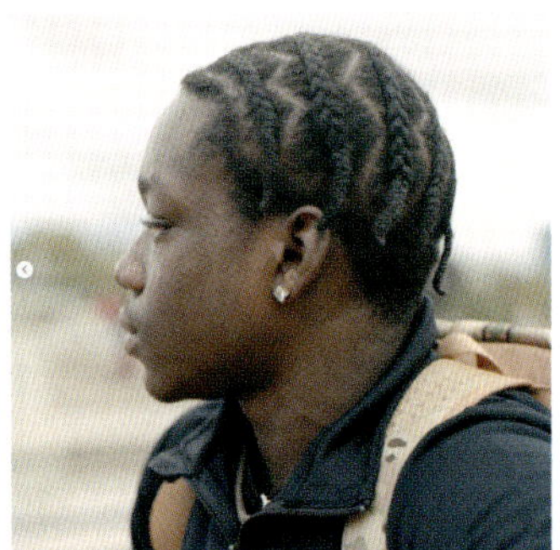
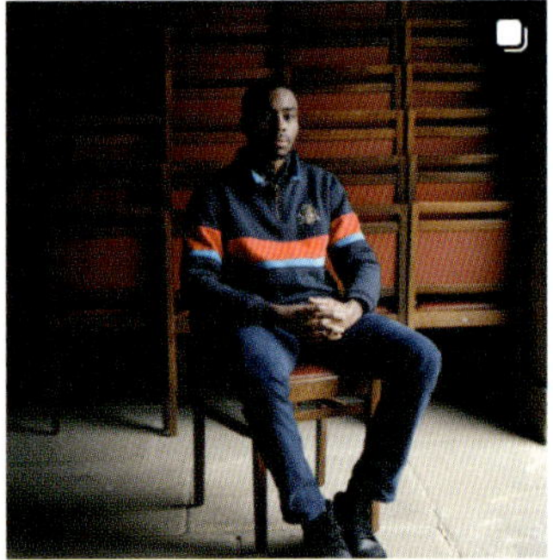

Screenshot showing the above photograph in situ with other photographs on Cian's profile 'grid'.

viewed on your profile. Here you can see an example of how one of Cian's photographs looks as an individual post and when cropped in a row of other images. The post of the boy on the bike, featured opposite, is one of the most popular on Cian's Instagram page. By including two images in a single post – one full-length portrait and another a close crop of the rider's face – he has improved the chances of engagement. The whole bicycle and rider also fit within the square frame, making this image look good in both ratios.

Many photo editors and those who commission photography use Instagram to find new photographers, make connections and even to reach out to you. It is advisable not to reach out to these people on the app yourself, as it's better to be polite and formal, and an email is usually the best way to do this.

Task

To best understand Instagram, it's important to look at what other people are doing. The first part of this task is to find the accounts of three photographers you think are using Instagram particularly well. These might be people you already follow or you might need to do some digging if you've not used the app before. Once you've found the three photographers, have a look at their profiles in depth. Then search for some key information about each photographer, which should be very easy to find. Make notes on how many followers they have; how often they post; what they write in their captions and how long these are; if they use hashtags; and how they use their stories in a different way to their posts. All this research will help you build a plan for how you post your own photographs. If you're stuck, have a look at photographer Liz Johnson Artur's profile. She has

been making work for many years longer than social media has existed, and her page provides a home for her archive, installation shots of her exhibitions and some selected commissioned photographs.

The second part of this task is to plan three posts for Instagram. Start by considering, as mentioned earlier, how you want social media to work for you. Find three photographs you haven't posted before and think about the best order for them, then plan when you are going to post them. There are third-party apps that will allow you to schedule the posts automatically, but you can also just write out the captions (don't make them too long) and set reminders on your phone's calendar. Post one image every four days.

Conclusion

If you use Instagram as a place to support the people whose work you love and are willing to put in more than you get back, you are on the right track to having a successful social media presence. Building an engaged following may seem daunting, and although getting lots of followers will not make you a better photographer, there are clear benefits to utilizing social media in the right way.
• Make sure your images are converted to sRGB (standard red green blue), so they look as good as possible online. Adobe RGB is okay too, but any CMYK profiles will make your images look flat.
• Some photographers have a practice account – with no followers and a false name – which they use to test a post to see how it looks before posting on their real account. **MF**

CHAPTER 2

The Self

The portraits we make are normally of other people. But many photographers like to use portraiture to photograph themselves. In this chapter, we will look at some of the reasons why.

Projects

In an essay on the painter Albrecht Dürer (1471–1528) in his book *Portraits* (2015), the photography and art critic John Berger comments that 'Dürer was the first painter to be obsessed by his own image. No other before him made so many self-portraits.' He continues with the question: 'Why does a man paint himself?' and suggests that one motive could be 'the same as that which prompts any man to have his portrait painted. It is to produce evidence, which will probably outlive him, that he once existed.' This is a wonderful way to think of photographic portraits – our desire to record our lives, holidays or school classes – and, more specifically, one of the reasons people photograph themselves.

When you consider the work of Francesca Woodman, for example, it becomes even more pertinent. Woodman first photographed herself at the age of thirteen and continued making self-portraits until her death by suicide at only twenty-two (see From Selfie to Self-Portrait, page 82). Today, Woodman's work receives the highest critical acclaim. In this way, the idea that the work left behind 'becomes' the artist after death can be regarded as true. Perhaps it is even truer when you spend your life photographing yourself.

As an educator, I have noticed that students and the new generation of photographers in general are making more inward-looking and introspective work, whether they are photographing themselves directly or their own communities, families and experiences. I think this is partly a result of conversations around ethics, with students worrying about making work that features 'the other', but there is also a wider shift to memoir in the world of filmmaking and to autofiction in literature. Perhaps people are becoming more

▶ *Self-Portrait at Twenty-Eight* by Albrecht Dürer.

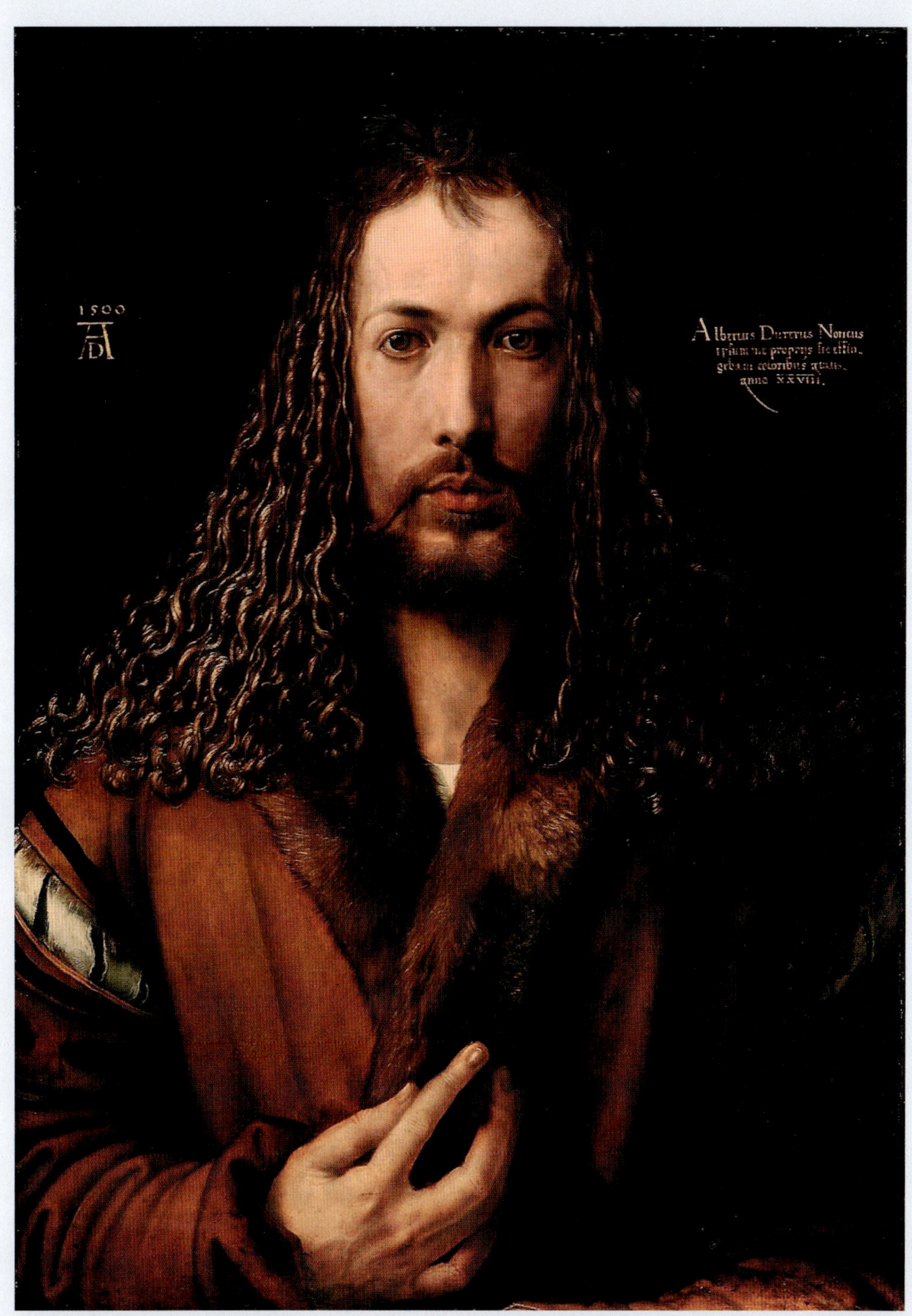

1500
Albertus Durerus Noricus
ipsum me proprys sic effin
gebam coloribus aetatis
anno XXVIII

interested in using art as a tool to unravel the threads of their own lives rather than presenting the world through snippets taken from those of others.

Self-portraits do not make up the entire practice of most photographers, but many will include a self-portrait within their work. Photographer Kaitlin Maxwell, for example, has spent years photographing herself, her mother and her grandmother in a body of work that examines the shifting matriarchal roles between them and how women are regarded by society. Both her mother and grandmother were involved in the sex industries. By including herself in the portraits and photographing herself naked, Maxwell creates equality between the three of them.

In her project 'Whispering for Help' (2020), London-based photographer Marie Smith made annotated portraits of the experiences of mental health of women of colour. One of the images is of Smith herself and, again, this bridges the gap between the subjects and the photographer. Looking at a final example, in her project 'Encounter' (2019), the Italian photographer Silvia Rosi recreates her family's history and migration from Togo, in West Africa, to Italy. She photographs herself dressed as both of her parents – in so doing, becoming them for us. In other words, the photographs can be regarded as performances.

For Kaitlin Maxwell, whose photographs I published in the first issue of *Granta* I was photo editor for, all her pictures form one long project. She uses a camera to reimagine and portray the lives of herself, her mother and her grandmother, who both worked in the sex industries. She talks of the power and role of matriarch shifting between the three of them. Often in the images she is portraying one of the others herself but here, as in some others, she is herself, lighting her mother's cigarette. It doesn't look posed. The natural moment, movement and intimacy all betray our expectations of a staged photograph. How does knowing she is in the photograph of two women sharing a cigarette change it? Does it? There is a wonderful essay by the American writer Lynne Tillman that accompanied these photographs when I published them, which can be read alongside Maxwell's work on the *Granta* website. One part of this text has stuck with me when I think about the work. Tillman writes, 'Voluptuous bodies wear casual or revealing clothes. The women appear not to mind being shot; Maxwell herself seems more tense or, as the photographer, less comfortable in front of the camera. Maybe the women were uncomfortable, they just know how to perform.' It's interesting that when we think about the relationship between photography, the self and how we view portraits, the comfortability of the sitter rarely comes in. Perhaps this is something to explore further in your own self-portraits.

Other examples are included within these pages, including images by photographer Juno Calypso who presents herself as a different character for the camera, but elsewhere in the book you will also find photographs by Zanele Muholi, Pixy Liao and Ronan Mckenzie that feature themselves. **MF**

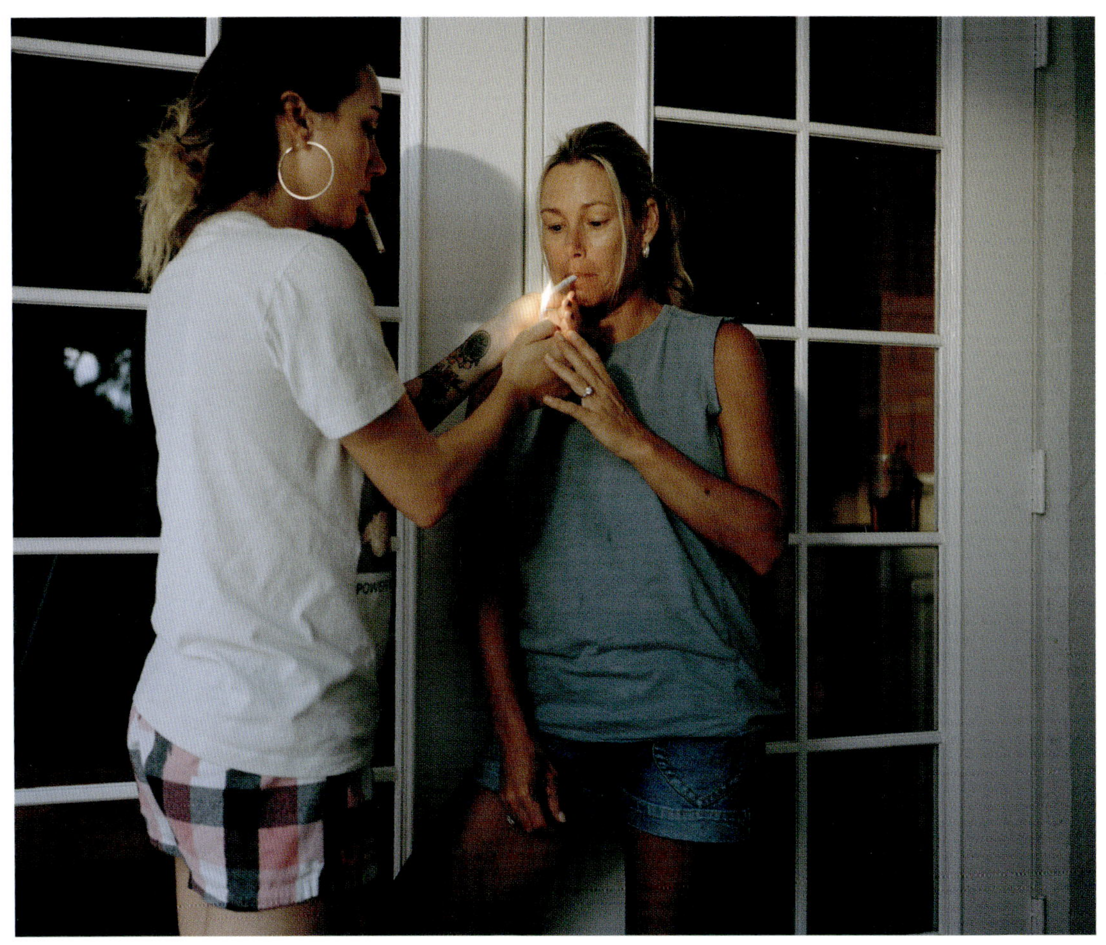

Kaitlin Maxwell. Me lighting mom's cigarette,
Florida, 2017.

Making Self-Portraits

This project will help you get started if you want to make self-portraits. Make the most of being alone and enjoy being creative while no one is watching.

Even if you have never considered photographing yourself, the practice of making self-portraits can be very useful when learning the skills associated with portrait photography and for pushing your creativity. Shown here is a self-portrait by the American photographer Frances Benjamin Johnston. It shows her dressed as a man, with a fake moustache and holding a penny-farthing bicycle. It was made in 1890. So for over 100 years, people have been working in this way.

Think carefully as you work through this task and try to have fun with it. Think of the photograph as a stage and the camera as your audience. When making self-portraits you are inevitably performing for the camera, and therefore the viewer, so think about how you want to be portrayed and perceived. The smallest changes to your clothes, hair or facial expressions may have a huge impact on how the image turns out.

Task

The steps outlined on these pages will guide you through the practicalities of making a self-portrait, but you should try to think about why you are making them too. For example, does including yourself in a photograph change its meaning in any way?

▶ Frances Benjamin Johnston. Full-length self-portrait dressed as a man with false moustache, posed with penny-farthing bicycle, facing left, 1890–1900.

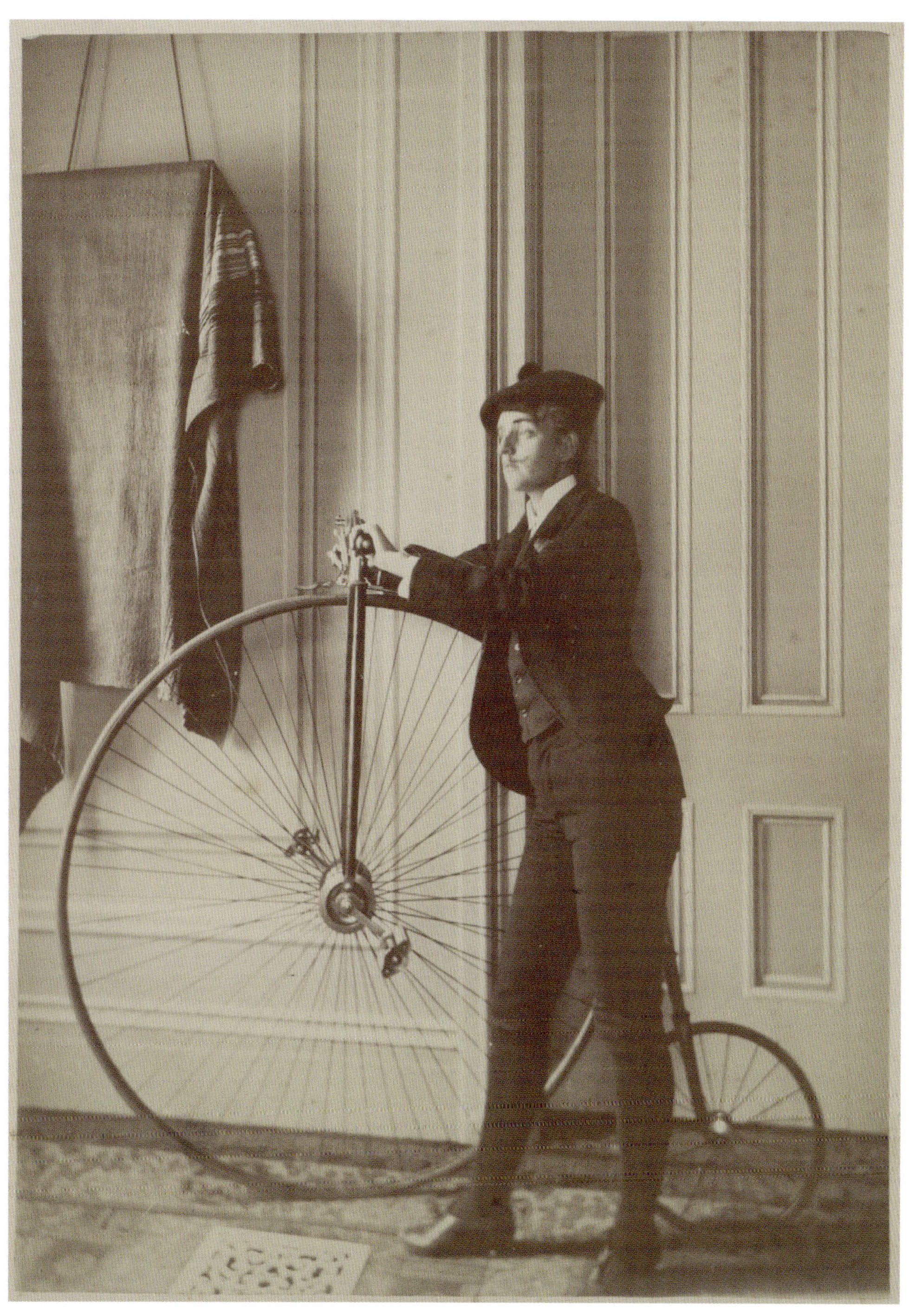

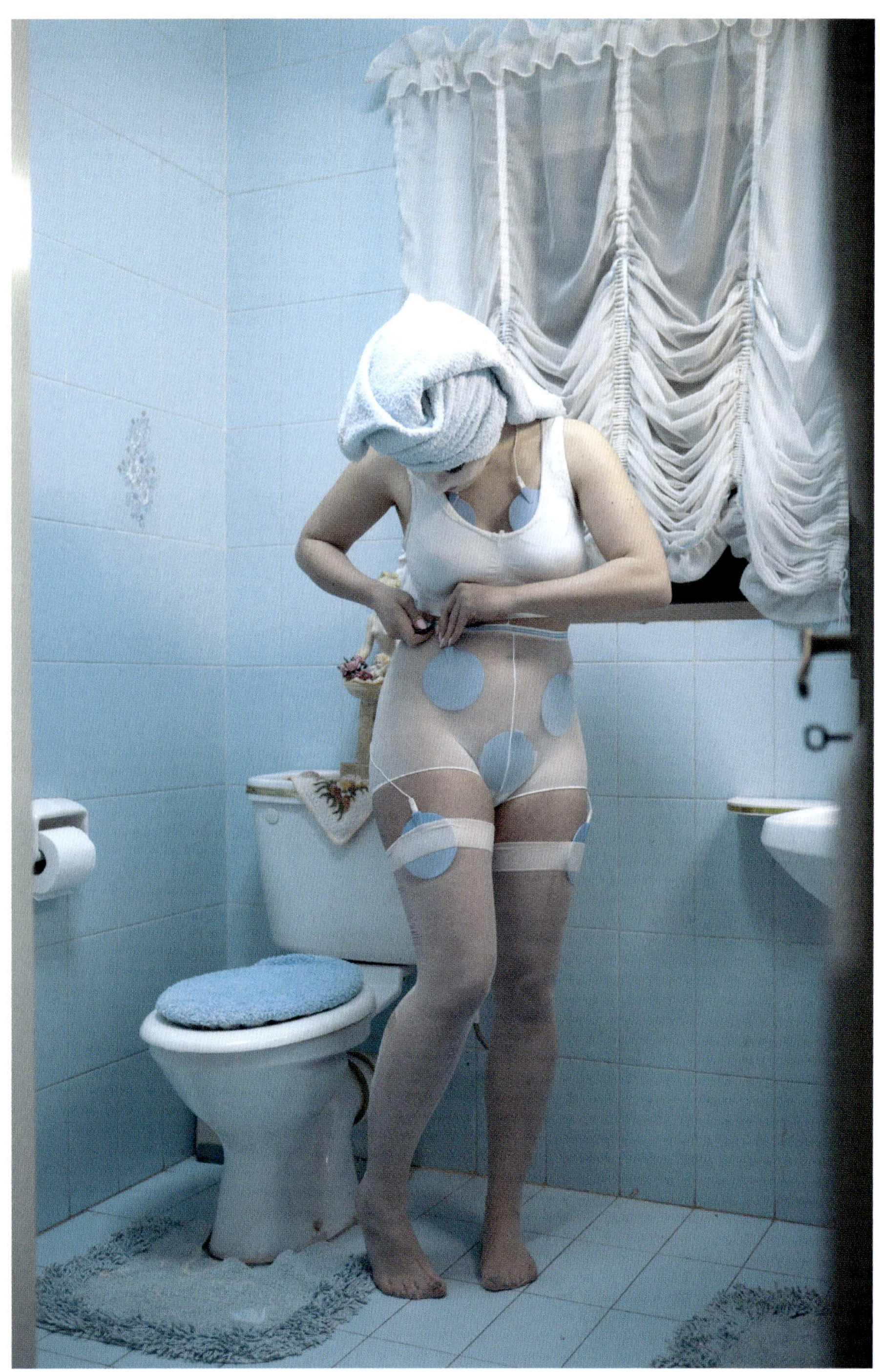

1. Find somewhere indoors that will work as a set for your self-portrait. This might be a place that means something to you, or perhaps you are inhabiting a character. It's important to think about the context and aesthetics of the place you choose – somewhere clean and simple will be the easiest to work with. If in any doubt, find a corner of a room because the edges of floors, walls and the ceiling will draw the viewer to the centre of the image, as shown in the self-portrait opposite by Juno Calypso.

2. You can also create the self-portrait outside, but if you choose this option, remember to think about where your camera will be. If you don't have a tripod, then find a platform on which to balance the camera. Make sure it's sturdy, though!

3. Frame and focus the shot as you would a normal portrait. The most difficult part of self-portraiture is framing and focusing your camera without someone sitting in front of you. Photographers often use a shop mannequin for this, which works well, but you are unlikely to have one at home. Alternatively, if you can convince someone to sit for you while you frame and focus, then that works well too. Failing that, any object you can place where your eyes are looking (or wherever you want the focus to be) will work as a placeholder.

4. You have several options for pressing the shutter while you're in the photograph. If you are using a digital camera, your phone or a modern film camera, it will almost certainly have a self-timer, which will (most likely) give you ten seconds to run back to your spot and pose. Remote shutter or cable releases mean you can stay where you are while you shoot. These may be seen in the final image, but photographers often like to leave them visible in self-portraits – a cable coming from the subject's hand reminds us we are complicit in the act of image making. **MF**

Conclusion

• Self-portraits can be a useful way to learn about the basics of photography without having to go through this process in front of other people.
• By putting yourself in front of the camera you are often performing *for* the camera. Think about how the background can become your stage.
• Focusing can be difficult, but by using something as a guide, you can get around this easily.

◀ June Calypso. Slendertone I.
From the series 'Joyce', 2015.

Juno Calypso

born 1989, London, UK.
junocalypso.com

Juno Calypso began making photographs of herself disguised as a fictional character – known as Joyce – while she was studying photography. She travelled across America in 2015, posing as a travel writer, staying in love motels and strange rooms in strange hotels, and creating a body of work called 'Honeymoon', some of the photographs from which are featured here. As is often the case in photography, the main subject of the images is not really what the photographs are about. In an interview with *Sleek* magazine, Calypso described the work as being about 'a woman's right to be selfish'.

Calypso is a master of crafting images within a defined space. She often uses symmetry, an approach that is shown to great effect in the two photographs featured here. In the image below of Calypso standing in a pink bath, the wall of vertical mirrors around the edge reflects her body, so we see her from a different

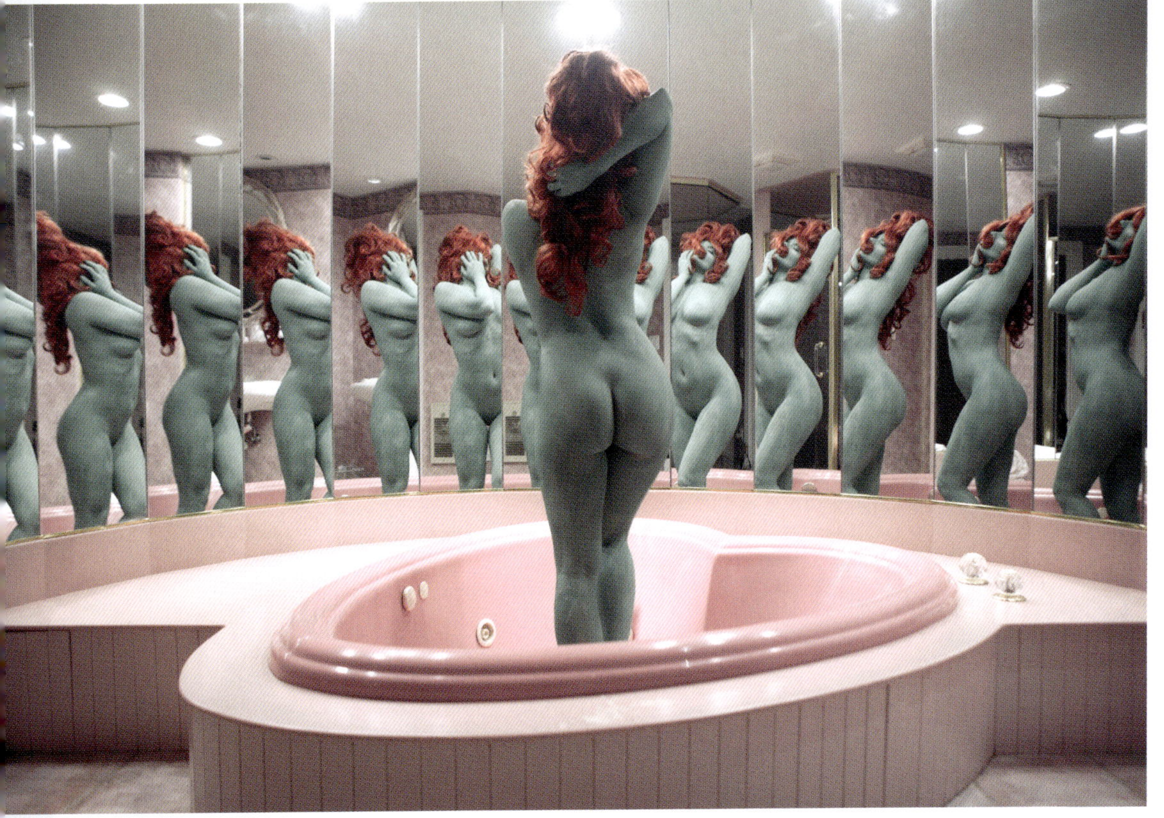

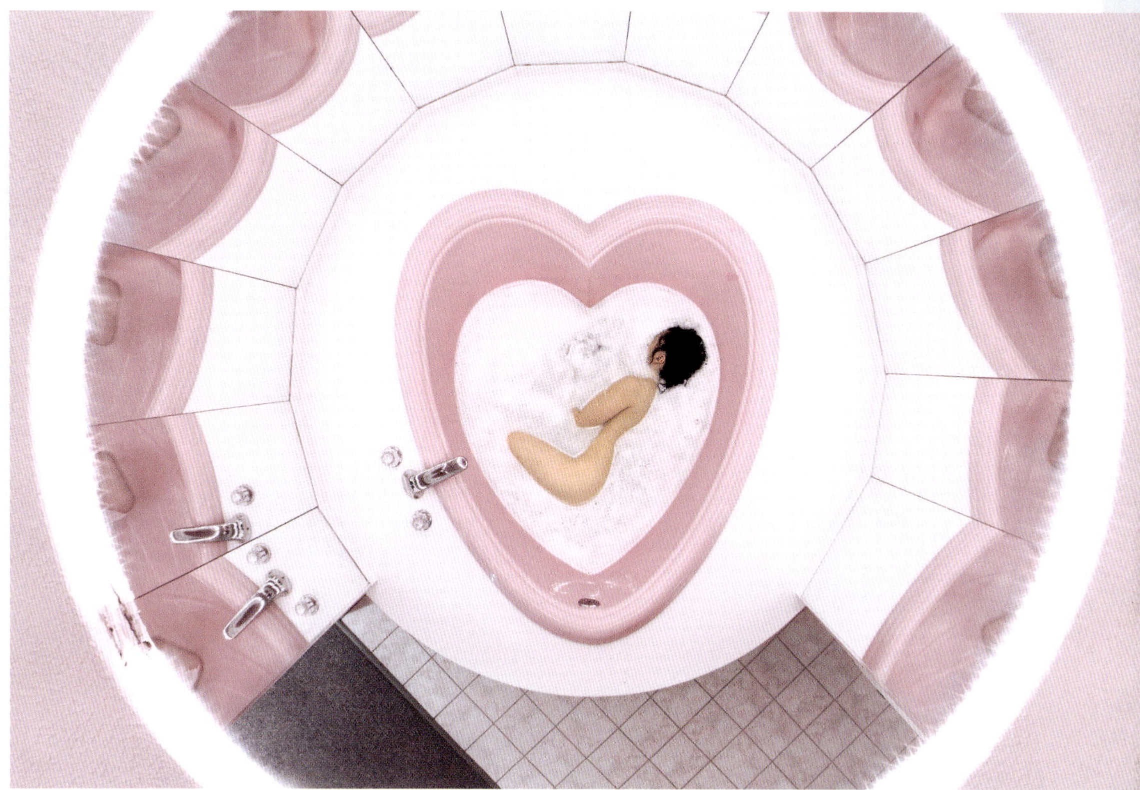

angle each time. It's not usual in photography to be able to view someone 'in the round' in this way, as most photographs only show one side of the subject. This device creates the illusion that we are seeing all of Calypso – she is very much on display.

The other image shown here is also of Calypso, although this time she is lying down in a different pink bath. Again, the bath is surrounded by a wall of vertical mirrors, but in this image, it is the heart-shaped bath itself that is the centre of the symmetry and the series of mirrors runs in a circle from one side to the other. Unlike in the first image, where we see Joyce/Calypso as being above us and powerful, here she is vulnerable, hiding from the viewer and lying as if asleep under a spell, half-submerged in the bubbles.

For Calypso, making self-portraits is not just about pressing a shutter, as she also plans her shoots and stays in hotels, motels and homes that can act as stage sets for her performances. Working completely alone, she sets up cameras and photographs herself with a remote shutter release. By not working with any assistants, Calypso is able to build on the intimacy of her photographs. The sets also become as important as the characters she creates. It is interesting that the photographic medium can be utilized to create these fictions as easily as it can be used as a tool of evidence or truth-telling. **MF**

Exploring the Self in Portraiture

A self-portrait does not necessarily have to include the photographer in the literal sense. This is because the photographer can be present in many other ways.

When we consider the portrayal of the self in portraiture, we often think of selfies or self-portraits. Although these are some of the most prominent forms of the self in portraiture, there are many other ways of expressing the self in photography. For example, the self can also be expressed conceptually, rather than literally or physically, in the form of a self-portrait or selfie. It can be shown through the subject matter or through collaboration, with the photographer leaving their imprint on the images even though they are not actually present. For example, in one section of the book *Ghetto* (2003) by Adam Broomberg and Oliver Chanarin, the photographers visited Rene Vallejo Psychiatric Hospital, in Cuba, and collaborated with the patients by creating self-portraits. Shot using large-format photographic film, the subjects were photographed against the same background. They were given a cable release and decided themselves when to press the shutter, therefore taking the responsibility and control of when the image was taken away from the photographer.

The resulting images, some of which are shown here, raise questions around authorship, identity and the ethics of making portraits in general, but particularly in the context of photographing vulnerable people. When considering the idea of self-portraits, we often think of control and having the ability to direct the image and how we are perceived – hence the rise in popularity of the selfie alongside the use of social media platforms, which allow people to curate their own image.

An interesting feature of the examples shown here is that they also represent a form of self-portraiture in which the subject is not entirely in control. This is because it is the photographers who have chosen the way the portraits are lit and composed, while the subject is only in control of the moment at which the image is taken.

Photographer Jemima Stehli is herself present in the images in her work 'Strip', although she is not the one in control of taking the photographs, as is the case with the images by Broomberg and Chanarin. For this series, Stehli invited male friends from the art world, including curators, collectors and critics, to sit for a portrait. They were each given a cable release and instructed to take ten photographs using this while they watched her undress. When viewing the images individually, it is not entirely clear that the photographer is present. It is only when the portraits are viewed alongside each other and the text is studied that the context becomes clear.

▶ Self-portrait by Mario, Rene Vallejo Psychiatric Hospital, Cuba, courtesy of The Goodman Gallery and the late estate of Broomberg & Chanarin. C-type print, 16 × 20 inches, 2003.

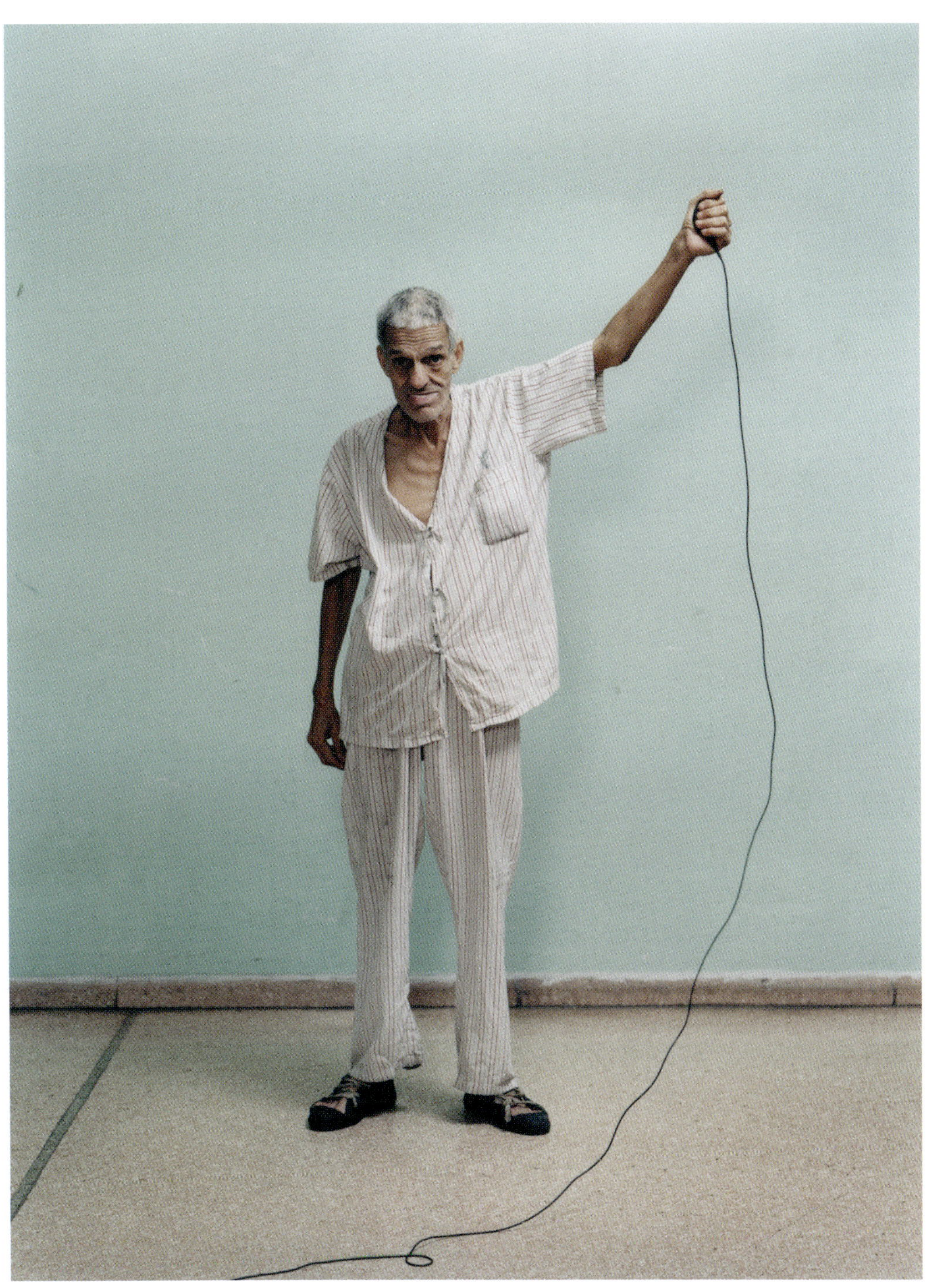

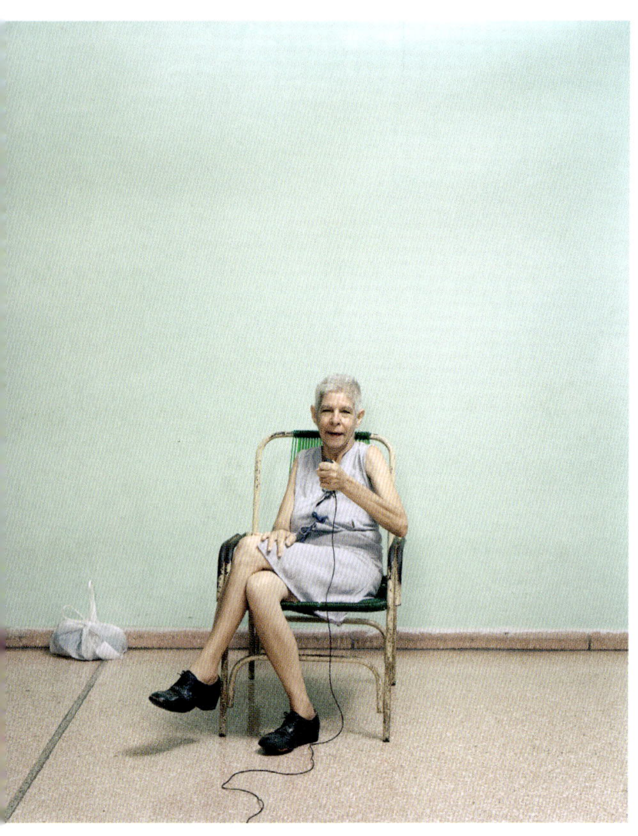

Self-portrait by Anais, Rene Vallejo Psychiatric
Hospital, Cuba, courtesy of The Goodman Gallery
and the late estate of Broomberg & Chanarin.
C-type print, 16 × 20 inches, 2003.

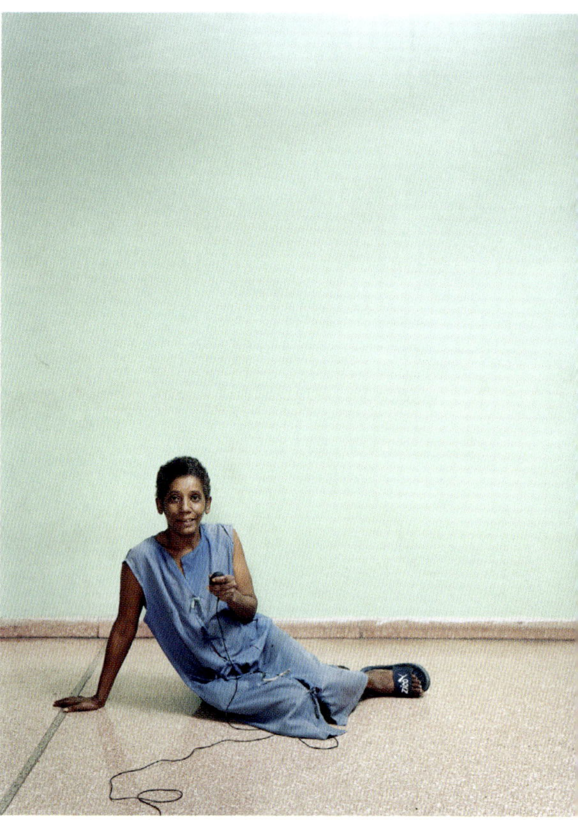

Self-portrait by Celia, Rene Vallejo Psychiatric
Hospital, Cuba Courtesy of The Goodman Gallery
and the late estate of Broomberg & Chanarin.
C-type print, 16 × 20 inches, 2003.

Stehli's portraits are interesting because she is almost anonymous in the photographs. She is facing away from the camera in all the images and thus our gaze is drawn to the expressions of the men. We are watching them watch her and analyzing their responses. This series of images poses important questions about the agency of ownership within a photograph and the impact that the photographer has on the outcome of a portrait. In these photographs, the impact is obvious because the photographer is present, and we can understand visually how she is influencing the images. However, it should be noted that the photographer is always present in the image in some shape or form, whether subtle or not. This series also highlights the photographer's experience as a woman in a patriarchal society and, in my opinion, it successfully takes the objectification that Stehli has experienced throughout her life and turns it back on the male gaze.

A common way in which photographers can explore the self is by creating work linked to their own experiences. Just as Stehli's work examines her experiences as a woman, so many other photographers choose to make portraits or projects centred on their own identity or experience. Although many photographers may not perceive this investigation of the self as self-portraiture in the literal sense, I think most would agree that making work that's deeply personal, or documents the communities you come from, is an equally valid way of exploring the self.

I made the portrait shown opposite of my brother Sé in March 2018, four months after our cousin Greg took his own life (see page 122). I've always found photography to be a cathartic experience; it's been a tool for me to process the intense experiences and traumas I've had to deal with in life. For this portrait my brother and I discussed our relationship with Greg, our bond with him and what we felt led to his passing. We went to Wormwood Scrubs Park in West London, a place where Greg had spent a lot of time, and made this portrait. I asked Sé to close his eyes and composed him in front of the plant, using a shallow depth of field to create the blurring in the background which to me signified the feeling of being caught up in our own thoughts and the business of our minds. **COS**

Conclusion

Self-portraits come in many different forms, as we have discussed in this project. Think about ways in which you can express yourself, both literally and conceptually. The self-portrait can be a photographic manifestation of your physical self; it can exist as a self-portrait of someone else, facilitated by you as the photographer; and it can also be a self-portrait in the non-literal sense, being more of an exploration of a subject matter that is deeply personal, with the photographer channelled through the sitter.

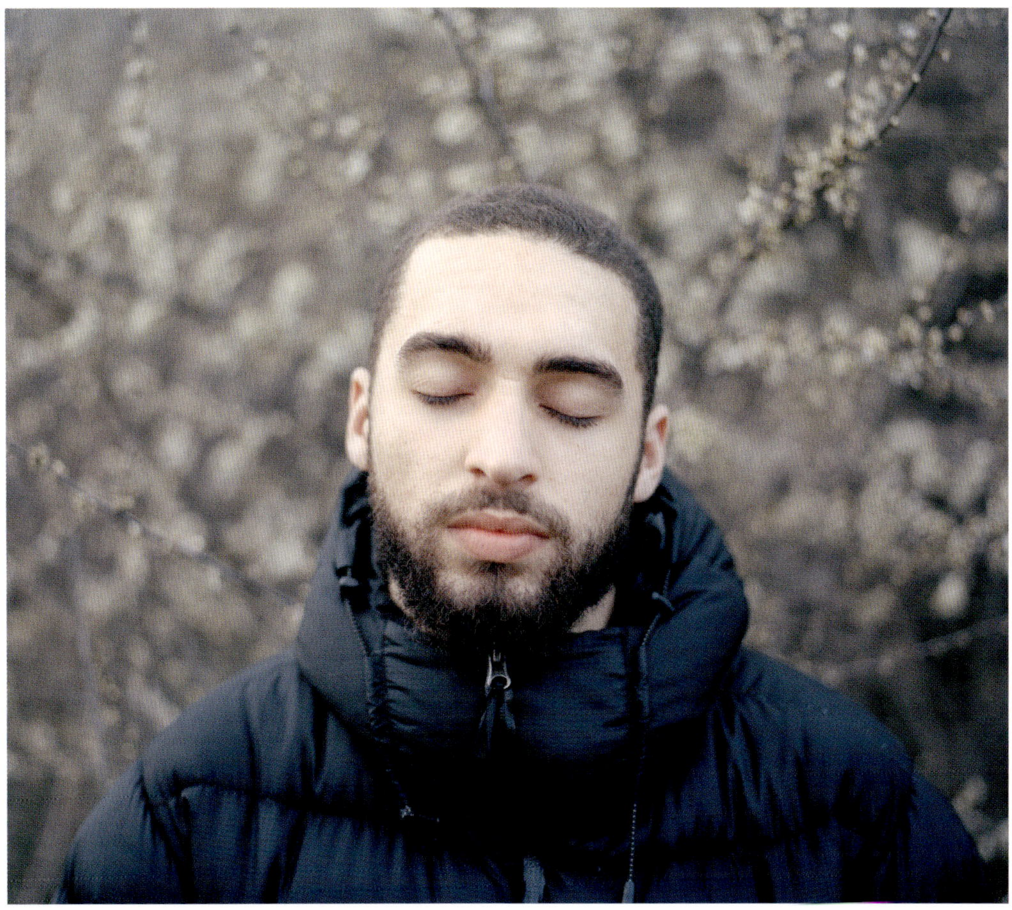

Cian Oba-Smith. Sé, Wormwood Scrubs Park, London, 2018.

From Selfie to Self-Portrait

Self-portraiture has a strong history in the art of photography. For photographers, such as the American Francesca Woodman (1958–1981), it might form most of their practice.

Sometimes people incorporate a self-portrait into a project, but these are often just random photographs, such as the one featured here that Cian took in March 2020 during the first lockdown of the Covid-19 pandemic in the United Kingdom. He appears to be preparing to take a photograph out of the window. If we did not know that Cian is a photographer, it would seem like a candid image of a photographer at work.

So, what is the difference between a selfie and a self-portrait? The answer is perhaps not that clear cut, but we could define a selfie as an image mostly taken on the front camera of a mobile phone and made quickly without much planning. Selfies are also often taken specifically for sharing on social media. In contrast, self-portraits are usually made with a camera rather than a phone (although the technology someone uses is perhaps not relevant). They are also more considered. In short, selfies are not traditionally regarded as portraits.

Such definitions can be frustrating, however. Why should an image that you have taken quickly, and on the 'wrong' camera, be less valuable than one taken by someone using a tripod, with a professional camera and lighting? There is, of course, no reason for the 'professional' photograph to be more valuable. In addition, there is no shortage of artists who have worked with the selfie aesthetic to significant effect.

Look at Valerie Phillips's book *I Had a Dream You Married a Boy* (2020). For this, Phillips photographed her friend Arvida Bystrom, who was based in Stockholm, via webcam, directing the images from her home in London. The images are mostly screenshots, video conversations and small thumbnails of photographs in a phone's image library. The aesthetic makes you think of selfies, of performing for social media and the camera – but, in reality, they are portraits

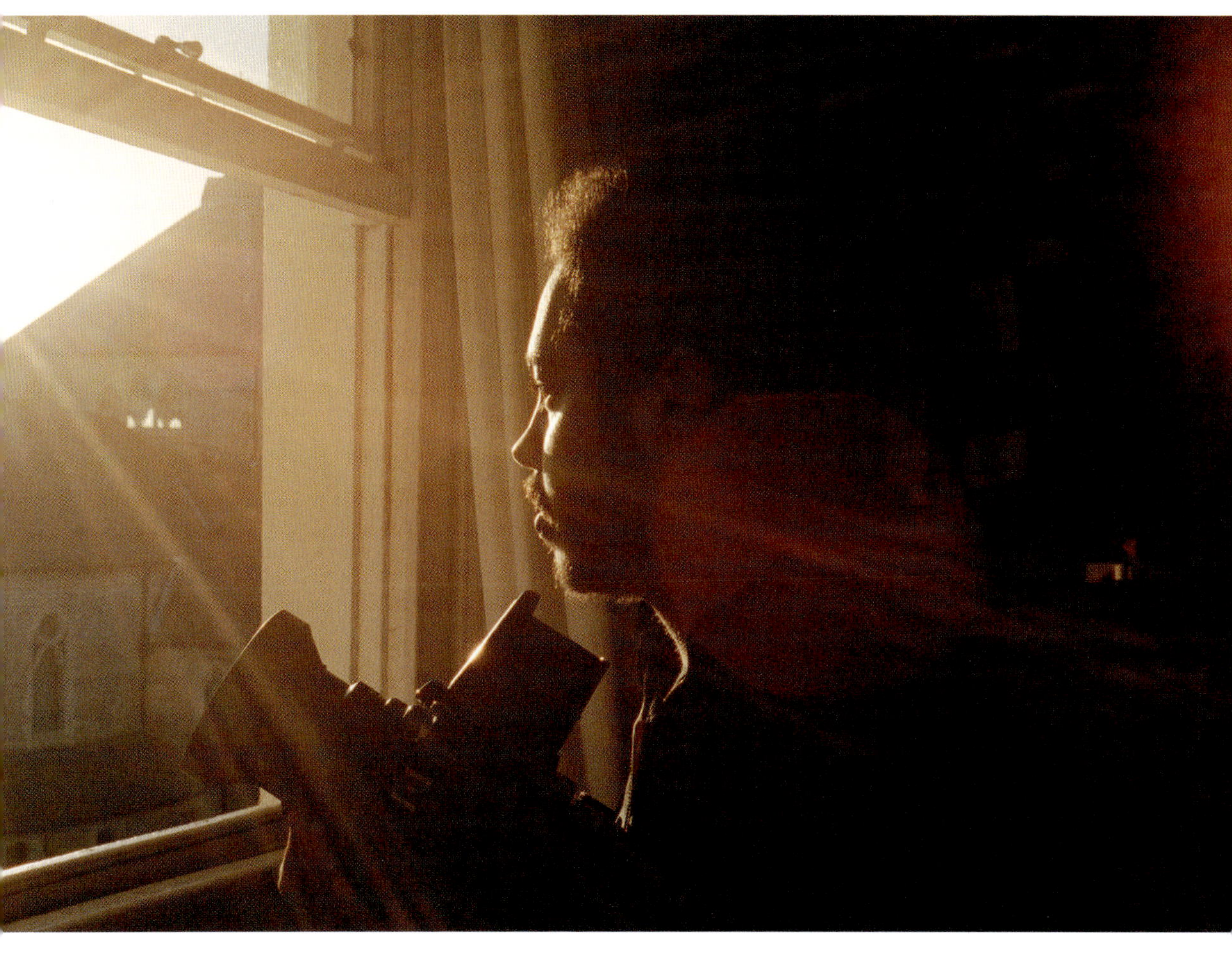

Cian Oba-Smith. Self-portrait during the first
Covid-19 lockdown, London, March, 2020.

taken by Phillips from many miles away. This book
blurs the lines between the aesthetic of a selfie, which
relies on the immediate availability of camera phones
and webcams, self-portraits (the subject is performing for her own cameras) and portrait photography
(Phillips is taking the photographs remotely). Clearly,
there are not always distinct lines between different
areas of photography, but a general understanding
of the boundaries can be useful and help you place
your work. **MF**

Conclusion

• Whereas selfies are usually taken on mobile phones or
webcams, self-portraits tend to be made with cameras.
• Selfies and self-portraits can cross over, with the
maker's intention usually being what separates them.
• Photographers like Francesca Woodman (see page 68)
have made self-portraiture popular in art photography.

Editing Photographs: From Darkroom to Digital

Editing is one of the most important stages when making a photographic portrait. The traditional equivalent of photo editing is the processing and printing of photographic film in a darkroom.

The processing and printing of photographic film is still a method used by some photographers with the added step of digitizing the print or film with a scanner or digital camera (I personally scan my negatives when I shoot film, which makes up most of my personal work). However, most photographers prefer to work with digital cameras.

Many image-processing tools are available to photographers, but the main ones used by professionals are Adobe Lightroom, Adobe Photoshop and Capture One. Lightroom allows you to batch edit large quantities of photographs and is great for cataloguing and exporting images. Photoshop isn't really designed for cataloguing and is better suited to retouching and more complex editing. Capture One is a great all-rounder, but it really excels during the image-making process – you can tether your camera to a computer with a cable and it will load the pictures instantly, allowing you to see them in greater detail as well as edit as you go (Lightroom also has this capability, but I think Capture One does it better). I prefer to use Lightroom and Photoshop when working with film and then Capture One and Photoshop when working digitally, although this is all a matter of personal preference.

▶ Cian Oba-Smith. Style poses for a portrait, Philadelphia, USA. From the series 'Concrete Horsemen', 2016.

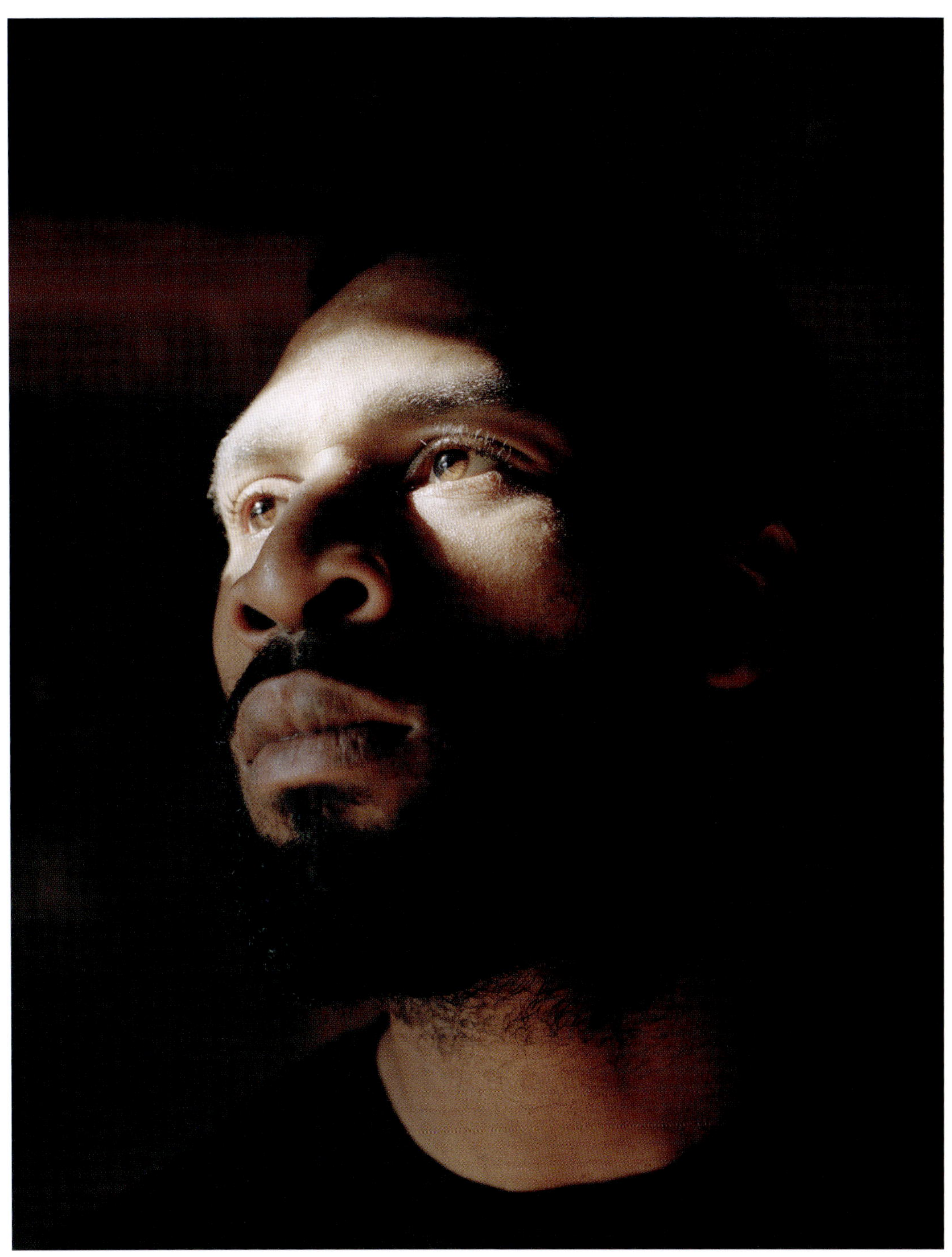

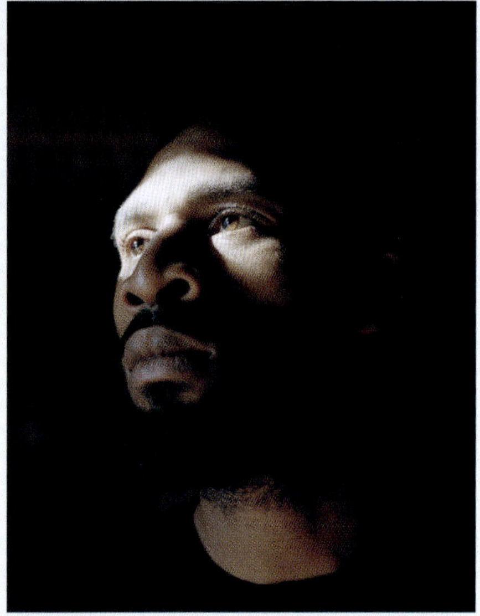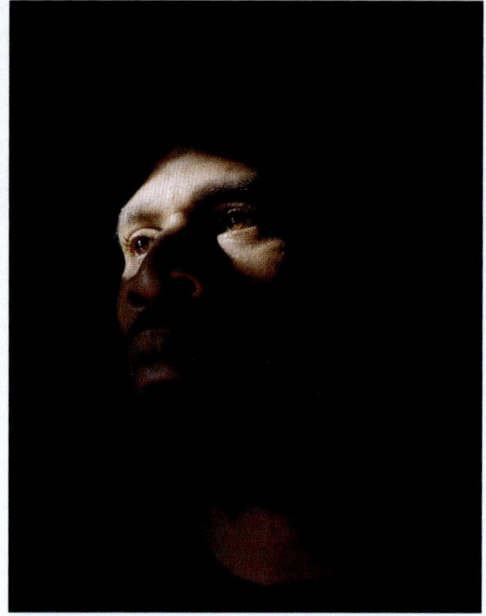

This edit is an example of poor colouring. It's a lot colder than the other images and has a blue/cyan tint. To fix this, you would use the Colour Balance tool in Adobe Photoshop to adjust the colour temperature.

This edit is too dark. All the detail has been lost in the midtones and shadows of the portrait. It is acceptable if you only intended to light the eyes. Otherwise, to fix it, you would adjust the brightness with the Levels or Curves tool.

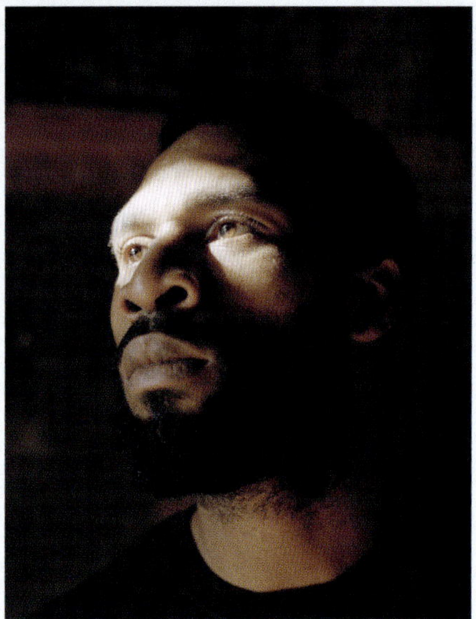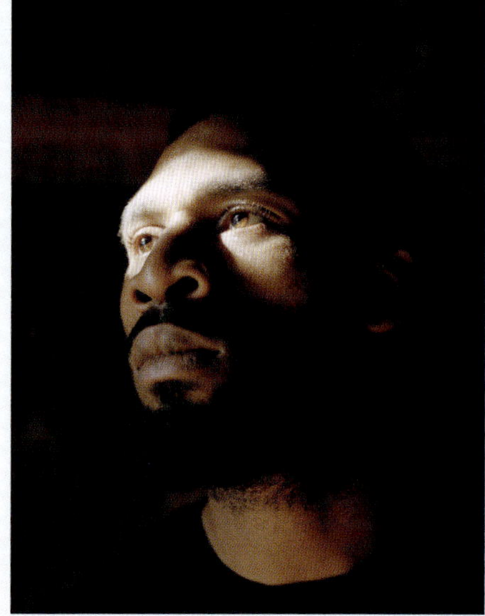

This edit is almost there, although it is a little too bright, which makes the image look washed out and grainy in the shadows. It has also blown out the highlights on the subject's eyes slightly. To fix this, you would use the Levels or Curves tool to adjust the brightness.

This is the edit I settled on. Although only subtly different to the first image, there is more detail in the highlights. In my opinion, this portrait works better because there are fewer details in the shadows.

Every photographer has a different approach to editing, since the result is entirely subjective. However, there is a basic workflow that applies to most situations:

1. *Cropping*: Crop your image, if necessary, and remove any dust or blemishes if you're shooting on film (this is usually done with the Spot Healing or Clone Stamp tool in Photoshop).

2. *White Balance*: Adjust the white balance to correct any colour temperature discrepancies or to produce your preferred colour temperature.

3. *Exposure*: This can be done by using the Exposure, Levels or Curves tool.

4. *Contrast*: If necessary, adjust the contrast of the image using the Brightness/Contrast tool.

5. *Saturation*: You may need to adjust the saturation of the image using the Hue/Saturation tool.

6. *Sharpening*: An image usually needs to be sharpened before printing or sharing it online.

Note: Bear in mind that the order of this workflow can change. If you're shooting on digital and using raw files, you'll want to do some of this in Adobe Camera Raw before fully opening your file.

The process of editing an individual image is a complex and specialized skill. Many photographers employ master printers/retouchers for this because it can take years to become proficient at editing images. Just as it takes practice to develop your photography skills, so the best way to improve your photo-editing skills is to dedicate time to the technical and creative process by experimenting with different approaches. Remember, editing is not a replacement for good technical proficiency. It's a tool for enhancing images. **COS**

Conclusion

Editing your images is a crucial part of the creation of a photograph, regardless of whether you're only tweaking them or working on them more thoroughly. The steps we've discussed in this project are a good starting point, but experimentation will provide you with a workflow that works best for your creative process.

Yushi Li

born 1991, Hunan, China.
yushi.li

Yushi Li creates work that questions many of the core structures of society. Issues of gender and race are heavily present, as is the photographer herself, whether physically or not. Woven into all Yushi Li's work is a critical questioning of the gaze, be it male or female. The gaze is ever present in, and central to, her work, as is an interrogation of art history and its associated power dynamics. Li uses the camera as a tool in striving towards creating gender equality through the reversal of the male gaze, a term coined by the late writer and art critic John Berger, who said in his book *Ways of Seeing* (1972): 'Men act and women appear. Men look at women. Women watch themselves being looked at.'

Many of Yushi's portraits feature nude White men. The choice to include White men specifically is interesting, given the context of Li's background as a young Asian woman and the cultural history of White men exoticizing and fetishizing Asian women. The objectification of women in general has been present in photography from the beginning of the genre. Li's work subverts this and turns the tables by creating self-portraits that place the man in the photograph as the object of scrutiny, rather than the woman.

The photograph featured here, titled 'The Nightmare' after the 1871 painting of the same name by Swiss artist Henry Fuseli, features Li looking directly into the camera. As is the case with many of her self-portraits, she is wearing a red item of clothing, in a nod to the Chinese colour of luck and happiness. In this image, the man is seen as object, both metaphorically and physically. The chiaroscuro-style lighting, which was utilized by painters such as Caravaggio and Rembrandt, creates an obvious comparison to classical portraiture where the focus was often on the woman as object. Chiaroscuro is an Italian term meaning 'light-dark', a style of lighting that uses the strong contrast between light and dark to create a three-dimensional effect within a two-dimensional image. For example, in this image, the subjects are lit by bright sunlight through a single window in a dark room, so creating the effect.

In this portrait, and in Li's work in general, she creates her own agency and identity through self-portraiture. As she notes: 'When I look through the viewfinder, I'm the photographer behind the camera, which hides me and protects me. On the other hand, when I look through the lens, in other words, looking at the viewer, I become both the looker and the looked-at.' **COS**

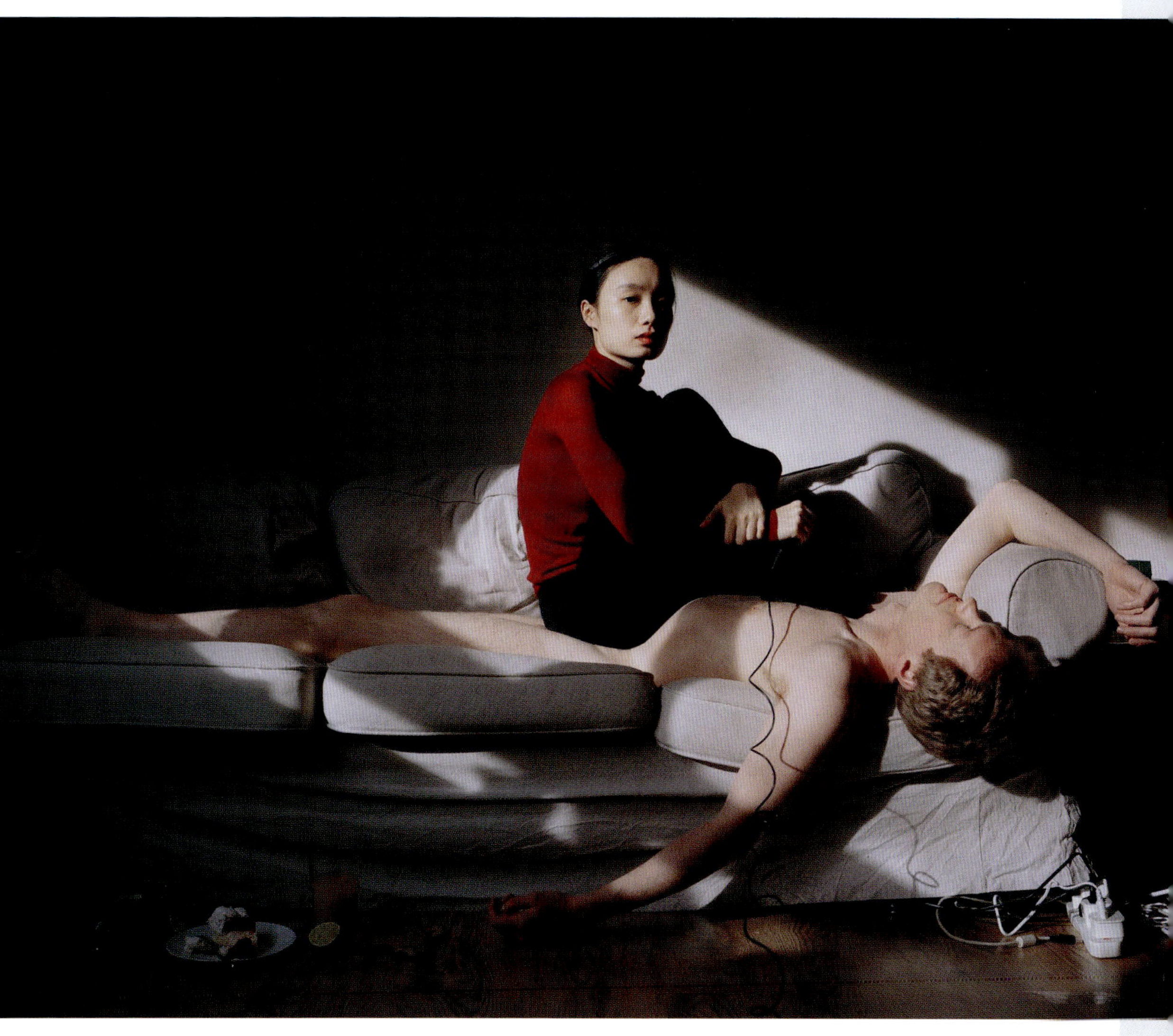

CHAPTER 3

Studio and Styled

Working in a studio and thoughtful styling can help you construct any image your imagination can conjure up. In this chapter, we explore studio-based and styled imagery in their various forms.

Projects

If we regard photography as being the child of painting, both in terms of the period in which it has existed and also of the influence painting has had on the development of portrait photography stylistically, then perhaps the photographic studio is the most closely related to the traditional portraiture of fine art and painting.

In some ways, the artificial environment of the photographic studio seems at odds with the basic concept behind photography, particularly in terms of how it is used as a form of documentary. This is because photography was originally perceived as a beacon of truth, something that over time we have come to learn is not the case. Rather, photography sits in a grey area between the truth and a lie. As photography and art critic John Berger wrote in his book *Understanding a Photograph* (2013), 'A photograph is not necessarily a lie, but it isn't the truth either. It's more like a fleeting, subjective impression.'

Unlike other areas of photography such as documentary photography, which purports to be the bastion of truth, studio work plays into the concept of photography as performance and leans into the idea of a constructed image. In Susan Sontag's seminal book *On Photography* (1977), she writes that 'The painter constructs, the photographer discloses.' Although I agree with this idea to a certain extent, I do not feel it applies to studio and fashion photography in the same way that it does to documentary photography. It should also be noted that for many photographers, studio work is synonymous with fashion photography. Although it is true that fashion photography

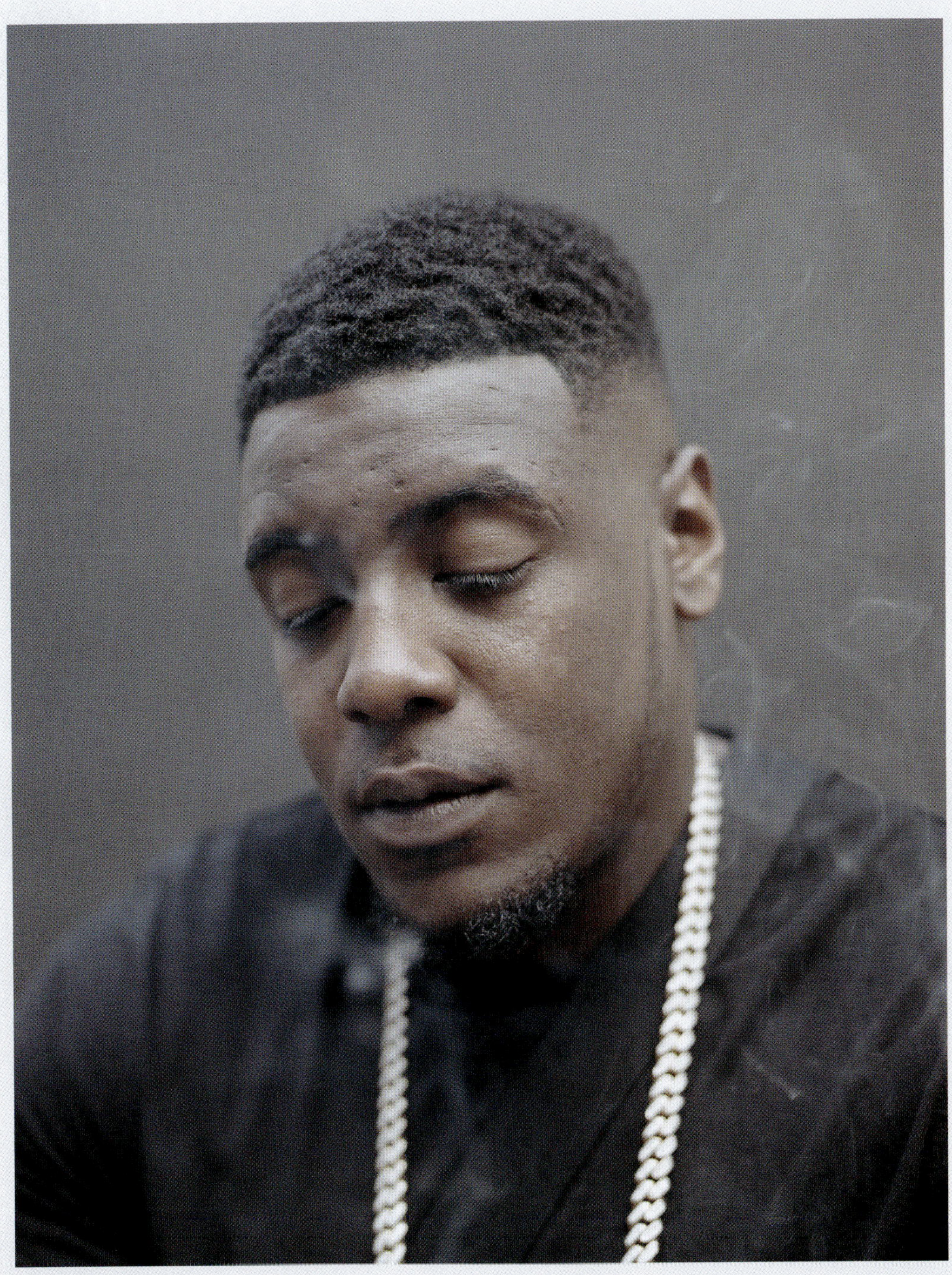

Cian Oba-Smith. Mist, for *Push Magazine*, 2019.

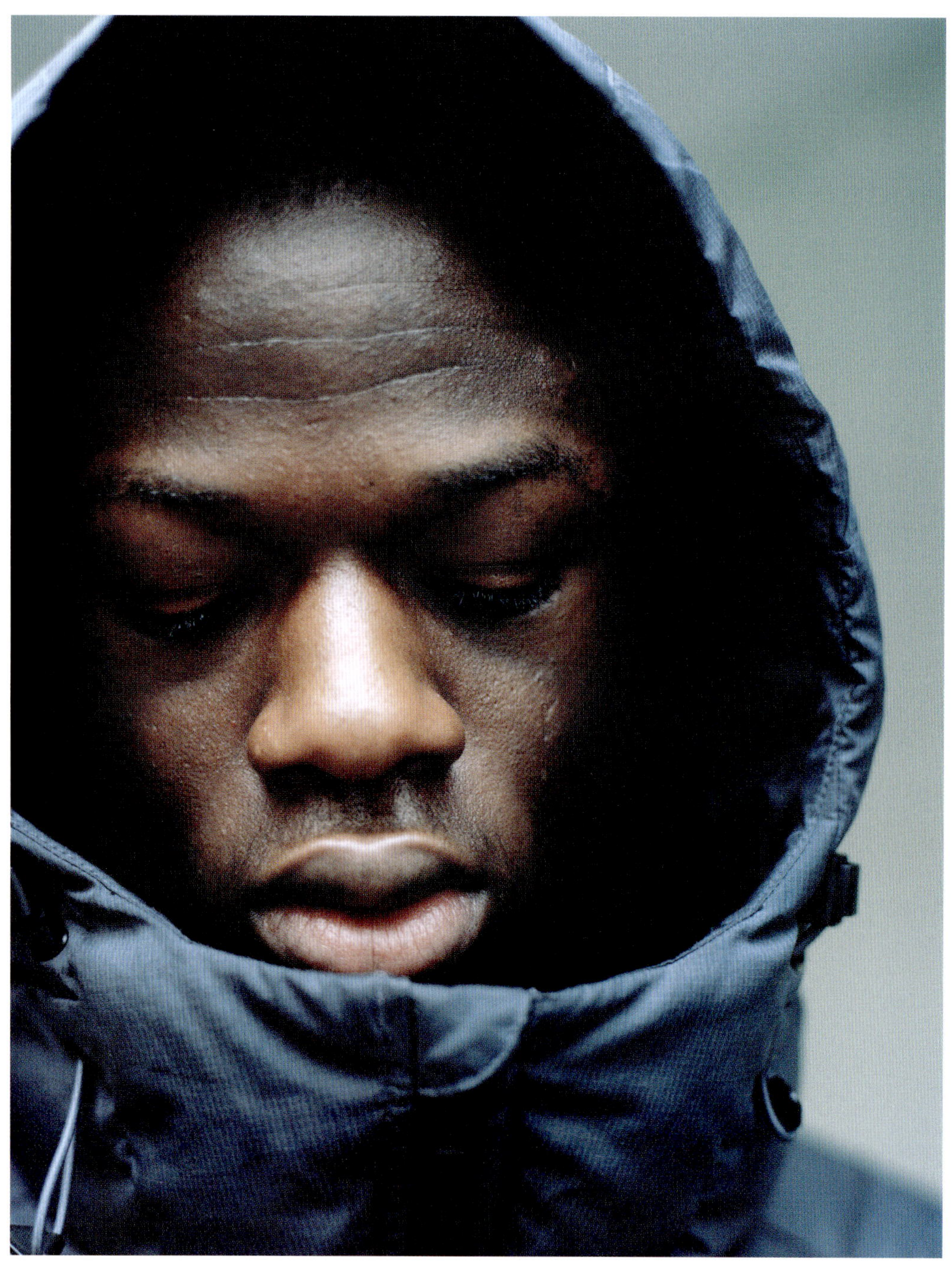

Cian Oba-Smith. J Hus, for *Crack Magazine*, 2017.

is sometimes used to sell clothing, this is not always the case. Photographer Nadine Ijewere (see page 94), for example, uses photography to celebrate diversity within society and to highlight people from her community who have historically been underrepresented in fashion photography.

What separates different genres of photography, such as documentary and studio portraiture, is that documentary is usually reactionary, while studio and styled photography is largely premeditated. With documentary portraiture, photographs generally present themselves through the act of looking, whereas with studio portraiture the photographer is fabricating and presenting us with an image from start to finish. The images of rappers J Hus (opposite) and Mist (see page 91), for instance, sit in an interesting place between both documentary and studio portraiture. There was an element of premeditation with the direction I wanted to take the shoot but at the same time they were created in reaction to the environment that we were shooting. The construction of an image allows photographers to curate every element of a portrait. This freedom from the idea of 'photography as truth' provides an opportunity for intense creativity and allows photographers to plan an entire image from initial idea to fruition.

Not all studio shots are heavily planned and orchestrated – in fact, sometimes the only element that is obviously constructed is the backdrop. For example, in the series 'In the American West' (1985), the late Richard Avedon utilized a plain background roll as a canvas against which he placed his subjects (see Create Your Own Studio, page 96). But the subjects that Avedon then photographed were normal people who he picked out while travelling across the American West, rather than models or people cast weeks in advance of

a shoot. Photographer Tom Johnson, who also features in this chapter (see page 100), takes a similar approach, but with a heavier fashion influence. He creates photographs that search for the commonalities among us and is drawn to community. He often creates fashion work that uses real people, working with stylists to blur the line between fashion and documentary.

Another photographer, Gregory Crewdson, takes the opposite approach, creating cinematic environmental portraits in which every element is elaborately planned. He builds huge sets and closes off entire roads to construct his images. For example, in his series 'Twilight' (1998), all the images exist in a surreal space between fact and fiction. The closer portraits appear more obviously constructed, while the wider images could almost be documentary photography.

The studio and fashion photography both provide a creative playground for many photographers and a sanctuary in which they can fabricate photographs from scratch. They offer a degree of protection from the harsh reality of the world, while also providing a means of showcasing the truths and experiences of the photographer and their community. The genre exists as a series of contradictions, blurring the lines of photography as truth and lie, in some ways synonymous and providing contrast in others. **COS**

Nadine Ijewere

born 1992, London, UK.
nadineijewere.co.uk

Nadine Ijewere creates beautiful portraits that celebrate diversity in all its forms. Growing up in London, perhaps one of the world's most diverse cities, Ijewere was frustrated by the lack of representation she saw in the fashion industry and sought to create work that actively challenges the prevalence of the West's standard of beauty. Her approach to making portraits reflects this intention. For example, she is heavily involved in the casting process for her fashion photography – particularly commissioned work – selecting suitable subjects herself. This allows her to create portraits that disrupt the historical beauty ideals upheld by the fashion world and so contribute to the changes she wishes to see in the industry.

As Nadine says herself, 'For me, it's always been about how I portray and celebrate those not considered part of the beauty ideals, and how I can present them in a beautiful way.' Portraits like the one featured here do just that. The subject defies so many stereotypes of what a model should look like. Her race and curves are not historically typical of a fashion magazine, but she is portrayed as being beautiful and vulnerable. Her posture mimics that of the goddess Venus in Sandro Botticelli's famous painting *The Birth of Venus* (circa 1480), the delicate pose as she emerges from the darkness giving her an ethereal feel. She appears to be floating in the abyss of Ijewere's lighting, the flowers dotted across her body creating pops of colour and separation from the backdrop.

Ijewere's consistent approach to image making landed her a coveted commission from *Vogue* in 2018, making her the first Black woman to shoot a cover for the magazine in its 125-year history. Although this is something to celebrate, Ijewere hopes that we will see more equality in the fashion industry as time goes on, a sentiment I echo for the photography industry as a whole. As Ijewere so eloquently says, 'I want everyone to be seen in my work. I want to kick down as many doors as I can. I want the younger generation to follow, for one day I hope the industry will be an even playing ground.' **COS**

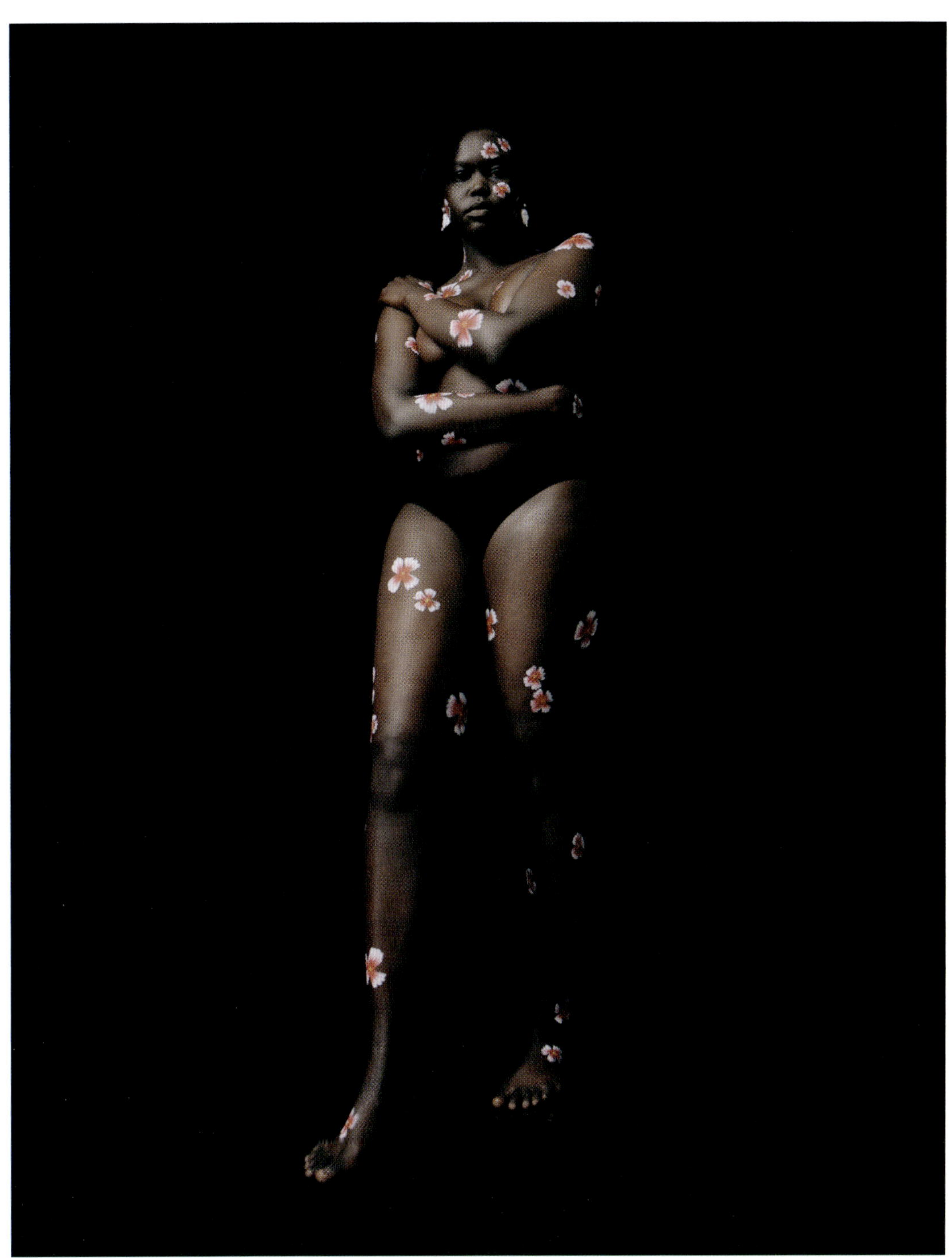

Create Your Own Studio

Creating a home studio doesn't have to be difficult or expensive. You don't need expensive or complex lighting setups, as the sun will provide a perfect light source in most situations.

You can create a basic studio either inside or outside with just a few simple pieces of equipment: a camera, a subject, a plain background and a light source – and that's it! Often when I create portraits with a studio-style background, I just use a plain wall and position the subject in front of it. If you move them away from the wall towards the camera and frame the portrait correctly, a shallow depth of field will give a soft background, which creates the impression that you've used a studio backdrop. This portrait of Jermaine (opposite) for example, shot on large-format film, uses the shallow depth of field that is naturally created by the format to its advantage, helping to create a softer background and giving the impression that the portrait could have been taken in a studio when it was, in fact, made on the street.

Another technique that's relatively inexpensive and is utilized by the iconic 20th-century portrait photographer Richard Avedon is to shoot against a section of seamless photographic background paper. This comes in around sixty different colours and costs less than £60 for a roll. My favourite colour for portraits is white or slightly off-white. Avedon would cut a section of the background roll and gaffer tape it to a wall to create a perfectly plain white backdrop against which to photograph his subject. The image on page 99 shows Avedon talking to a cowboy (one of his subjects), while his team sets up his large-format camera and dark slides. You can see his makeshift studio behind him utilizing the background paper and gaffer-tape technique. **COS**

▶ Cian Oba-Smith. Jermaine,
Syracuse, USA, 2019.

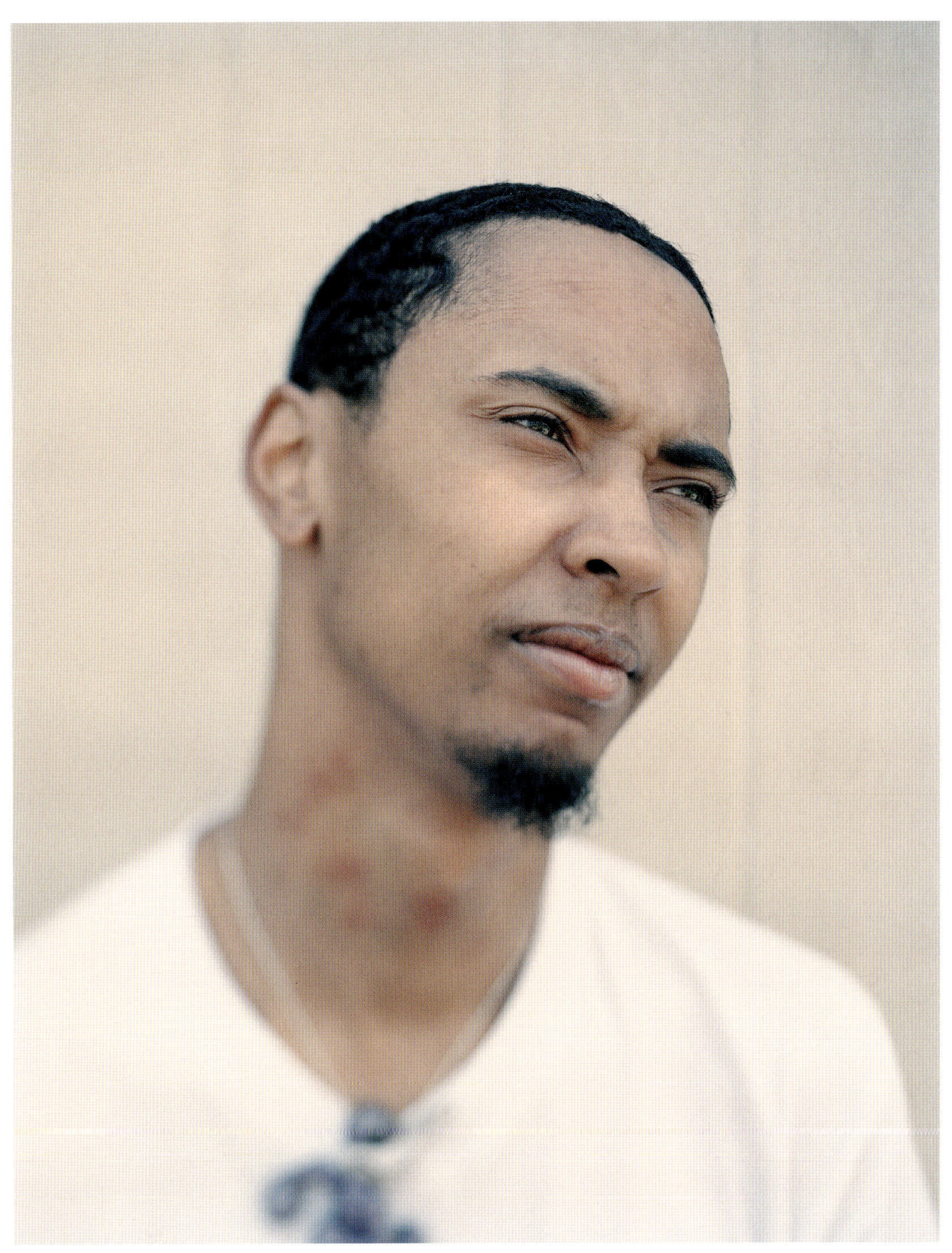

Task

Take your camera and background roll out onto the street (you may need help from friends for this) and look for a section of wall that's either south- or north-facing. A south-facing wall will provide sunlight all day long whereas a north-facing wall will provide shade throughout the day.

Decide which aspect you'd prefer to use, bearing in mind that a south-facing wall will provide more interesting lighting but on a bright day without clouds the sun can create harsh shadows and you will get a lot of changes in the lighting throughout the day. In contrast, a north-facing wall will create softer, flatter light with fewer shadows and more consistency. It's worth experimenting with both aspects to see how they affect your portraits and decide which you prefer.

Once you've settled on a spot, set up your background by gaffer-taping the paper to the wall with help from your friends. You want the paper to be nice and flat with no creases or marks. Do some test images of your friends to make sure everything looks fine in camera, then once you're happy with the setup, you can start asking passersby if you can take their portrait.

Most photographers find it very scary to ask someone if they can take their portrait. When I first started making pictures of strangers on the street, I was terrified to approach them, but you quickly learn that most people are open to being asked and if they're not interested, they'll politely let you know. The best approach is just to be polite and explain what you're doing and why you'd like to photograph them. It gets easier the more you do it, so put yourself out there a few times and your confidence will follow!

Conclusion

Setting up a studio in the street can be a great way to create a series of portraits with a common thread that ties them all together. The removal of the environment isolates the subject and allows us to see them in a different way. Creating a studio outside can be done cheaply, even for free. Remember to follow the steps we outlined in this project:

1. Decide on a north- or south-facing wall. The first will be shady, the second sunny.

2. Tape your background roll into place with the help of a friend or, alternatively, choose a plain-looking wall with little texture.

3. Take some test images of your friend.

4. Once you're happy with the setup, start asking passersby if you can take their portrait.

5. Remember to be conscious of everything we discussed in the project on Taking Better Portraits (see page 52).

6. Don't forget to note down people's contact details, so you can send them their portrait afterwards.

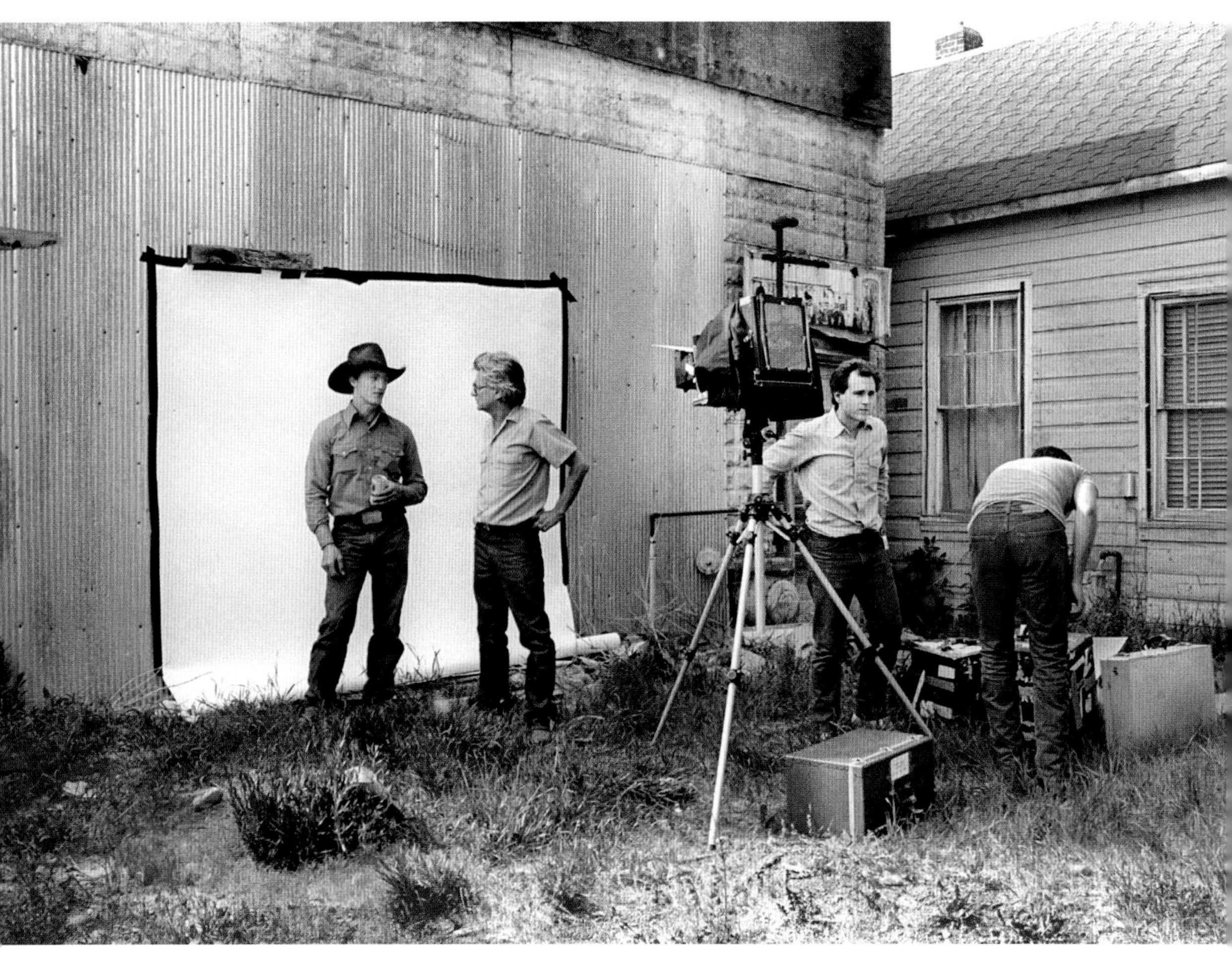

Laura Wilson. Richard Avedon talking
with a cowboy in Augusta, Montana.
From 'Avedon At Work', 1983.

Tom Johnson

born 1991, Oxfordshire, UK.
tomjohnson.studio

Tom Johnson's work sits in an interesting space photographically, blurring the lines between portraiture, fashion and documentary photography to produce a unique portfolio of images. Unlike most fashion photography, in which the subjects are models or those cast specifically for their looks, Tom Johnson's work mainly features people chosen because of who they are as a person, whether that is a stunt rider, monk, acrobat or member of any community that draws him in. For Johnson, photography is an excuse to explore the world and satisfy his curiosity – it is his route to understanding the world.

Johnson's motivation for creating photographs of communities of every kind comes from a place of wanting to highlight the connections between humans and find the commonalities among us. As he explained: 'I like to tell stories of real people and how they are connected together. Community is a very important aspect of my work.'

The photograph opposite is of stuntman and *Globe of Death* rider Peter Pavlov and his partner. Johnson spent some time with Peter Pavlov, travelling with him and the circus he performs with. The portrait appears to have been lit using natural light from the left-hand side. If I were to hazard a guess, I would say that the image was made in the late afternoon, due to the warmth and slight softness of the light. This light is similar to that of golden hour lighting, a term used to describe the quality of light shortly after sunrise or before sunset.

At first glance, the portrait seems to conform to gender stereotypes, with the woman sitting on the man's lap leading us to think this is the case. However, on further investigation, we notice the subtler details – the woman's left hand is resting on top of the man's hand and her right hand is placed gently around his neck, pulling him in and providing comfort. Interestingly, Johnson has directed the subjects to close their eyes for the portrait. This is unusual because the eyes are normally an incredibly important part of how the viewer connects with a subject. In this portrait, the lack of eye contact and the position of the subjects creates a sense of vulnerability – it feels as if we are witnessing a captured moment of intimacy in the couple's life. **COS**

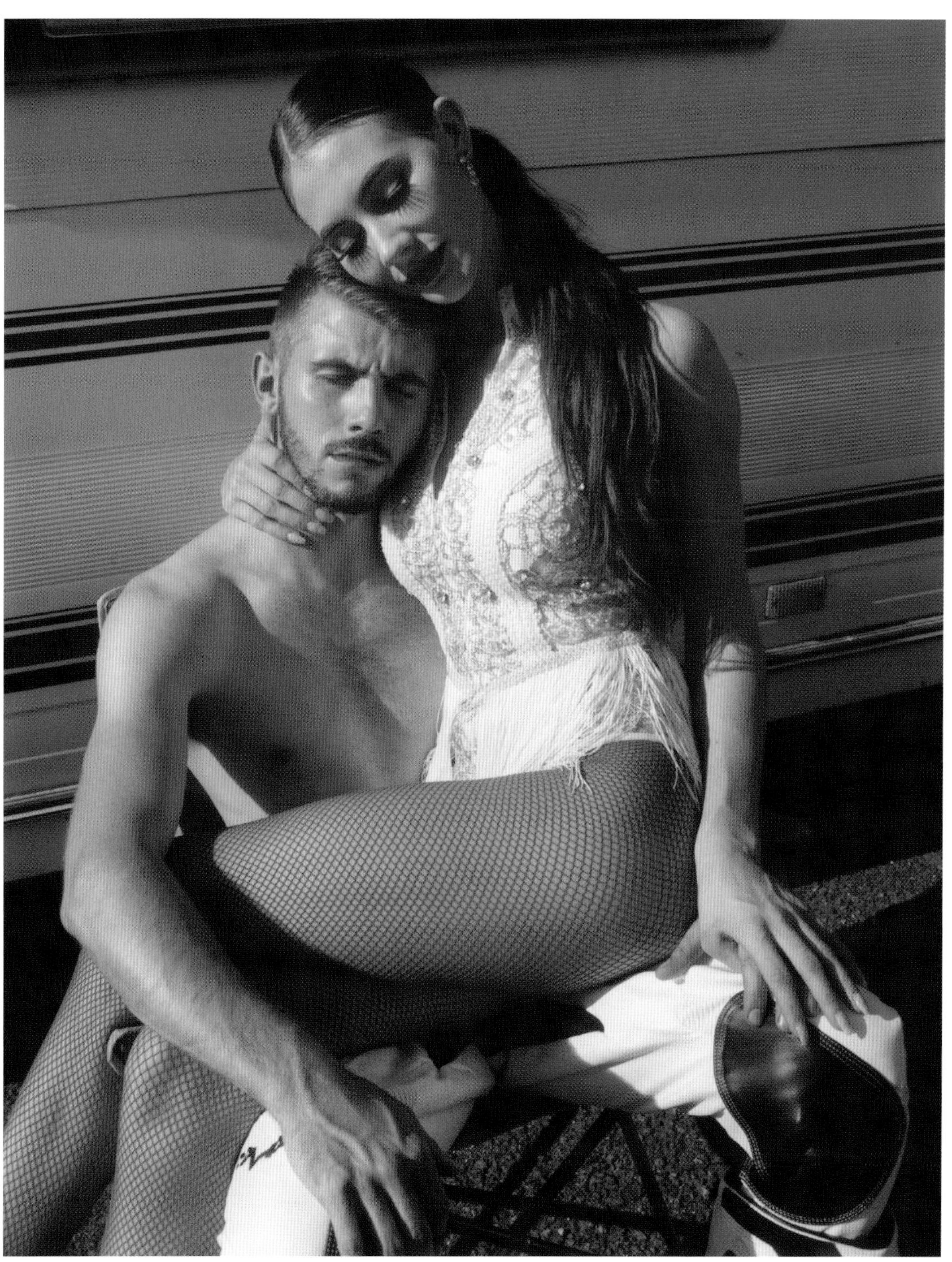

Experimenting with Poses: Tom Johnson

Photographic subjects have their own autonomy, of course, as individual people with their own identity, but with the right direction they can also become objects within the frame, forming part of the composition.

Regardless of your approach to photography, posing your subject is an important part of the process of creating a portrait. Documentary photographers tend to spend less time posing their subjects, whereas fashion photographers will give a lot more direction. The majority of my work fits into the documentary category, so when I'm making project work, I will only direct the subject slightly, telling them to stand in a specific spot, so I can compose the portrait, or asking them to look in a certain direction. If they're doing a cheesy smile or something similar, I suggest that we try a slightly more 'serious' one. However, I try not to give my subjects too much direction because I want the person that I'm photographing to present themselves how they would naturally.

Tom Johnson, whose work we discussed in the preceding profile, takes a similar approach to his documentary-type work. The portrait seen opposite of a mother and her daughter was made as part of a series on the Semeneyek family in Southern Ukraine. Throughout 2020, Tom spent time with the family's 347 members, photographing them and capturing the special bonds that exist between each generation.

One of the key aspects of directing your subjects effectively is creating trust between them and yourself. This was something Johnson had to build before he could photograph the family. As he explained:

'I originally found a translator in Ukraine who went and made contact with the family, as I couldn't find them on the Internet. It took a long time for them to trust me. We had to drive across Ukraine from Kyiv

▶ Tom Johnson. The Semeneyek family, Ukraine, 2020.

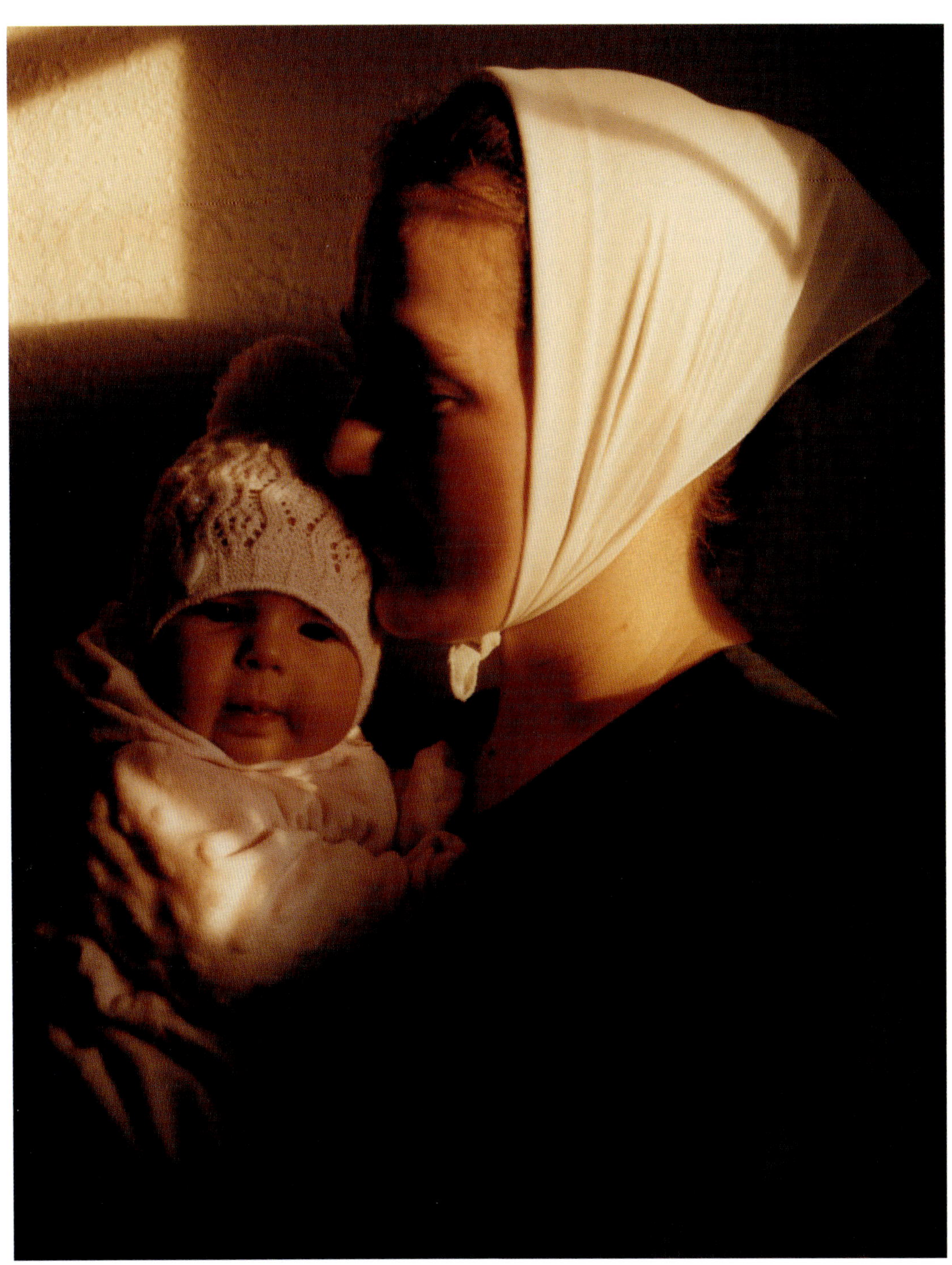

to below Odessa, which took seven or so hours. When we got there, even though he made contact and we did have some kind of permission, we still had to come back over multiple days and I had to do a speech in front of the entire church (this was very nerve-racking), so they could understand what I was doing before we could start taking any photos.'

Johnson provided more details on how the photograph was made, saying:

'This photo was taken after a few days of shooting. One of the elders of the village was showing me around and invited me into his shed to eat some pickled tomatoes that he had made and was very proud of. I wasn't planning on taking any more photos, as it was the end of the day, but I saw this mother and her daughter in the house, and asked permission to take some photos of her and her baby. I couldn't speak Ukrainian and she couldn't speak English, so I think the translator helped me. I moved her into the light, and we shot fast as it was going. I just wanted to portray this closeness and intimacy. In these moments, I try to be quieter and calmer than on my fashion shoots. I will direct my subjects to an extent, but I still want to portray reality. This is not a fashion shoot. I want them to be comfortable and treat them respectfully.'

The portrait on the left was made by Tom Johnson in India for *The Plant* magazine.

'Everyday I would sit down and storyboard what I wanted to create, and we would go around local shops and buy random props and objects. I would work with my friend/assistant to play around with them and figure out what we could do with them. We'd just try and be loose and fun with it. We would then have a boot full of fabrics, flowers, and shiny and colourful things for the subjects to interact with.

When you pull a massive camera and a bunch of flowers out the back of a car, people are often quite confused, but they are also very interested, and it kind of makes them more comfortable. When driving down the road we saw this group of schoolkids and teachers, and asked them if we could take their portrait.'

The portrait featured above opposite shows a different approach, when Johnson was working on a studio fashion shoot in London for *T* magazine, which marked a change of pace for him as he prefers to work outside. Here Johnson explains in detail how he made this portrait:

'For this shot, we wanted all of the five models in the shot, and focused on the dark makeup around their eyes. It was about uniformity. I would then place them all very close together, almost on top of each other, and got them to get as close as they could to each other to fit them all in the frame. I've often asked people to close their eyes, it makes you look at people in a different way; for me, you can look further into them, giving them a sense of stillness. I would try variations of having their eyes open, ask them to move their heads around to make sure the symmetry feels right. I wanted to have a huge studio for this one, so we

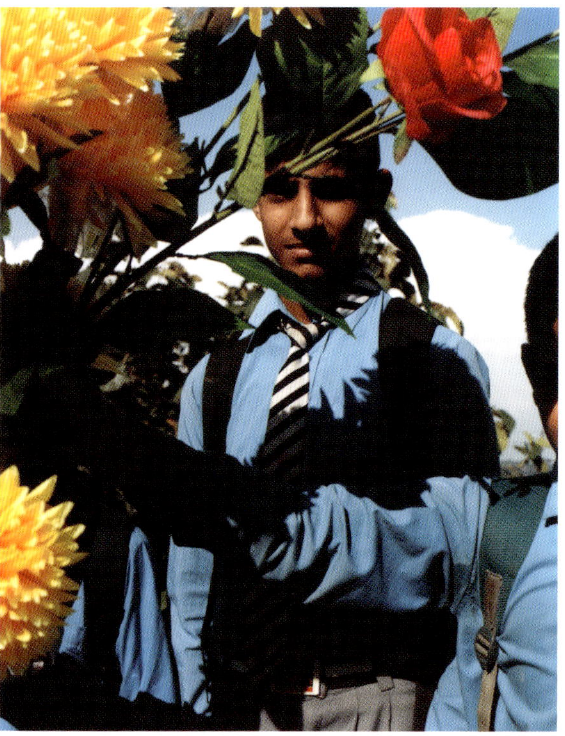

◀ Tom Johnson. *The Plant* magazine, 2018.

could play with perspectives and treat it like I would a huge landscape.'

Energy is often the key to getting the most of your subjects, whether that's a mellow energy to match their mood or a more upbeat energy to lift it. Johnson described how he approached the photograph below right of the group holding flowers:

'In this portrait made for *Re-Edition Magazine,* energy was the key. There were about six people holding this huge, billowing parachute behind and it was windy, so it was blowing all over the place. I often end up very muddy after shoots, as I roll all over the floor to get the image, often climbing trees and running around. Sometimes you have to act like a kid to get the shot, and have this child-like curiosity.'

Looking at this portrait you wouldn't necessarily know that all of this was going on behind the scenes – indeed, part of the magic of photography is that it can freeze a moment of beauty in the broader chaos. **COS**

Conclusion

Your approach to posing your subject should be tailored to the image you're making. Some pictures call for a tranquil approach, whereas others require more of an energetic atmosphere. Communication between yourself and the subject is key, as is creating the right atmosphere to allow the picture to happen.

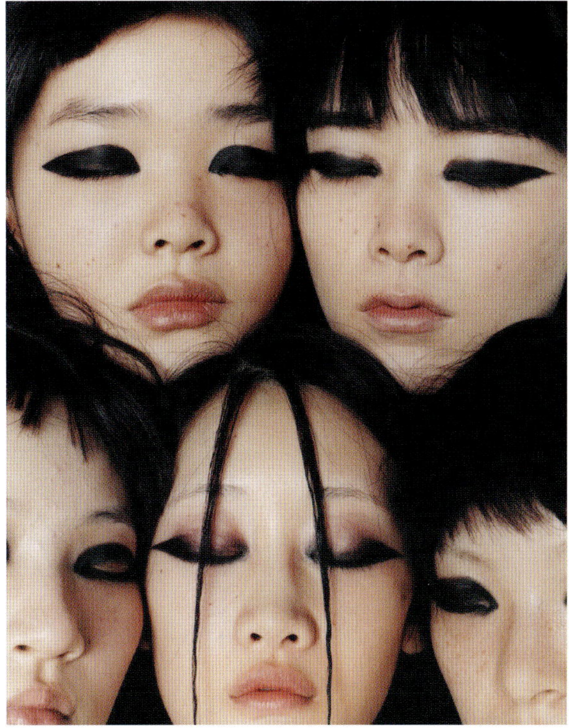

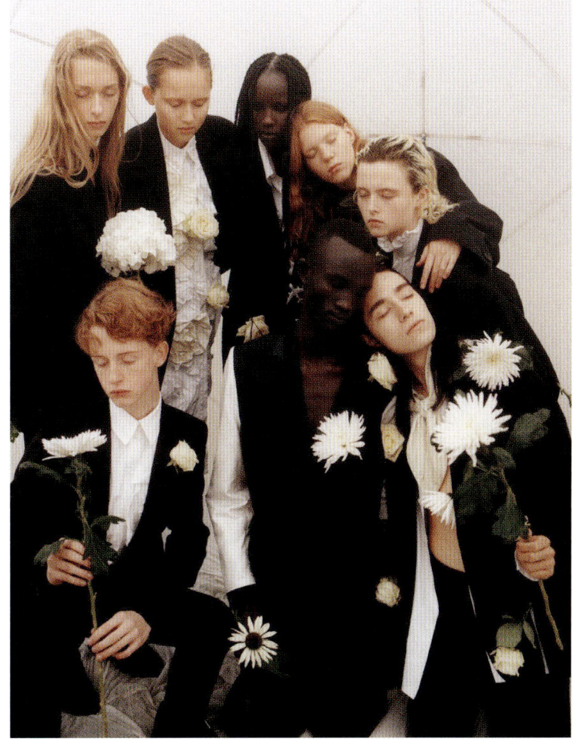

Tom Johnson. *Re-Edition Magazine,* 2019.

Zanele Muholi

born 1972, Umlazi, South Africa.

Zanele Muholi has described themselves as a visual activist rather than an artist – and when you view their work, it is easy to see why.

Despite the censorship that Zanele Muholi has faced, they have managed to create some incredibly powerful black-and-white portraits that document and generate conversations around the plight of South Africa's Black LGBTQI+ community. Muholi views their work as collaborative, being a member of the LGBTQI+ community themselves and having documented the community since the early 2000s in order to raise awareness of the issues faced by its members.

The self-portrait shown here, titled 'Phila I, Parktown, 2016', draws our attention instantly. Muholi's unwavering gaze locks eyes with us and allows us no respite. It is usual in black-and-white photography to have a broad spectrum of black through to grey and on to white. However, Muholi's decision to use high-contrast black and white makes it seem as if there are hardly any grey areas, an approach that helps highlight the texture of the gloves, with the slightly deflated ones almost looking like human hands. This effect is something of a trademark, consistently appearing throughout their various bodies of work as a stylistic choice.

In this 2017 collection of photographs, 'Somnyama Ngonyama' (Zulu for 'Hail the Dark Lioness'), Muholi created a series of 365 striking self-portraits. The project evolved as a result of a racist incident involving a hotel manager in New York in 2012, which led Muholi to create a self-portrait in their hotel room. This self-portrait then became the catalyst for when they returned to the project in 2014. Muholi made 365 portraits to represent a year of their lived experience. In Zanele's own words, 'You live as a Black person for 365 days. There are a lot of events and experiences that you go through in a year and I wanted to map those important or specific moments.' **COS**

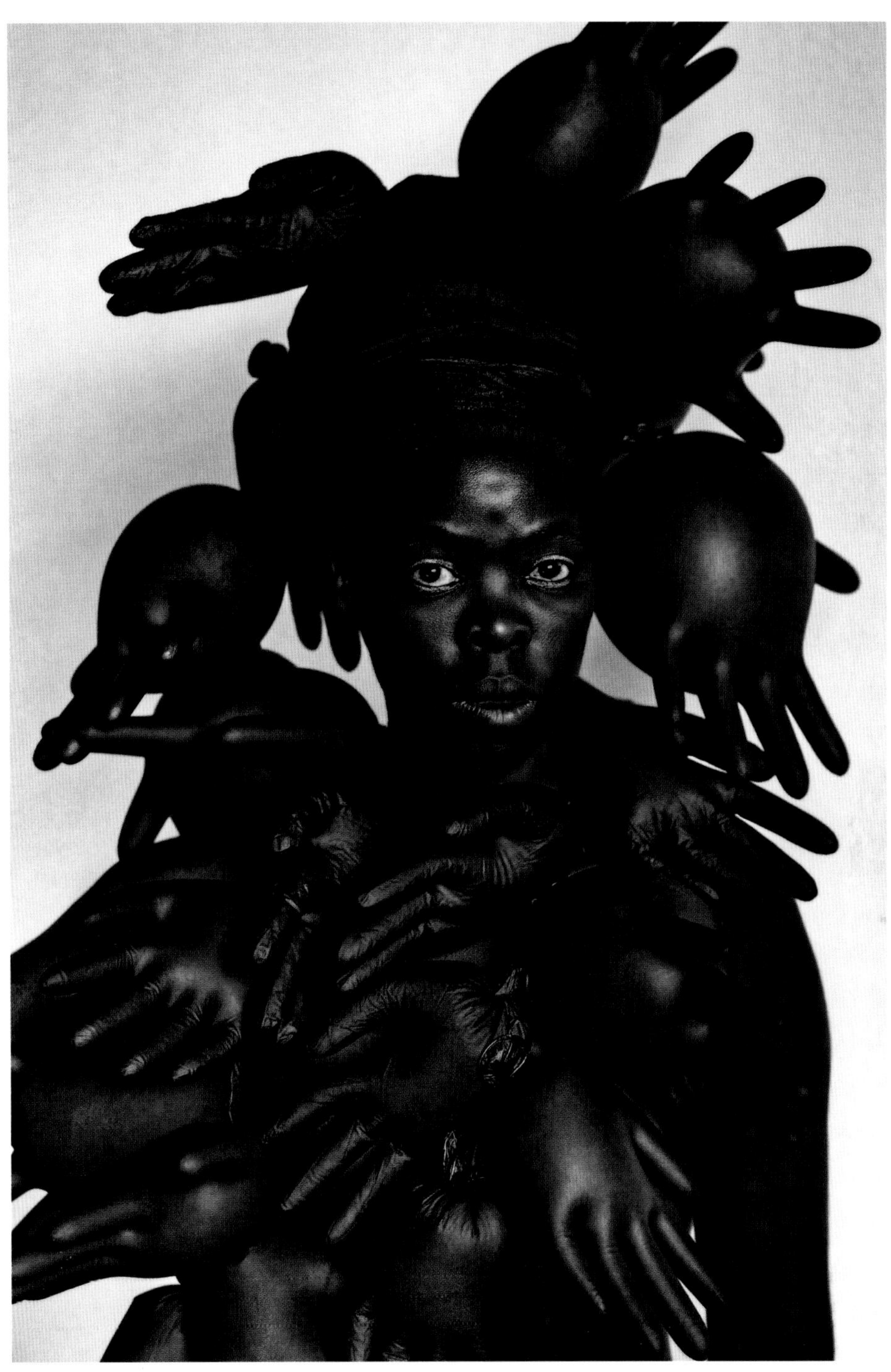

Playing with Lighting

Lighting is one of the most important elements of creating a great portrait, influencing how an image is read and, if used correctly, transforming an average portrait into something incredible.

In this project, we look at a few basic lighting ideas and how to implement them. First off, it's important to be aware that there are two main types of light: natural light (the sun, for example) and artificial light (whether flash or continuous lighting). Artificial lighting gives you more control, and in theory anything is possible with enough lights and a big enough budget.

Flash lighting works by firing a short burst of bright light when the camera shutter is triggered – it might be a flash gun attached to the camera or one or more strobes set up externally. Continuous lighting is simply lighting that stays on. There are three main types of bulbs that fall under this category of artificial lighting: fluorescent, tungsten and LED (light-emitting diode).

Fluorescent lights are the type of lighting you see in offices and commercial buildings, for example, but they are not generally very popular among photographers. They produce a low light output with a green/blue cast and don't create particularly aesthetic results. However, there are some advantages to using them, namely their low cost and energy efficiency, but I personally would not recommend them.

Tungsten lights are traditionally used in the film and TV industries, but they are also useful for photography. They emit a yellowish glow similar to sunlight, which is complementary to skin tones – so great for portraits! There are various advantages to using tungsten lights: for example, they are brighter than fluorescent lights, reasonably priced and versatile. The disadvantages are that they get very hot and use a lot of power, the colour temperature can be inconsistent after lots of use, and the bulbs can be fragile and do not have a very long shelf life.

LED lights are starting to rival tungsten lights as the industry standard for continuous lighting. This is because you can easily control the colour temperature of the lights and the bulbs also have a much longer shelf life than tungsten or fluorescent ones. They're not without their disadvantages, however. Good-quality LED lights are expensive, can have poor battery life and are not as powerful as tungsten lights; they are good for lighting indoors, but not especially useful

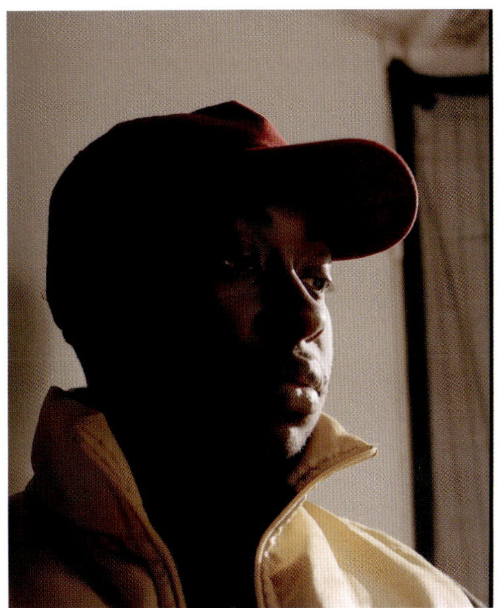 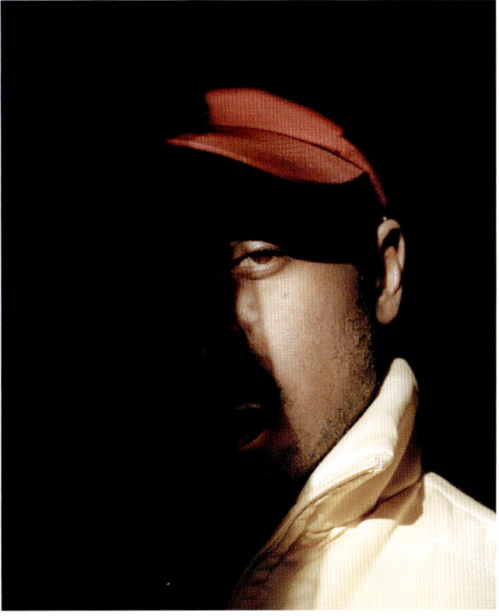

Taken inside Oscar's home, the main light in
this image is coming from outside the door on
the right. The sky is clear, so bright sunlight is
directly hitting the left-hand side of his face.
Another window behind me, the photographer,
is creating a small amount of ambient light,
which fills in the shadows on the right-hand side
of his face. I often use my hand as a point of
focus for the subject, directing them to look at
it and then moving it until the light is positioned
correctly for the portrait.

This image is lit by a single light source.
I've now swapped places with Oscar and am
standing in the doorway to his right in the first
image. The light is coming directly from the sun
through the doorway, and you can see the edge
of the curtain creating a soft shadow across the
right-hand side of his left eye. I've positioned
Oscar so that the background is a dark room
in the house. The contrast between the bright
sunlight and the dark room creates the effect
seen here; it gives the impression that Oscar has
been photographed against a black backdrop.

Here Oscar is lying on the ground in the snow. The sun is also behind the clouds in this image, but the fact that Oscar's hood is down and he's lying on the floor with the sun directly above him helps to fill in more of the shadows on his face. The surrounding snow bounces additional light from the sun onto him (white reflects light; black absorbs light), softening the shadows further.

outside. They can also produce flickering and banding on some settings with certain cameras, which is something you want to avoid.

The advantage that continuous lighting has over flash is that it enables you to see what the light is doing without having to take a test picture. They're also great if you want to shoot video as well as take pictures. However, flash lighting is more portable than continuous lighting, as well as more powerful.

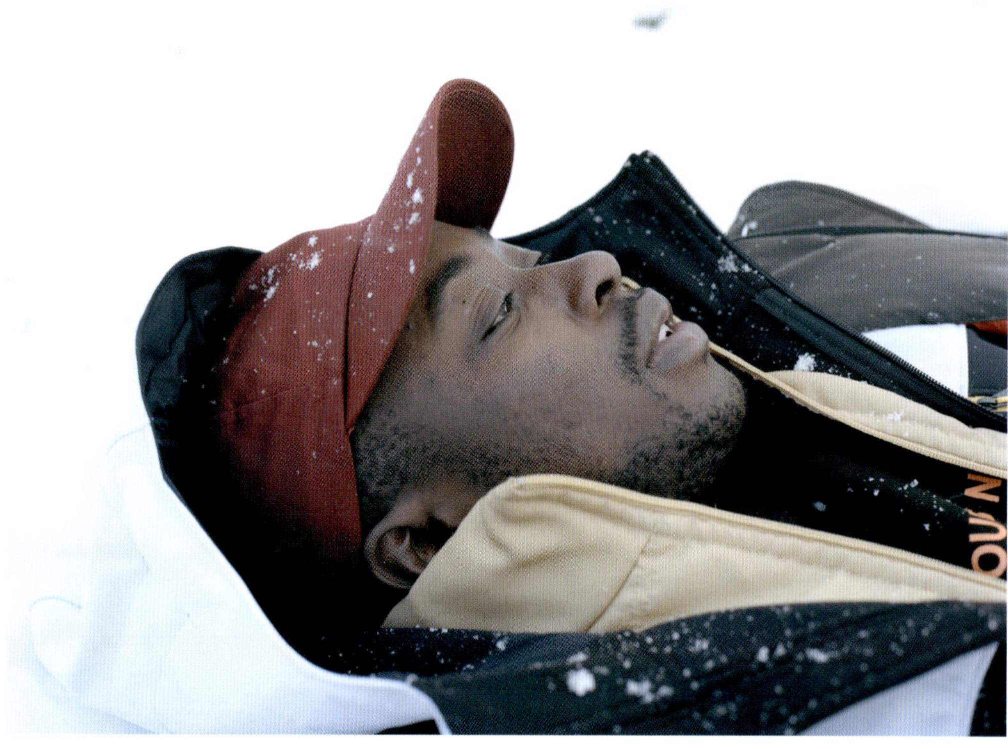

When it comes to purchasing lighting equipment, the old saying 'buy cheap, buy twice' couldn't be more true. Good lighting kit is not cheap. Cheap lights have inconsistent power and colour rendition, which is why we feature examples of photographs here that have been lit with natural light, which is free, of high quality and almost everywhere!

The portraits of rapper Oscar #Worldpeace on these pages were all taken for *Brick* magazine. They were shot with one or two sources of natural light in one afternoon. You can use these examples to create similar lighting in your own work.

Task

This project has looked at just a few of the ways you can use natural light to create compelling portraits. It's important to experiment and find what works for you, so have a go at the following task: look for different light sources throughout your home or local area (these could be windows or doorways, for example). How can you use these spaces to create different lighting setups? Try using the same space to create portraits at different times of day and in various weather conditions. Take note of where the sun is positioned during each portrait and how this affects the image. **COS**

Conclusion

The images in this project highlight just a few of the different ways in which you can light a portrait using natural light. There are almost unlimited options when it comes to lighting, both with artificial and natural light. Try out different ways of lighting your subject and don't be afraid to make mistakes!

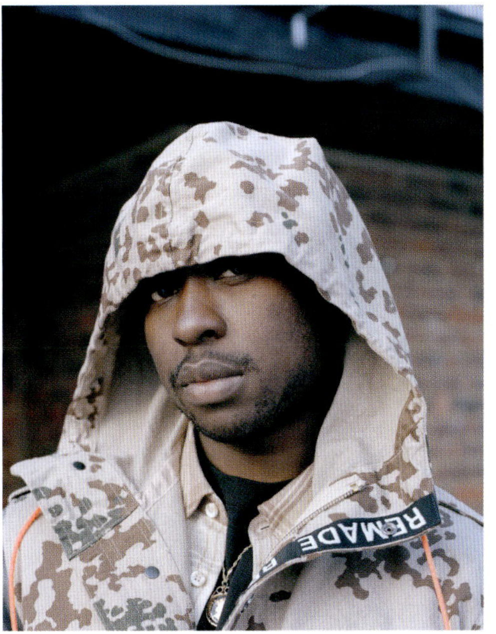

This portrait was made outside in the early afternoon in winter. The sky is overcast, which produces the effect you see here. The sun is above us to the left and in front of where Oscar is standing. The sun is shining through a layer of thin, light grey cloud, which filters the light to create a slightly softer effect. This type of lighting tends to be more flattering since it gets rid of harsh shadows, smooths the skin and lowers contrast.

Seydou Keïta

1921–2001, Bamako, Mali, West Africa.

Although Seydou Keïta primarily took photographs in the early to mid-20th century, they still feel modern and exciting, rather than dated. Keïta worked at his studio in Bamako, Mali, from the 1950s to the 1970s, but almost all the photographs we know of are from the 1950s. They reveal the day-to-day lives of the people who came into his studio. The props featured in the portraits were supplied by Keïta's studio and would change every few years, creating an interesting chronology in his works.

The photograph featured here shows a young woman sitting on a Solex bicycle. These motorized cycles were the height of cool in the early 1950s. I have given the crop Keïta used in this image careful consideration. It is a little curious and doesn't quite fit the rule of thirds – the subject's eyeline is high up in the image and there is quite a lot of ground visible at the bottom of the frame. These features specifically drew my attention and encouraged me to include the photograph in the book – they are also proof that breaking the rules of photography works time and time again. These are studio portraits but not as we think of them. Keïta bought the outside in to the photograph. The motorized bicycle, the uncovered ground, a bag draped over the handlebars might always make us question where she is going. But the Solex is stationary, sitting on its stand and a backdrop is hung behind her. Perhaps then these photographs are best considered as wonderful windows into Keïta's Bamako half a century ago.

In other images made by Keïta at around the same time we see people posing, usually on their own but occasionally in groups, and again with various props. For example, a woman leans on a radio. A couple sit astride a moped. Often, it is the backgrounds that become the props. Bright and patterned fabrics rendered for us only in black and white create dramatic patterns, sometimes blending, sometimes clashing, with women's dresses and men's sharp suits.

Keïta's photographs came to prominence outside Mali in the 1990s when galleries and museums in the United States and Europe began to pay attention to West African studio photography. Photographers such as Keïta, Sanlé Sory (b. 1921) and Malick Sidibé (1935–2016) were all making work in their own studios in different countries. They are probably still not given enough credit for how much they have advanced portrait photography. **MF**

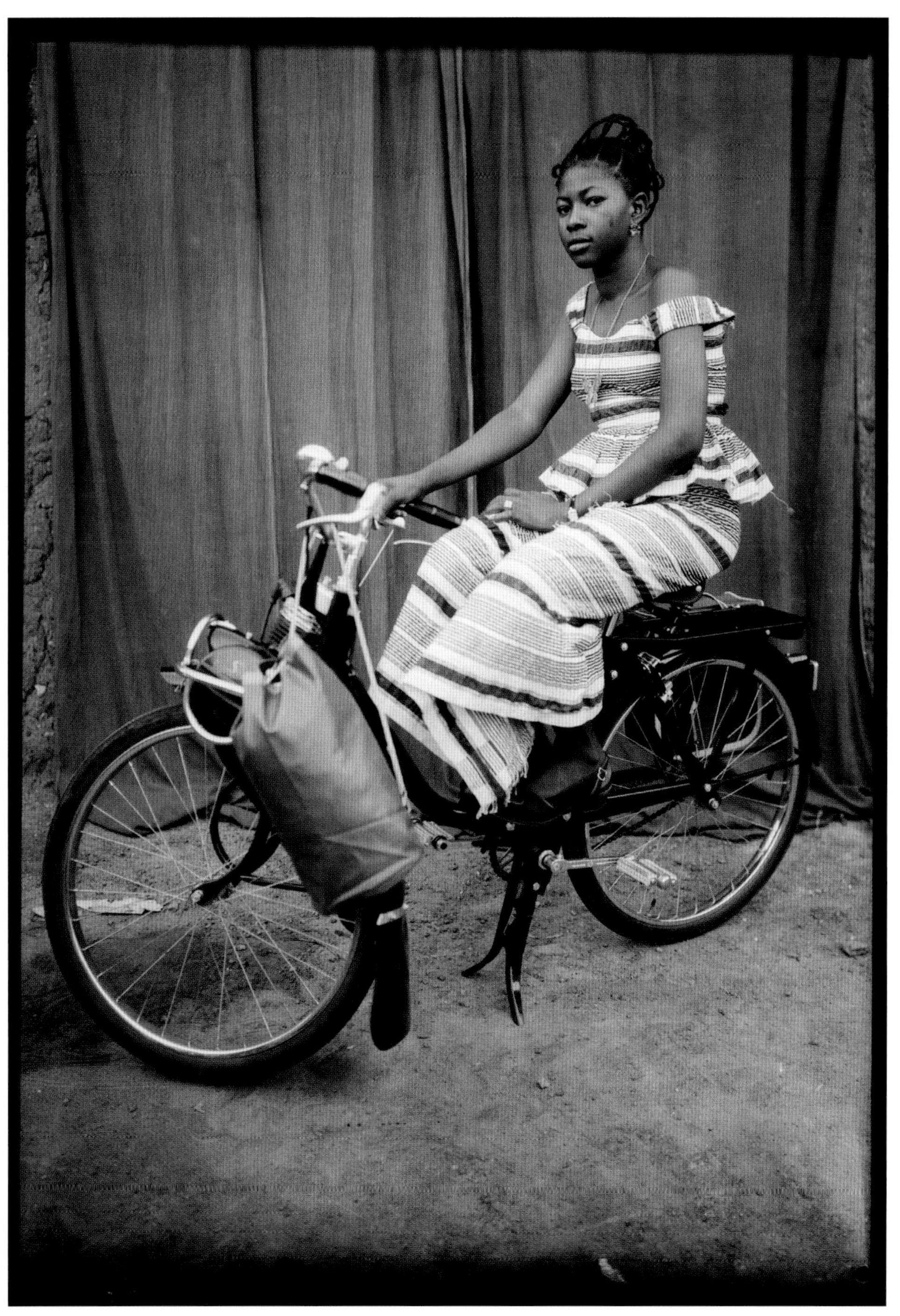

CHAPTER 4

Family and Friends

Turn the lens on those who are closest to you – your family and friends. Explore how other photographers have documented their own loved ones too.

Family portraits were originally formal affairs, similar in style to the traditional portrait painting seen over the centuries and something only the wealthy could afford. Having your photograph taken was unusual and the subjects of the portrait would often dress up for the occasion. As time went on and photography became more accessible, the style of family portraits shifted. In general, the manner in which the subjects posed for photographic portraits became more candid and less formal.

Although, on the surface, photographs of family and friends may seem mundane – for example, these pictures of my mum (opposite) and Maura, a family friend in Ireland (see page 116) appear on the surface as everyday snapshots – time has given meaning to the images, serving as a record of a specific moment in time. This is the power of photographing your family and friends. The resulting images provide an intimate historical insight into how people lived and how we have arrived at where we are today.

Photographer Carrie Mae Weems's 'The Kitchen Table Series' (1990) is successful at doing just that. The work provides a record of life as a Black woman in the United States, showing mutually shared experiences while simultaneously documenting her own personal journey. 'This woman can stand in for me and for you; she can stand in for the audience, she leads you into history. She's a witness and a guide,' Weems told

Projects

▶ Cian Oba-Smith. Mum, London, 2014.

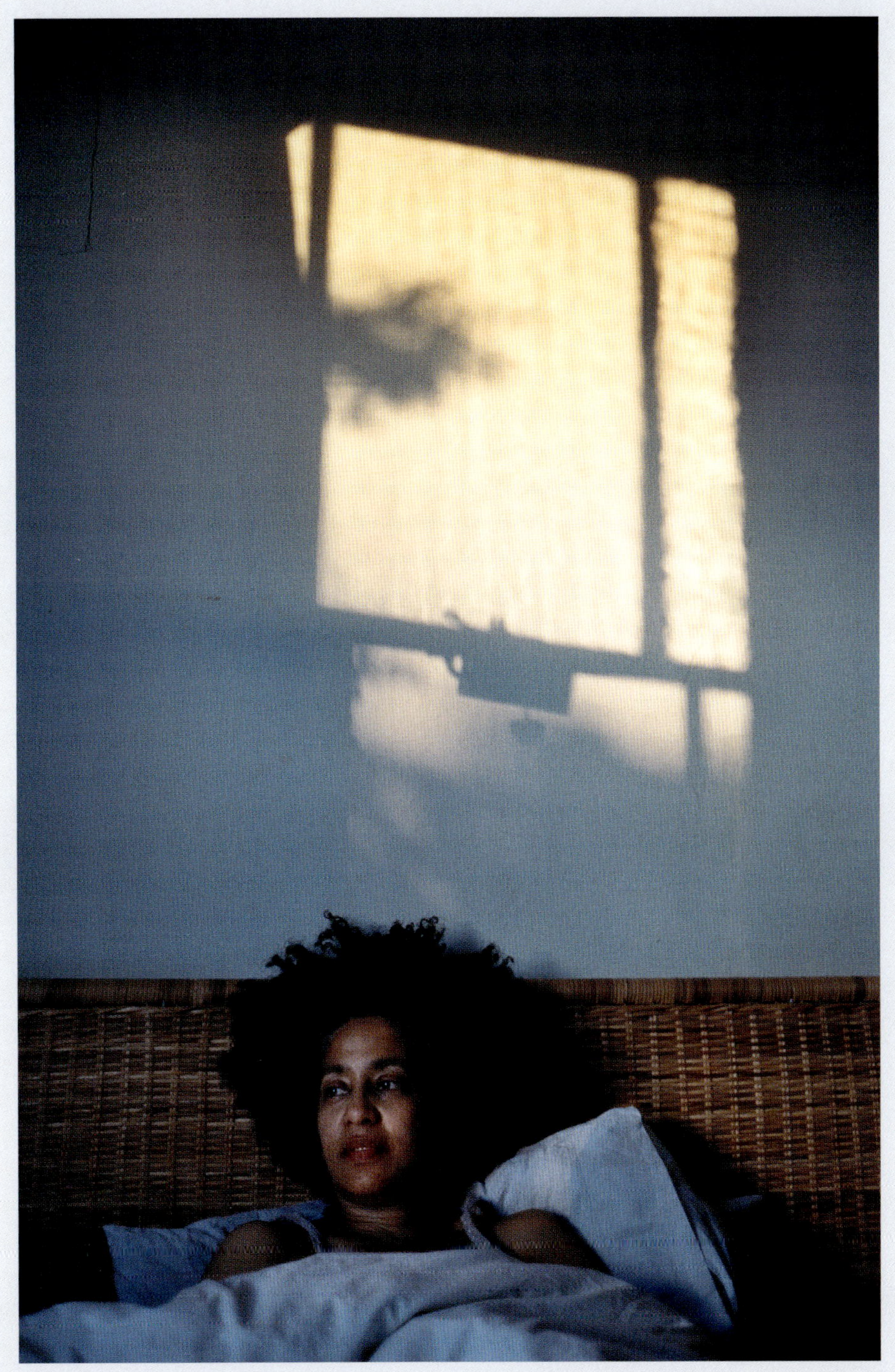

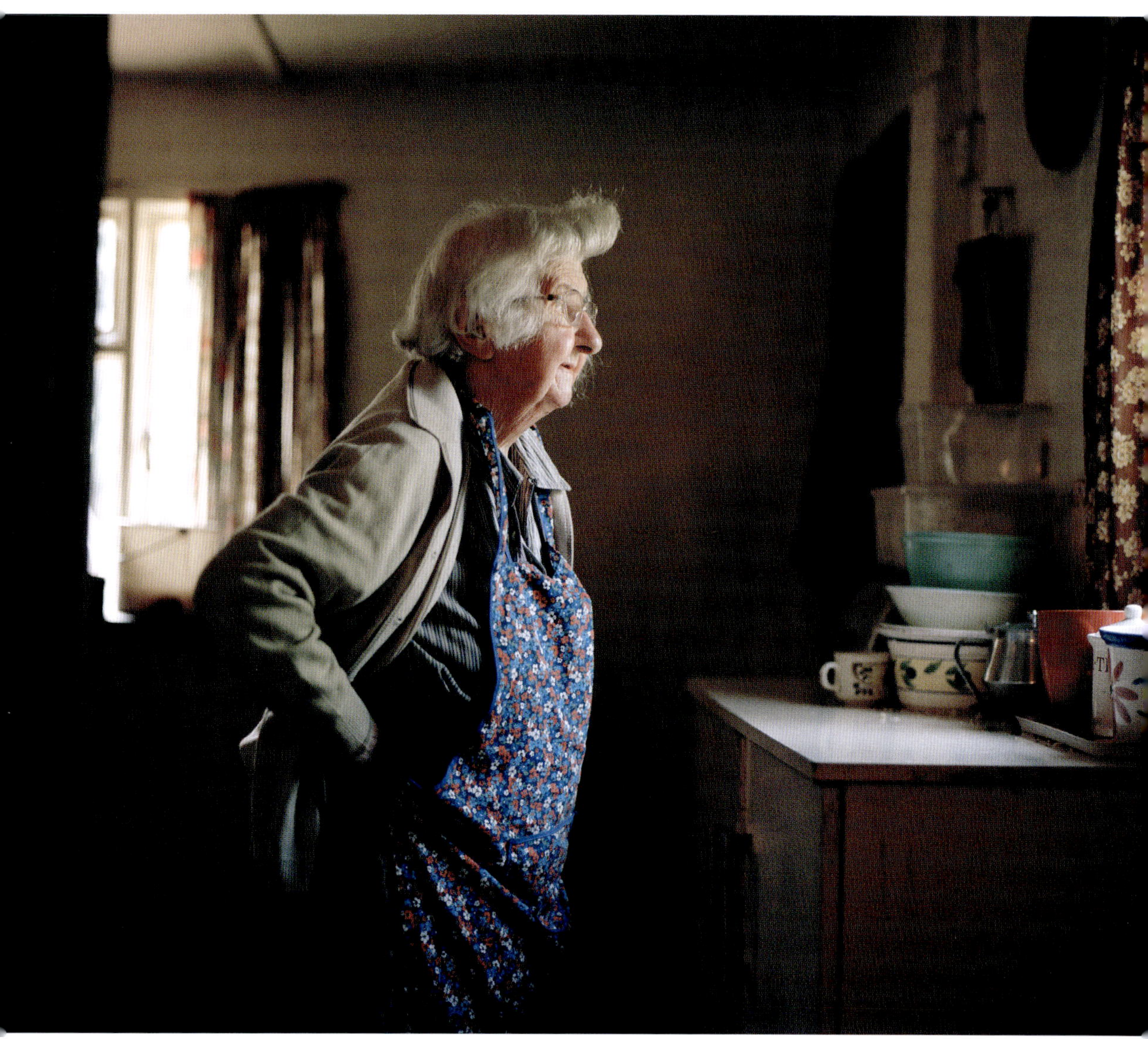

Cian Oba-Smith. Maura, County Meath, Ireland, 2015.

fellow photographer Dawoud Bey in a discussion for *BOMB Magazine* in 2009. Similarly, in the book *I Can't Stand to See You Cry* (2021) by photographer Rahim Fortune (see page 8), this autobiographical approach – pairing pictures of family and friends with broader social events – is utilized to extremely emotive effect. The project documents the passing of his father against a backdrop of the George Floyd uprising and what both events meant for him and his family and friends.

Photographs of family and friends can also be a way of sharing a window into the intimate areas of our lives. For instance, Pixy Liao's playful portraits (see page 128) from her series 'Experimental Relationship' (2007) subvert and reverse the assumed expectations of gender roles and the male gaze. Her partner often appears in portraits in more submissive roles, with Pixy being the nurturer, although throughout the series there is a common thread of intimacy and mutual support.

It is difficult to discuss photographers who have made portraits of their family and friends without looking at the work of Sally Mann. Mann's project 'Immediate Family' (1992) depicts her family life in rural Virginia, in the United States, and her three young children, Jessie, Emmett and Virginia, in particular. Shot on large-format (8 × 10 inch) black-and-white film, which is an unusual choice for family photographs, Mann was driven to photograph her children, because in her own words: 'Every parent thinks their child is the most amazing, marvellous thing ever on earth. I use my photographs to reflect that astonishment and gratitude.'

Mann's work was controversial when it was first published, especially because many of the photographs featured nudity, with critics saying that the portraits sexualized Mann's children. Despite this, Mann and her now adult children contest that the work was taken out of context and the critics were seeing what they wanted to see rather than the truth behind the photographs. Personally, I see images of a childhood spent in nature and the freedom that comes with that. Photography can be interpreted in so many different ways and often the interpretation is a reflection of the viewer themselves.

For many contemporary photographers, their first subjects are family and friends. Just like all humans, their world view is shaped by their environment, which consists of family and friends as well as other people around them. Therefore, it is only natural that photographers should begin by focusing on them. Moreover, for many photographers, family and friends are present as a consistent subject that weaves through the span of their lifetime. However, this is not to say that they are also not of great interest to us. **COS**

Tereza Červeňová

born 1991, Bratislava, Slovakia.
terezacervenova.com

I first saw Tereza Červeňová's photographs while she was studying for a BA in photography in London. Since then, we've worked together on commissions several times. I've always been struck by the similarities between the commissioned portraits she makes for magazines and her personal work. It sometimes seems as if she is unable to separate the two. And I love that about her work.

At roughly the same time that Červeňová started her master's degree at the Royal College of Art, the United Kingdom voted to leave the European Union. Červeňová spent the next two years working on 'June' – a body of work that is deeply personal, giving us an insight into what Brexit means for a young Slovakian artist living in London – and shooting the people around her and the places in which she found herself. The images are arranged chronologically. Each image is also titled and dated. Photographs of buildings, fences and animals become as significant as the people that appear in her photographs.

The work Červeňová makes could be described as diaristic or autobiographical. She likes to shoot tender moments – often photographing those closest to her. I love this photograph of her brother. It is a slightly unusual portrait because we can't see his face and, usually, a lot of our reading of a portrait comes from the subject's facial expressions. When I asked Červeňová about this picture she explained:

'This was one of the first images that I took and that I actually knew I wanted to take photos of. My brother's back, which was covered with quite deep stretchmarks from how fast he grew up.'

Then, continuing in greater depth, which is indicative of Červeňová's thoughtful approach to photography, she added: 'The thinner skin, where the skin broke apart, reminded me of the symbol of strength in unity. That by breaking apart we become weaker and leave scars. But then also as an acknowledgment that growth and separation are a natural part of life.'

When we look at this photograph, all we see is a young man's back. But in many ways everything that Červeňová explained to me is also a part of it. Maybe that's the magic of photography? **MF**

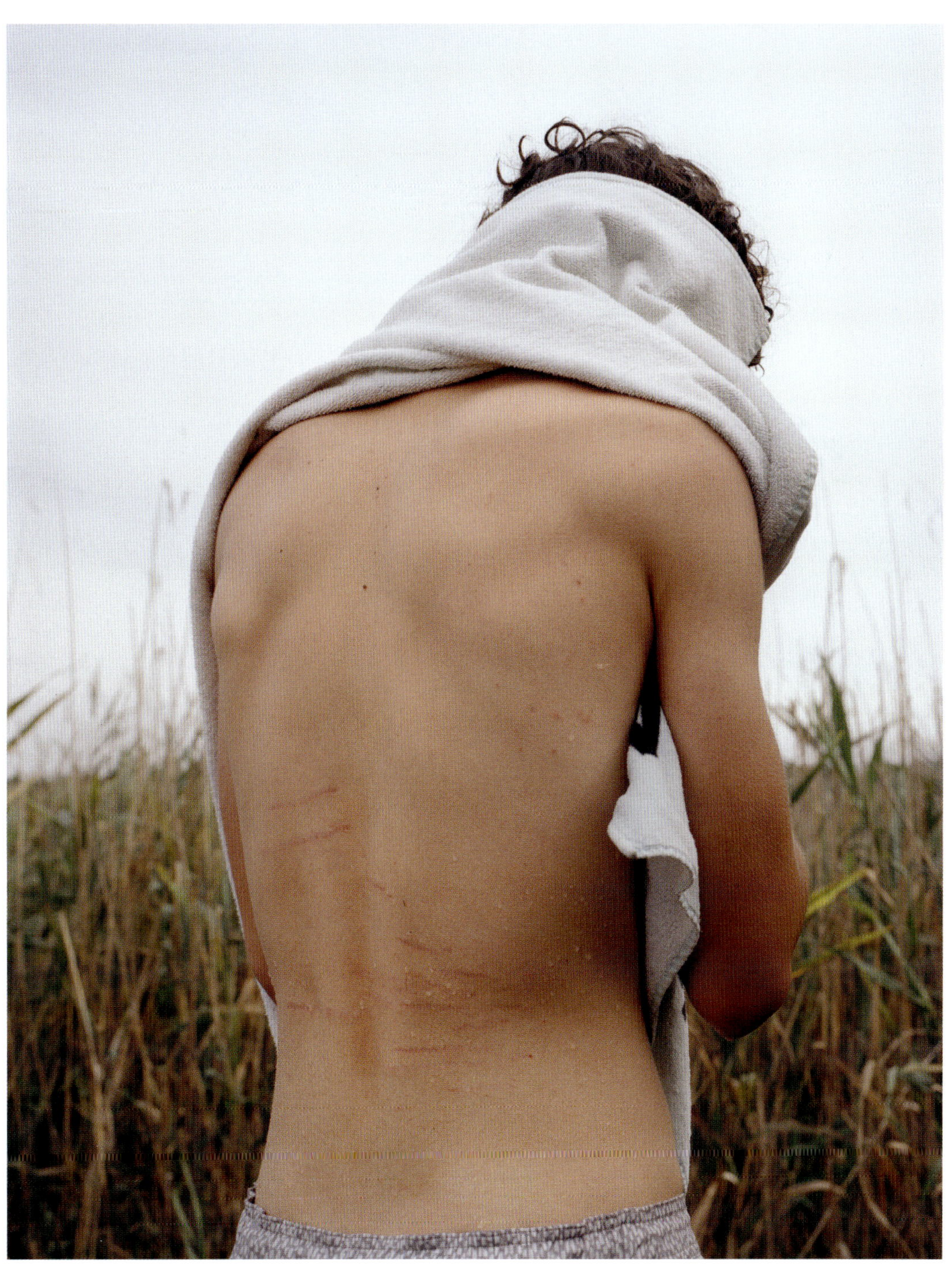

Capturing Personal Moments

Incredible portraits can be found anywhere – look to those closest to you for inspiration.

If you ask photographers who their first subject was, they will nearly always tell you that they started by photographing their family and friends. This is because the people who are the closest to us usually make excellent subjects: they are patient and take direction well and the affection we have for one another often comes across, which helps to create a portrait with more depth. Friends and family allow us to tell the stories that no one else can. You will not have the same unique relationships with any other people on earth as those you have with your family and friends.

Most of my personal photos are taken with a 35mm film camera. This is because the camera is compact and I carry it with me most of the time, which includes when I'm just hanging out with my family and friends. The other film cameras I use, a Mamiya RZ67 and a Toyo 45AII, aren't very practical for day-to-day use. I only really use my Sony A9II digital camera for commissioned work, otherwise I mostly shoot on film.

The portrait of my partner Aurore shown opposite was taken on holiday in France, the summer after I graduated from university. I woke up early in the morning and the sunlight was filtering through the window, illuminating the room as well as her. I metered for the highlights and then chose to slightly overexpose so

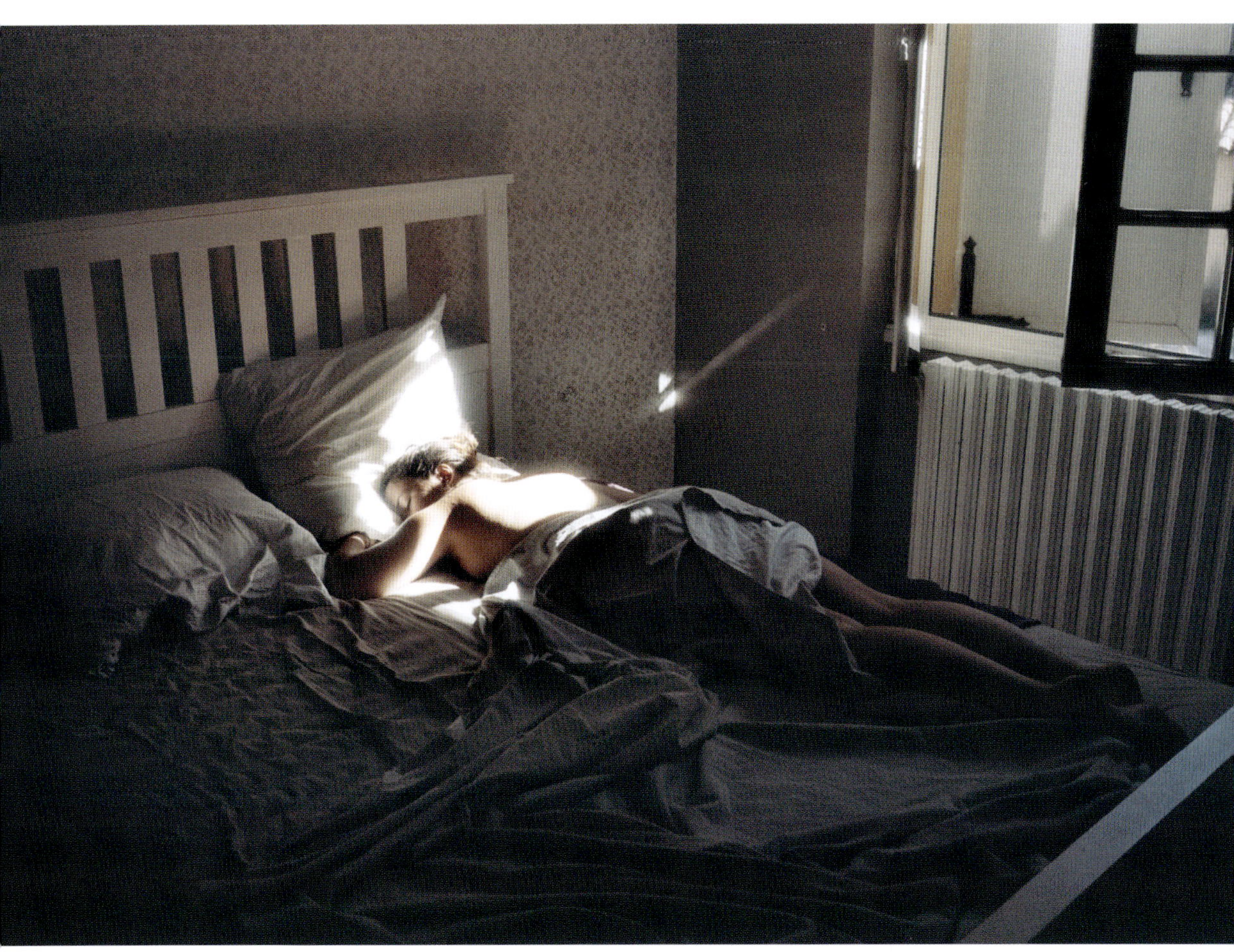

Cian Oba-Smith. Aurore, France, 2014.

that I got more detail in the shadows. The other image featured here is a portrait of my cousin Greg, which was taken on our way back from Notting Hill Carnival in London. It had rained all day and we were getting the train to my mum's house. When we came out of the station, I asked Greg to pose for this portrait. I chose to frame him slightly off-centre and left space above his head to allow the various vertical and horizontal lines to intersect and then lead the eye off to the right side of the frame where there's a hint of natural light.

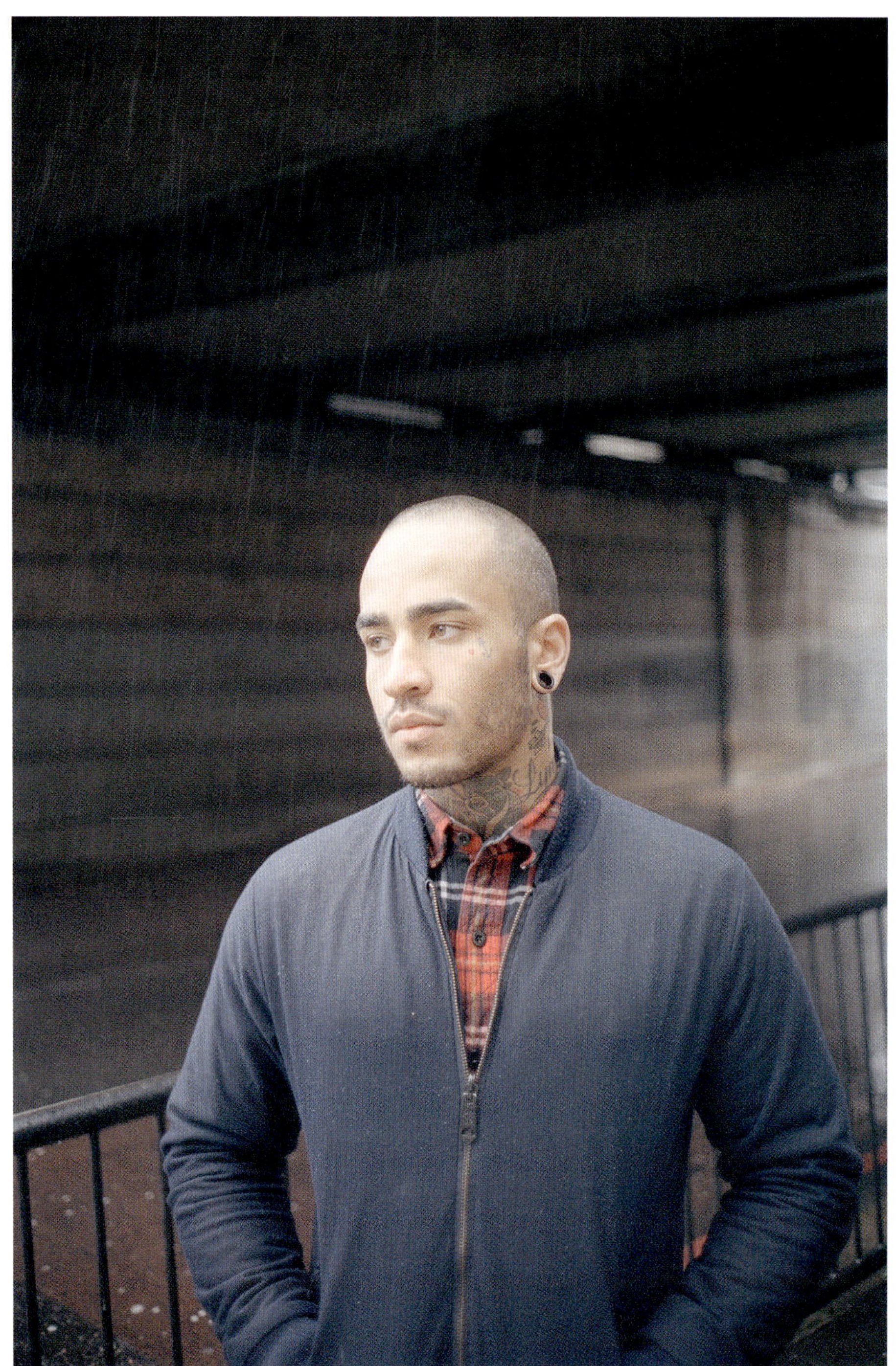

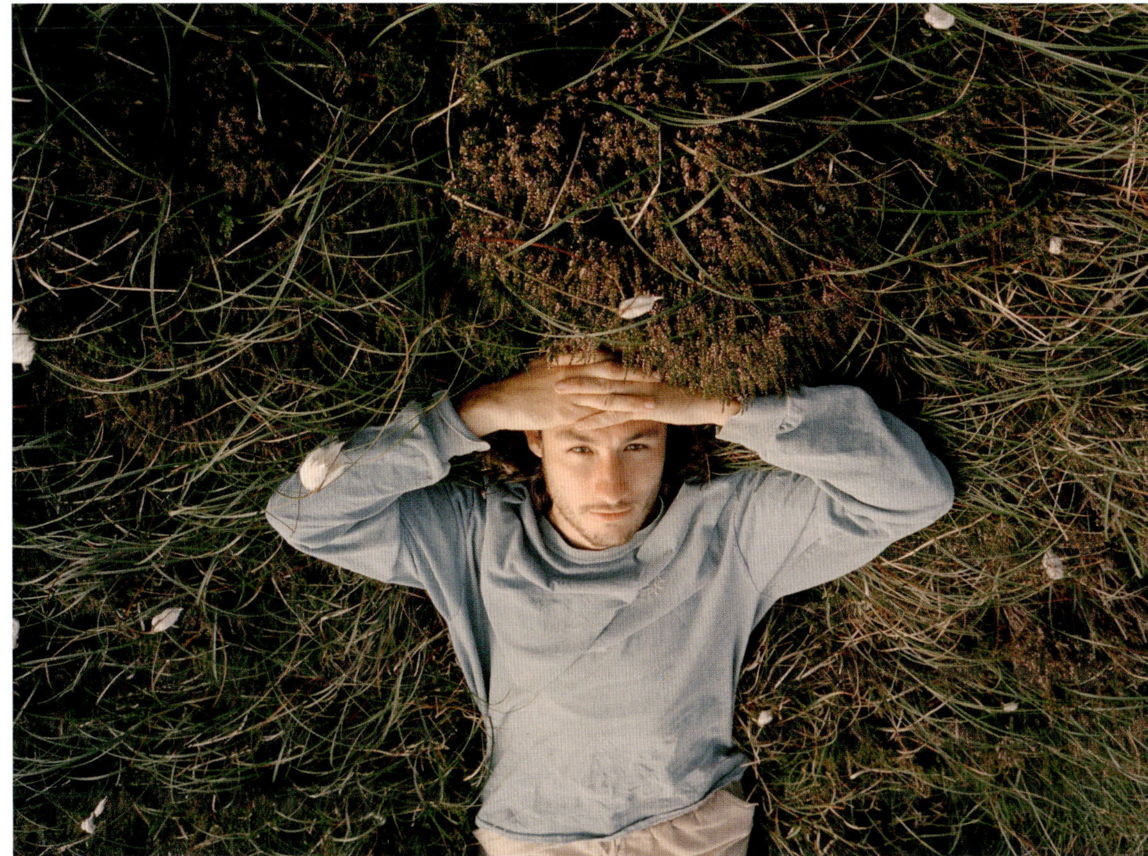

What's interesting about photography in general, but in particular with photographs of family and friends, is that as the images age they take on new meaning. Greg sadly passed away in 2017, but the photographs I took of him over the years now have another layer of meaning for me. They served as a portrait of him at the time I made them, but now they also serve as a record of his life and the experiences we shared together. **COS**

Conclusion

Start where most photographers begin: by shooting those around you. Always carry a camera with you; that way you'll never miss an opportunity to capture a portrait. The photographs you make of your family will become images that you'll look back on and treasure for the rest of your life.

Sian Davey

born 1964, Brighton, UK.
siandavey.com

Sian Davey turned to photography later than most, taking a master's degree at the University of Plymouth, after a fifteen-year career as a psychotherapist. Few people have kept their photographic practice as close to home as Devon-based Davey, where she almost exclusively photographs the lives of her children. For her first book, *Looking for Alice* (2015), Davey photographed her youngest daughter Alice, who has Down's Syndrome. The photographs take us beyond our preconceptions into a space of love, laughter and sometimes brutal reality.

Working in colour film and using a medium- or large-format camera, Davey builds a world around her children that is a mixture of both fantasy and reality. Some of the photographs feel like paintings by the Italian Renaissance artist Botticelli – namely, the teenage bodies draped across each other. But this isn't make-believe; this is Davey's life. Davey's children. Dreamy summer days spent swimming with friends in the river, nights out on the town, hangovers, cuddles and haircuts.

What I find so interesting about Davey as a portrait photographer is how little she photographs someone alone in the frame. Even in this book, which features a wide range of our favourite photographers, it is uncommon. Photographs in Davey's books are almost always of several people, and often of many, and while she makes it look easy, we can be certain that it's not.

Look at Davey's photographs carefully. How does she use natural light? How does she frame her subjects? Sometimes she combines a shallow depth of field with a delicate choice of where she focuses, masterfully guiding us around a photograph. The image shown here is a good example of this. It is of her daughter Alice, who is in the centre of the frame, but behind a collection of limbs, bodies and phones. In spite of being half the size of the other girls, she is dominant in the picture because she's the only one in focus. I love this picture. It is complex in terms of content, but really all the mess leads us straight to the key subject in the middle – who, like us, is watching the scene unfold. **MF**

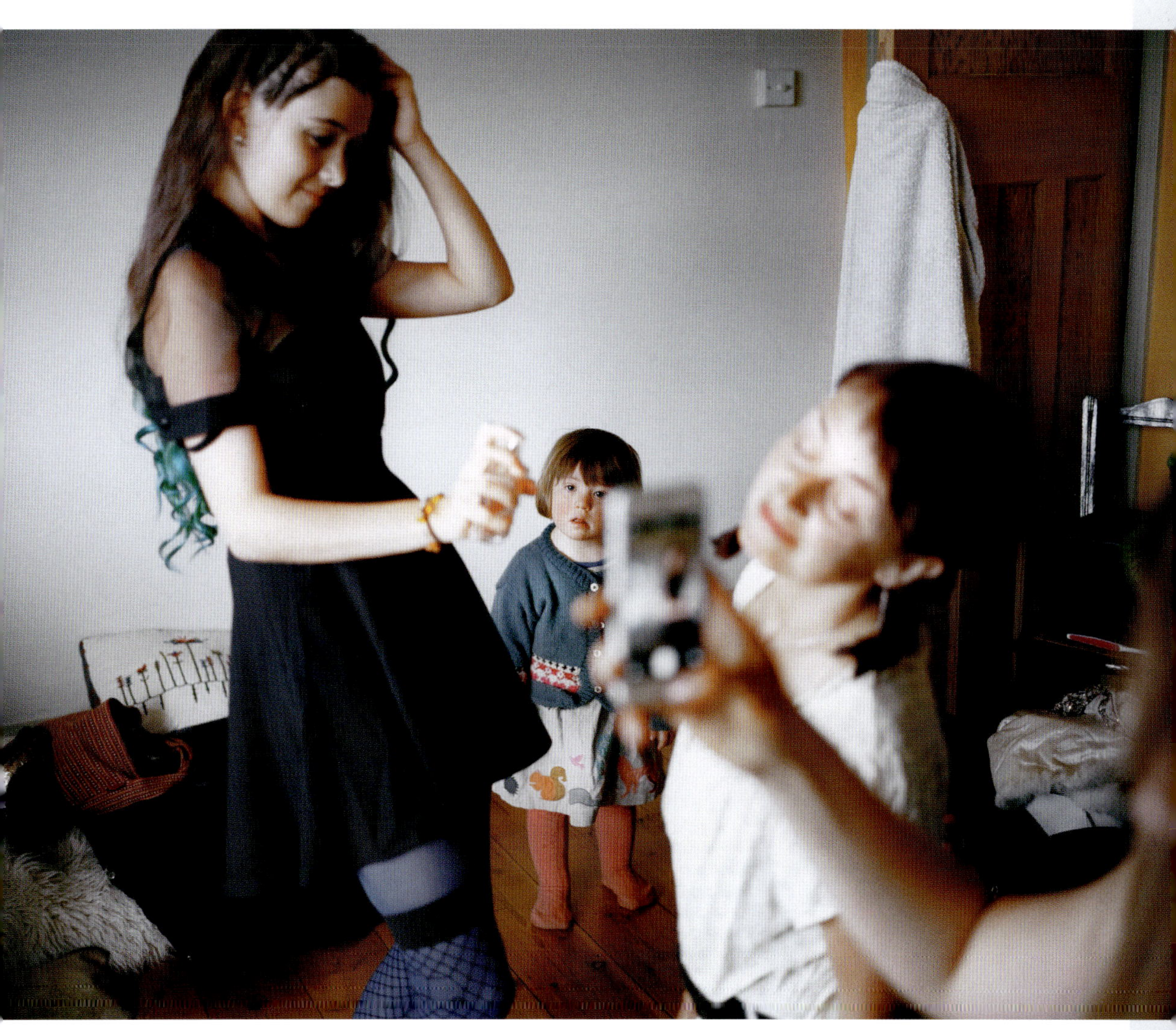

Family and Friends Studio

A enjoyable way to practise making portraits and to improve quickly as a photographer is to take photographs of your friends and family in a homemade studio.

Although making portraits of strangers is a great way to learn about photography quickly, it can also be intimidating, and sometimes the added pressure of photographing someone you do not know can lead to more mistakes. Carrying a camera around with you to make spontaneous portraits when they present themselves is a useful approach, but it can also be good to plan a shoot in advance by creating a studio at home and inviting your family and friends round to sit for a portrait. This can be a great way to make meaningful portraits in a pressure-free environment. You can create a studio at home using a background roll or use a section of wall (see page 96), whatever you prefer.

This image of my brother Sé was taken on a 35mm film camera in my living room in the late afternoon. The room faces south, so it gets a lot of light throughout the day – the sun in this portrait was quite low in the sky when the photograph was taken. The lower part of the window is frosted, so the light was filtered through the top section, creating a patch of light surrounded by interesting shadows. I asked Sé to sit in the light and then instructed him to look towards the light. I held my hand up and asked him to look towards it. I then moved my hand until the front of Sé's face was illuminated with the sides hidden in the shadows.

Task

Try to find a part of your home with interesting light and position your subject there. Alternatively, look for an area that has consistent light throughout the day and have a go at creating a range of portraits with similar lighting. Doing this will highlight the differences between your subjects and allow their personalities to shine through. After you've finished, reflect on the portraits that you've created. What do these images say about the people you love and what do they suggest about your relationships with them? **COS**

Conclusion

Practising making portraits with your friends and family is a great way to improve without the fear of rejection from strangers. Be conscious of how the time of day affects the lighting throughout your home and search out different spaces that work well for your portraits. Although it can be fun to book in some time to make portraits of your chosen subject, it's good to always be ready to make a portrait when the moment presents itself at any given time.

▶ Cian Oba-Smith. Sé in my living room, London, 2021.

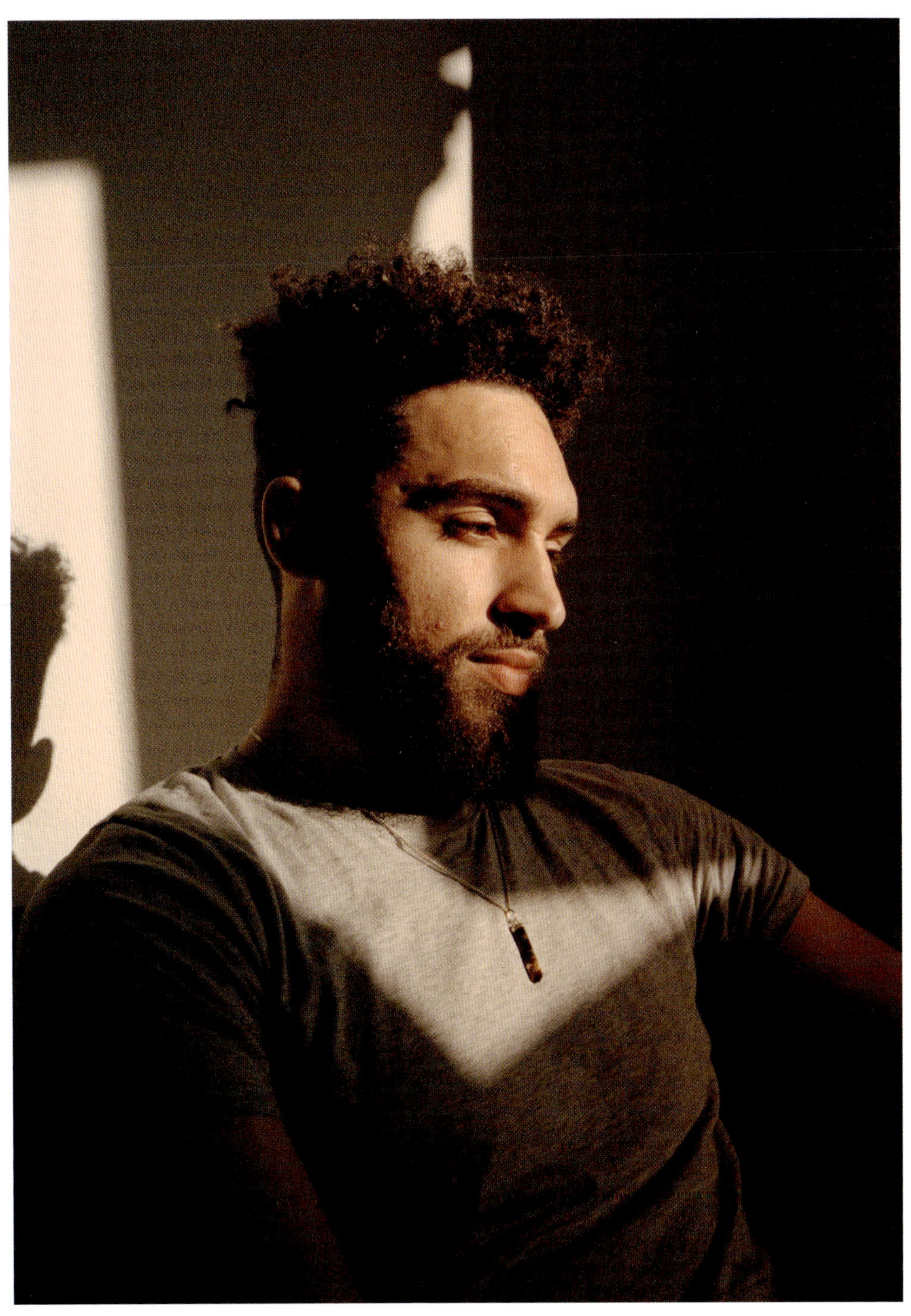

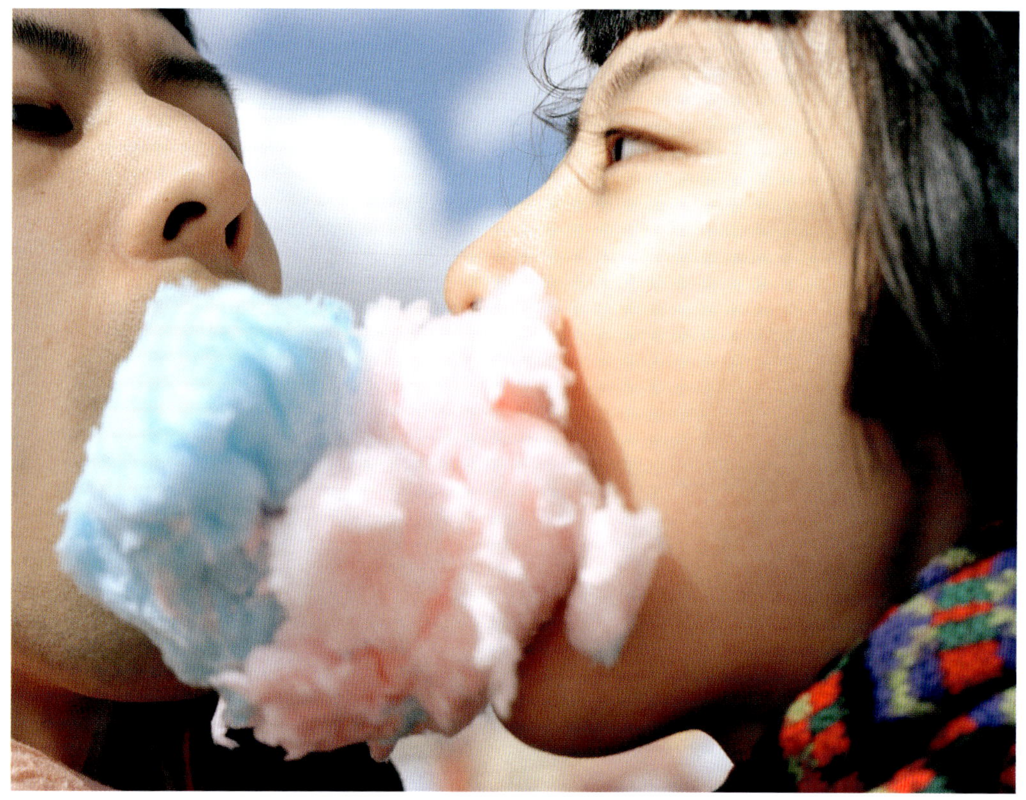

Pixy Liao

born 1979, Shanghai, China.
pixyliao.com

Pixy Liao is a multidisciplinary artist based in New York. Her work often uses humour to challenge the expectations society places on women and on heterosexual relationships. She first met her partner Moro while they were both studying at the University of Memphis. They have collaborated on her work from the start. The two photographs featured here are from her long-term – and probably most well-known – project 'Experimental Relationship' (exhibited since 2007). The photographs are of Liao and Moro, sometimes together and sometimes on their own. The poses are often unusual: they are photographed sitting and lying on top of one another, for example. They are often close or touching each other, which, despite their usually deadpan facial expressions, makes the moments feel very tender. It can seem as if Liao and Moro are 'performing' their relationship for the camera and the fact that the cable release also sometimes appears in the image adds to this. Incidentally, in both 'Experimental Relationship' and another of Liao's projects, 'For Your Eyes Only', she focuses on combining intimacy with the mundanities of life.

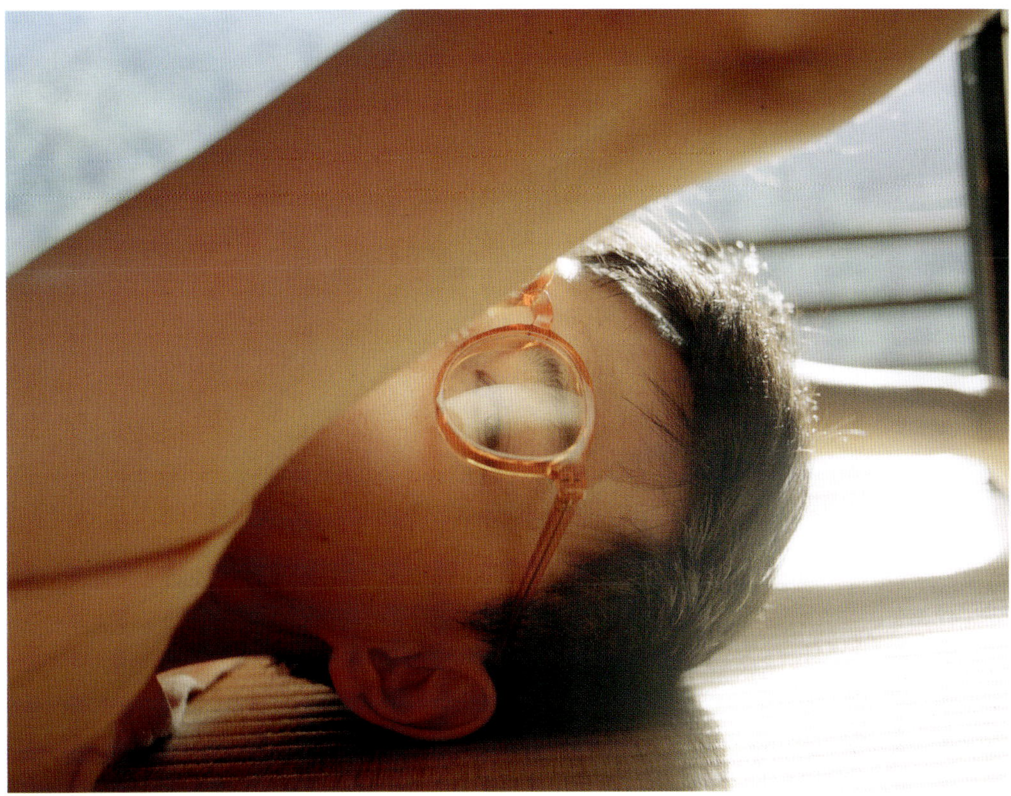

Both the images shown here are cropped close in on the subjects. In one photograph, we see Liao and Moro sharing some blue and pink candyfloss. You can almost taste the sweet, soft strands giving way to a wet crunch. The positioning of the subjects within the frame is interesting too. They're off-centre, towards the bottom left of the frame, which echoes the feeling of chaos and wonder found at places that sell candyfloss, such as fun fairs, theme parks and the seaside. There is also something to be said about the stereotypical gender roles portrayed in the photograph, since the pink candyfloss is on her side and the blue on his, although in her photography Liao often challenges these, presenting the female as dominant in a relationship and portraying herself as the one in control. Her thoughts on this idea are telling: 'Damn right! That's exactly what I'm doing, and why not!'

In the other photograph, we see Moro again, but this time he is lying on his back in what appears to be an image of intimacy and mundanity. By his left arm, which nearly obscures his face, we can just make out his left eye behind the glare on the tortoiseshell glasses. The arm, folded across his cheek, is protecting him from the viewer's gaze. The close crop means there is so little context in the image, and I cannot help but wonder at the vulnerability and intimacy that we are being allowed to see here. **MF**

Selecting a Portrait

Selecting your best portrait to show can be complicated. It will come down to taste, but understanding the purpose of your images can help you choose.

Consider the photograph opposite of Florence Owens Thompson from 1936 by Dorothea Lange. It's one of the most famous portraits ever taken and is better known by its ambiguous title, *Migrant Mother*. The version shown here is the only one most people will have ever seen. But Lange shot many photographs of Thompson, and her seven children, that day when working on an assignment for the Farm Security Administration (FSA).

To understand better why this image was chosen, it's important to think about the context in which the photographs were taken. During the Great Depression, the FSA commissioned many of the United States' most well-known photographers to photograph the resettlement camps set up as part of President Franklin D. Roosevelt's New Deal policies. These images – many of which became the foundation of photojournalism for decades – were also used as propaganda for the United States government. That said, there are some wonderful photographs by Lange, Walker Evans, Gordon Parks, Esther Bubley and many more, which can be viewed online in the Library of Congress archives.

Let's focus on the photograph chosen of Thompson and two of her children. The children are standing on either side of her, shielding their faces, perhaps shyly, and framing her. A third child, a baby, is just visible on her lap. In this version, Thompson is not paying the children any attention – instead, she is staring into the distance, looking at something behind Lange. Her brow is furrowed, and she is ever so slightly pulling

▶ Dorothea Lange. *Migrant Mother*, Florence Thompson, aged thirty-two, photographed in Nipomo, California, 1936.

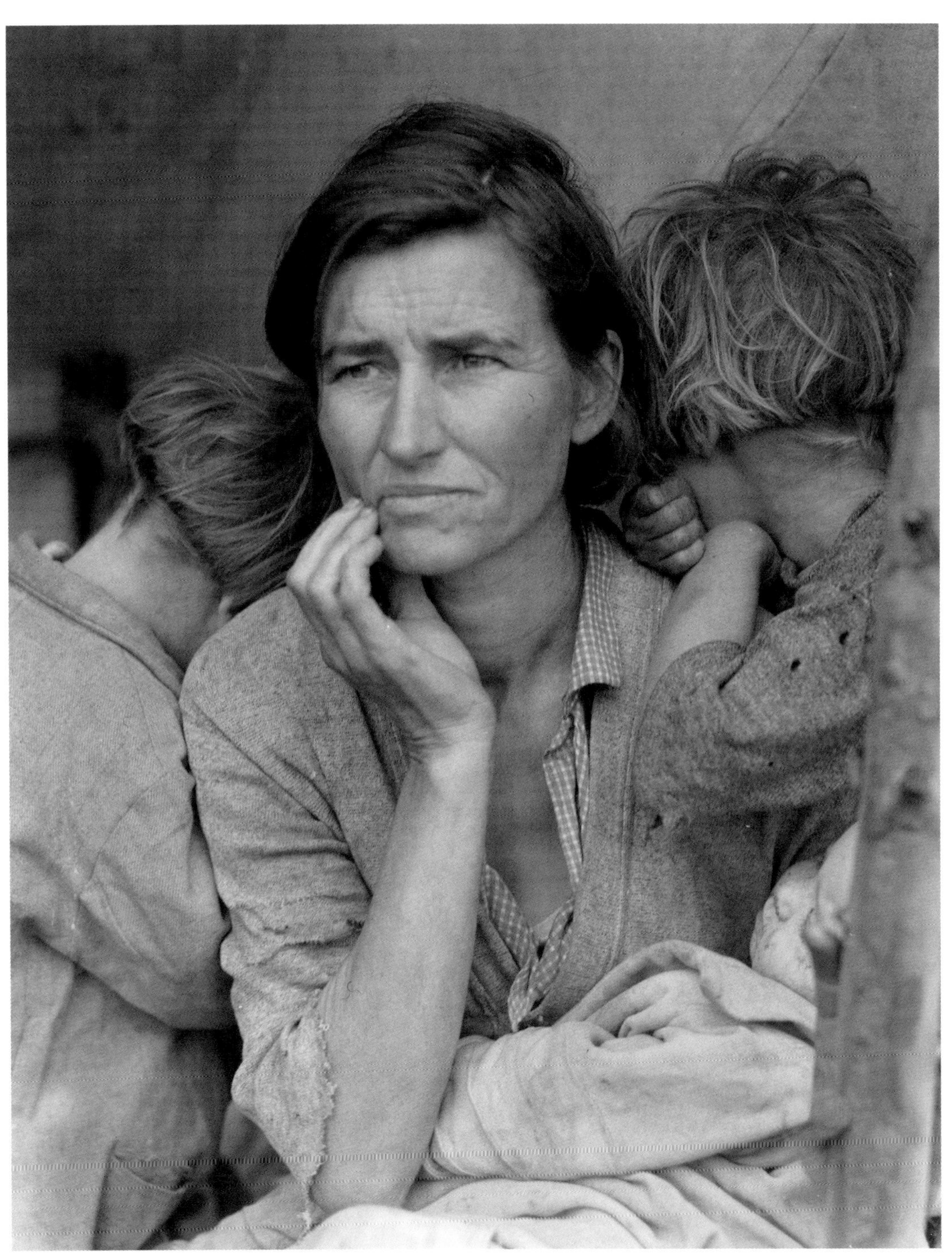

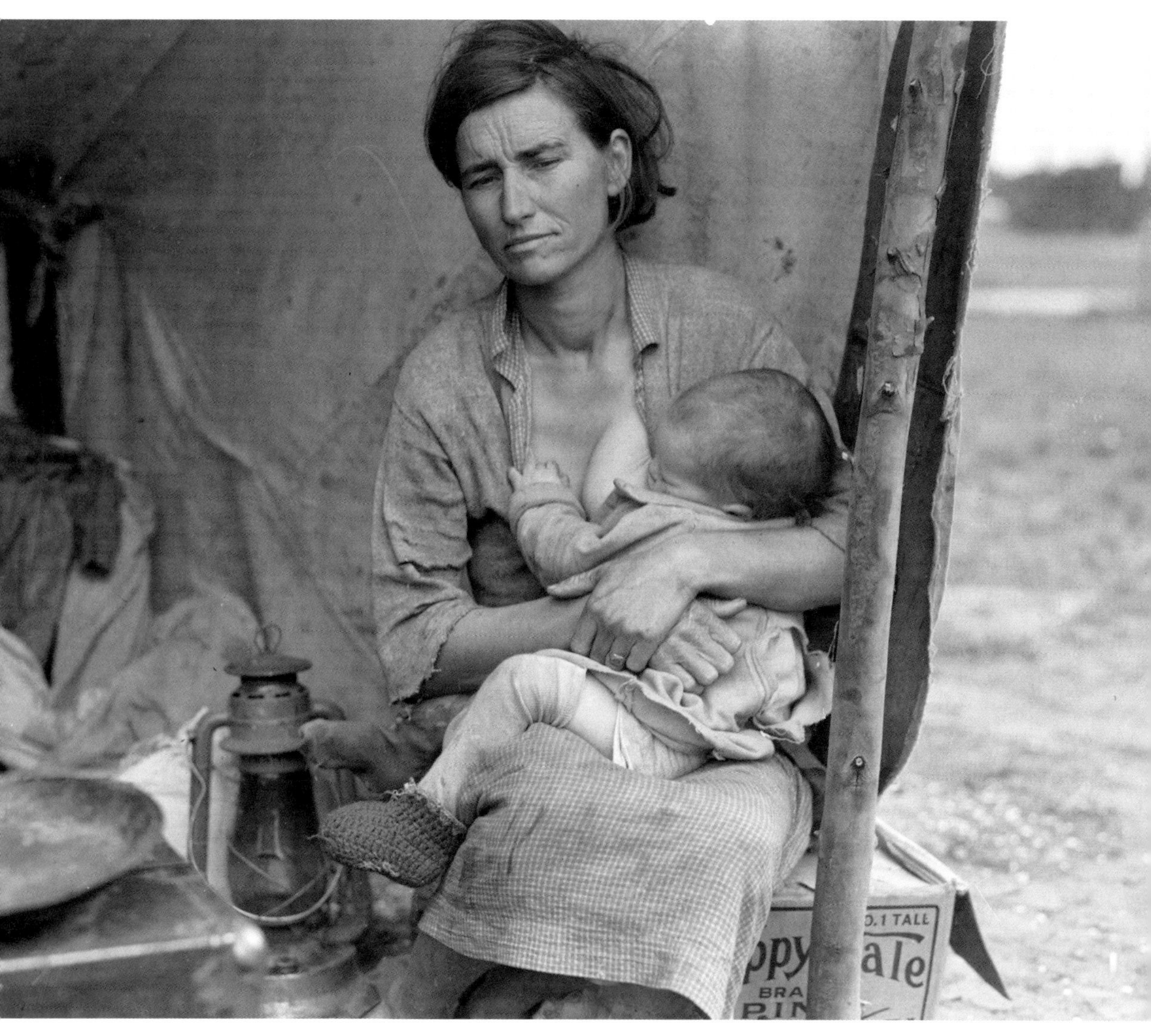

Dorothea Lange. Florence Thompson with one of her children, as part of the 'Migrant Mother' series, 1936.

at her face with her right hand. If you look carefully at the bottom right-hand corner of the image, you can see the ghost of a thumb, which has been mostly removed in the darkroom. This alone shows the level of thought the FSA put into selecting the images from their photographers.

On the opposite page is another photograph Lange took that day. In this image, Thompson is sitting in the same seat, at the entrance to the same tent. Here, she is breastfeeding and cradling her baby. It's an altogether more tender moment. But perhaps it didn't fit the motives of a government that wanted to show how destitute some of the poorest people were. I suspect Thompson's iconic image wouldn't be talked about as much if they had picked one of these other versions.

Of course, it's unlikely you will be taking photographs with such an obvious political agenda. But the reasons why the first photograph was chosen, making it infamous, are relevant to the decisions you should take when selecting yours. In the notorious Lange photograph, the framing of Thompson is key – the crop is tighter on this version than on the landscape photograph. The child on each side and the baby on her lap mean Thompson is boxed in on three sides. This, along with her arm, all lead our eyes to her face. And her stare – not at us, but at something in the distance – allows us to consider her without the confrontation of her locking eyes with the viewer.

Apply these ideas to your own work and think about a portrait you've taken more than one version of. How does the portrait change depending on where the subject is looking or how tightly you have cropped them from their surroundings? When shooting it's a good idea to try different approaches – one close crop of the head and shoulders, one from the waist up (this is called a three-quarter crop) and one where you can see the subject's feet and head in the shot. This will give you a good selection to choose from when working on your edits. If you have photographed a few people as part of a series, then you can mix up these selections to avoid being too repetitive. **MF**

Conclusion

• Famous photographs are probably part of a larger series of images that we never usually see.
• Photographs taken at the same time might be read completely differently.
• Small details can change the meaning of a photograph in unexpected ways.
• Much of what constitutes a good photograph is down to taste, so practise thinking about what it is you like in photographs. This will help you choose which of yours is 'best'.
• Sometimes your gut feeling – about an image you love – will be right. So go with that feeling. Asking people for their instant reactions can be really useful too. The photograph you choose might have a big impact on the end result.

LaToya Ruby Frazier

born 1982, Braddock, Pennsylvania, United States.
latoyarubyfrazier.com

American artist and photographer LaToya Ruby Frazier uses photography, filmmaking, installations and performance as tools for activism. She works on long-term, community-based projects that look at working-class identity in the Rust Belt states of the United States (Indiana, Illinois, Michigan, Missouri, New York, Ohio, Pennsylvania, West Virginia and Wisconsin).

The photograph shown here is from 'Flint is Family,' a 2016 project by Frazier that documents the communities in Flint, Michigan, who were affected by the Flint water crisis. Tens of thousands of people were exposed to dangerous levels of lead in their drinking water when the authorities switched the water supply to the Flint River to cut costs. Thousands of children, who are most at risk of the long-term effects of lead poisoning, including a reduced IQ and increased risks of Alzheimer's disease, were exposed to the contaminated water.

The photographs we see in 'Flint is Family' are split up in the book *Flint is Family in Three Acts* (published by Steidl in 2022) into three 'acts'. Act 1 introduces us to Shea Cobb, a Flint native. She's shown on the left in the image featured here, with one hand resting on her daughter at the front and the other on her mother's shoulder. In Acts 2 and 3 Frazier follows Cobb first to Mississippi to live with her father and then back to Flint to document the installation of an atmospheric water generator.

The question I find so interesting about documentary photography is this: what can photography add to the discourse around real-world issues? For me, Frazier's work is one of the best examples we have of moments when photography actually helps. Through community work, spending time with local people and constant dedication, photographers can make a real difference within communities. By utilizing her position as a renowned photographer, Frazier is able to further conversations around social issues and bring awareness. But I'm not sure that's all her work achieves. The images we see in Act 1 of 'Flint is Family' show protest, community, family, direct action and resilience. They reveal the people fighting for what they should already have. In a more recent body of work, 'The Last Cruze' (2019), Frazier shows us the workers at a General Motors plant in Lordstown, Ohio. It's another place, another state, another community. But the fight and struggles feel remarkably familiar in Frazier's photographs. She is constantly reminding us that the struggles of working-class people against governments that continue to serve the richest in society are sadly continuing. **MF**

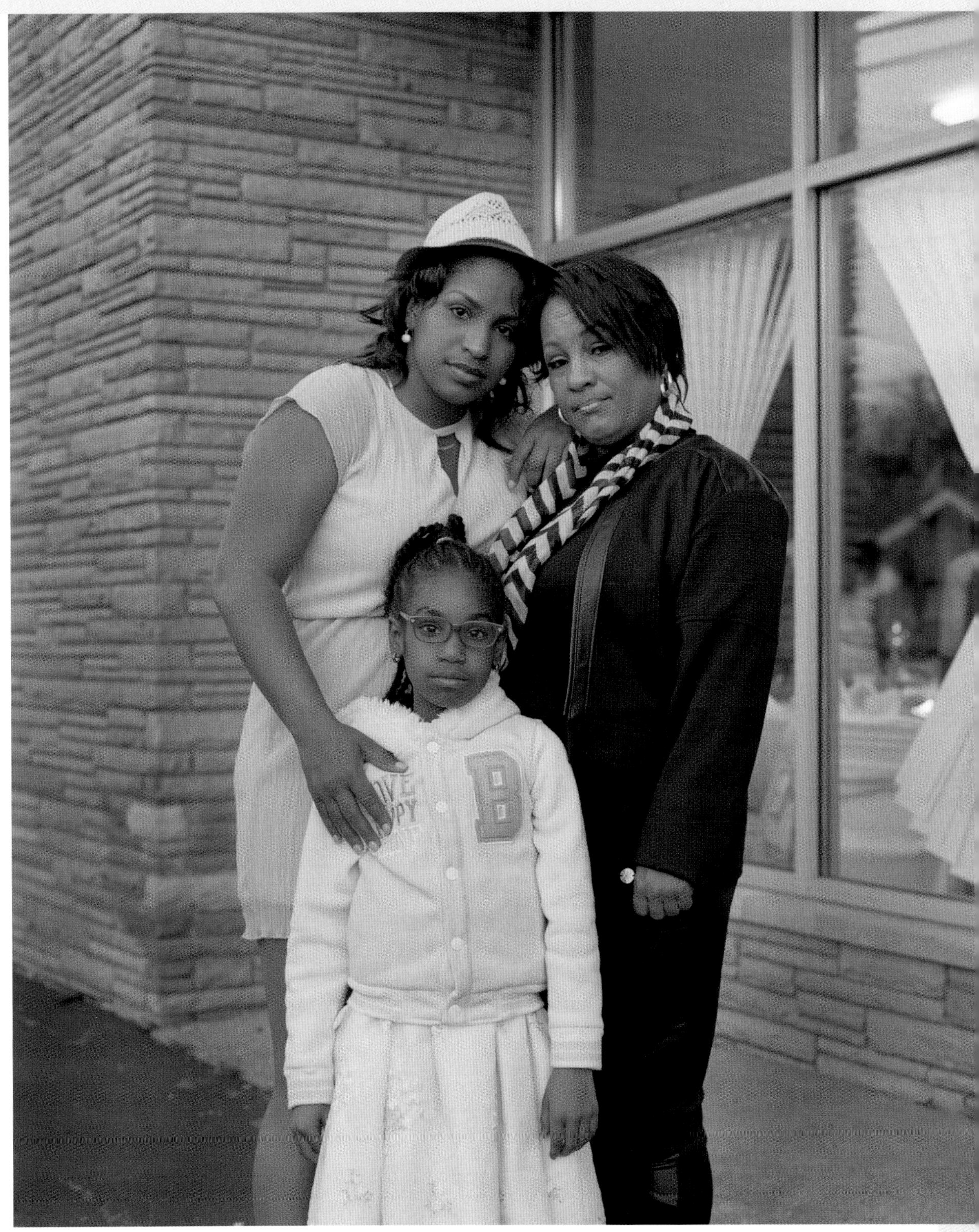

Zora J. Murff

born 1987, Des Moines, Iowa, USA.
zora-murff.com

Zora J. Murff was one of the first photographers I ever worked with, when I published him in the second issue of *Splash and Grab* magazine (Cian, incidentally, also featured in the same issue). I have since seen Murff continue in his career and become one of the most important contemporary photographers. The work we published then was called 'Corrections', a series of photographs made while Murff was employed at Iowa's Linn County Juvenile Detention Center. He was providing community-based services for the young men housed there and also photographing them, without revealing their identities, for 'Corrections'.

Murff is an American artist and educator who relies on photography as a key part of his practice. He uses photographs to examine white supremacy and its effect on Black people's lives. The photograph featured here shows a Black man holding a small child in his arms. His hand is cradling the child's head. The image is from a body of work called 'At No Point In Between', in which Murff uses archival images, citizen journalism and his own photographs to bring together a blistering investigation of the Near North Side neighbourhood of Omaha, Nebraska. The image is titled 'Jerrod and Junior (talking about fatherhood)'. This is an interesting title because it both confirms what we can see in the image while also giving it a wider context – a father holding his child becomes a metaphor for fatherhood in America.

I've always been struck by how effortlessly Murff uses the camera against itself in his work – he is constantly critiquing photography. Whether it is the part photography has played historically in racializing communities or documenting lynchings, or as a tool of surveillance, it is rarely viewed as wholly innocent in his work. However, photography is the tool to which Murff most often turns in his own artwork. While this may seem contradictory, it is, in fact, a rare and more truthful assessment of the complex nature of photography. **MF**

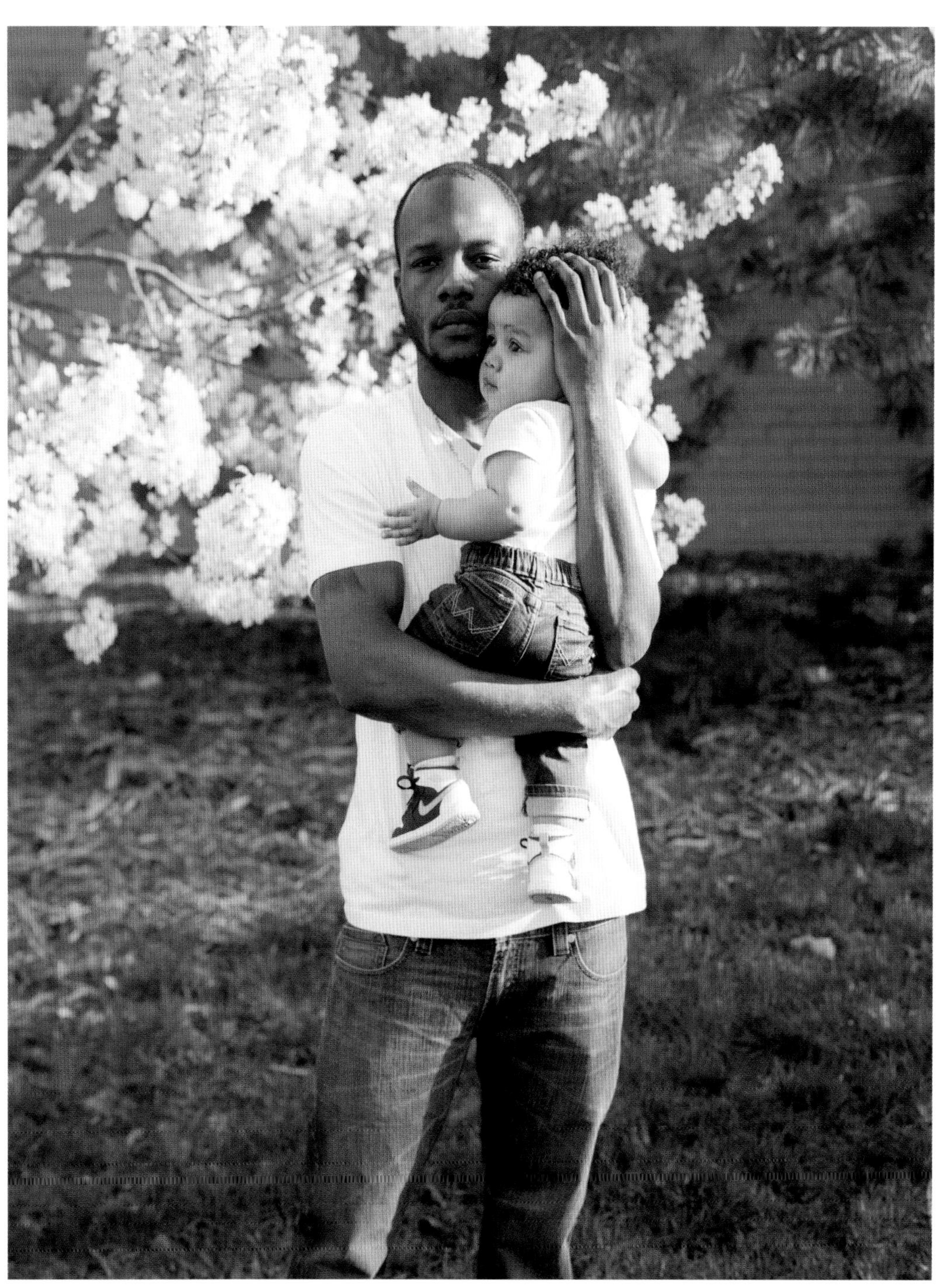

CHAPTER 5

Abstracting Portraits

Portraits often show someone's likeness in a realistic way. But there are many reasons to abstract, distort or obscure someone's likeness in a photograph.

What do we mean by the term 'Abstracting Portraits' and why, in fact, would you want to distort someone's likeness? Although a photographer may intentionally distort a subject's likeness, this can also happen whenever a photographer strays from the norms of formal portraits. A close crop, an unusual angle or pose, or distortion added after the photograph has been taken, for example, can all be used to abstract a portrait.

Photographers can have many creative reasons for abstracting the subject when making a portrait. But aesthetics clearly have an important part to play in all decisions made by photographers. In fact, since the camera was invented, photographers have battled with the dilemma of how 'honest' their depictions of people should be. At the end of the 19th and beginning of the 20th century, pictorialism in photography gained huge popularity. Pictorialists such as American photographers Edward Steichen (1879–1973) and Alfred Stieglitz (1864–1946) were making images of people rather than attempting to produce faithful reproductions of them. More concerned with the aesthetic qualities of their pictures, such as the tones and shapes, their photographs would typically be sepia rather than black and white, often have a soft focus, and even sometimes have brushstrokes from darkroom manipulations. Although pictorialism has mostly vanished from mainstream photography, their ideals, soft focus and loyalty to beauty remain.

Projects

▶ László Moholy-Nagy. Portrait of his wife, Lucia Moholy, in around 1924–1928.

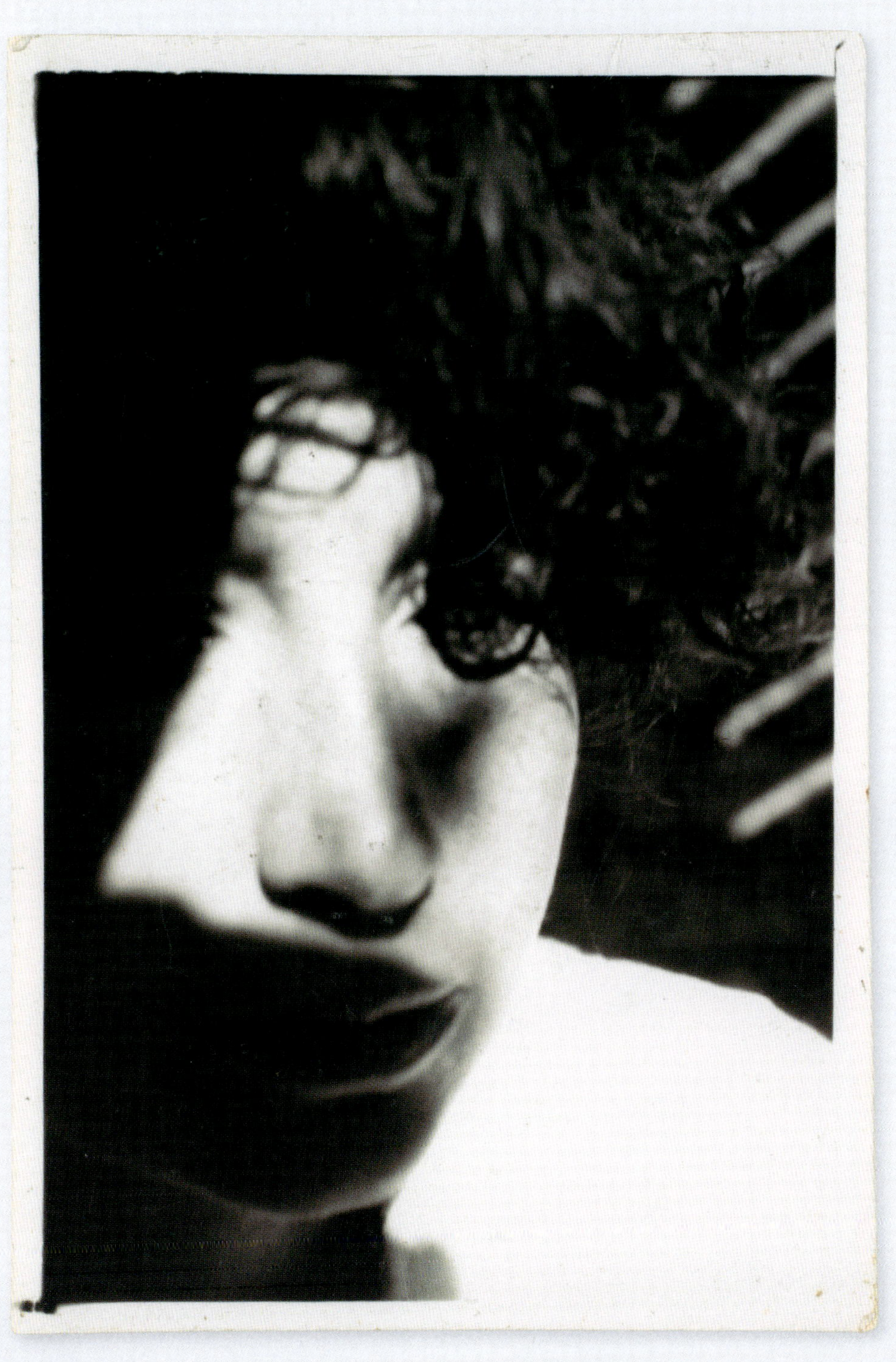

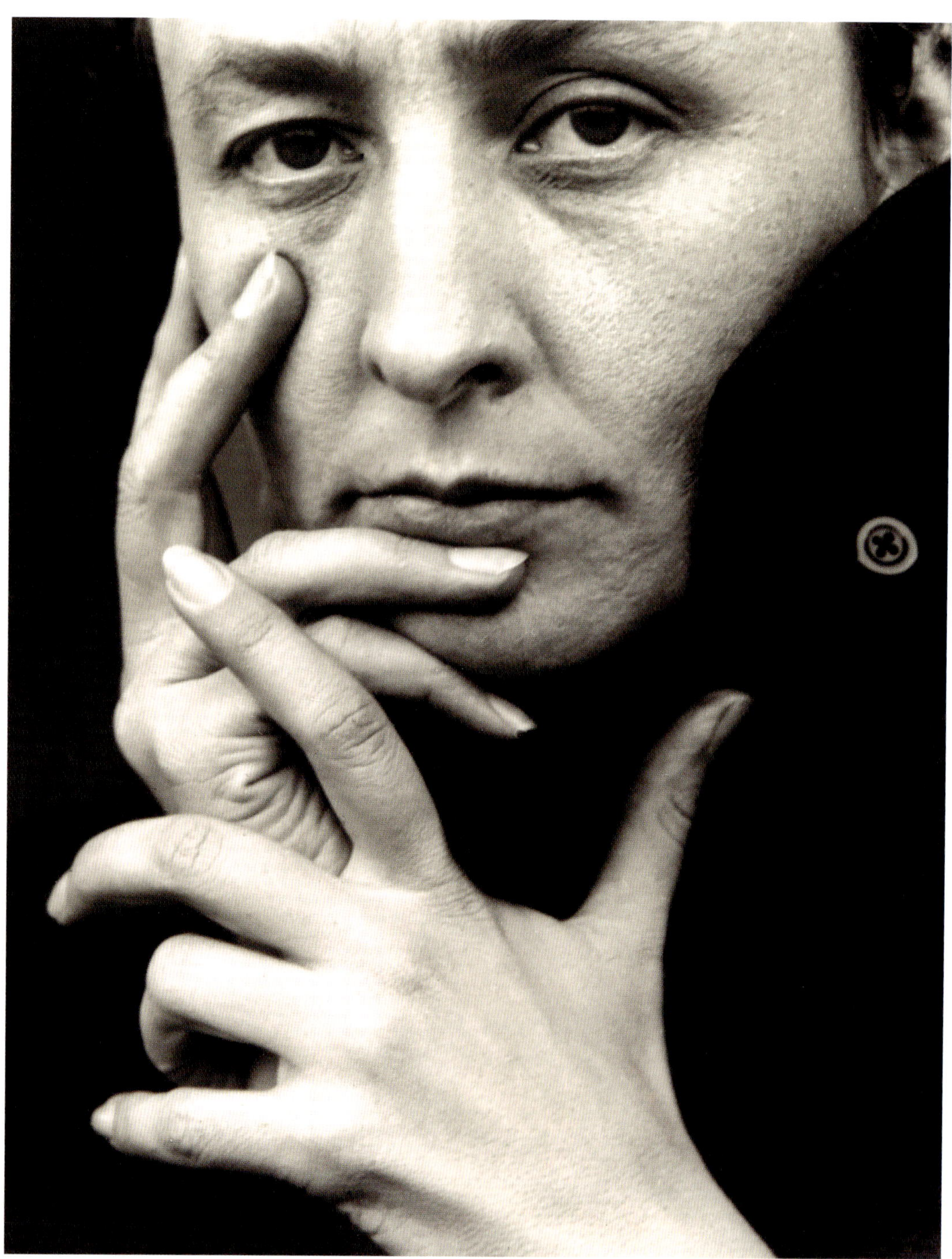

In the photograph shown here, on the left, of modernist painter Georgia O'Keeffe (1887–1986), who was his partner, Stieglitz has cropped the top of her head, which makes the hands key to the image. The fingers are entwined against O'Keeffe's chin and cheek, creating abstract shapes. What I love here is how much space the fingers take up in the image. More than the face. But bear in mind that this is a photograph of a painter, so the hands are important and something that Stieglitz photographed many times. It is strange to think that this photograph was taken over a hundred years ago in 1920 because it feels so modern.

Interestingly, photographers who like to use film have become frustrated with the environmentally unsafe chemicals required to process and print images. The Sustainable Darkroom in London runs courses on how to use alternatives to traditional developers and fixers. For example, coffee can be used instead of developer – and some of the images made in this way recall those of early pictorialists like Steichen and Stieglitz.

Photographers such as Man Ray (1890–1976) and László Moholy-Nagy (1895–1946) pushed portrait photography further towards surrealism. Investigate their photographs because it is worth seeing how far you can abstract faces, figures and portraits and still keep them recognizable. On the previous page we see a portrait of Lucia Moholy, the famous surrealist artist's wife. She was a professional photographer herself and taught him her craft. Here she's pictured between 1924 and 1928 in an incredibly modern image. Cropped close, most of her face is in shadow. It becomes graphical and we see shapes rather than a likeness.

There might also be practical reasons for abstracting photographs. For instance, when I was commissioning photographs at the *Financial Times*, we often ran stories in which we could not reveal the likeness of the person we were featuring. However, by photographing them in the shadows, with their face turned away or obscured by an object or even some smoke, we were able to include them in the story without compromising their safety. Whatever your reasons for abstracting photographs, and there are many, this chapter should inspire you and give you some of the skills you need to start bending the formalities of your portrait making. **MF**

◀ Alfred Stieglitz. Portrait of his lover, the painter Georgia O'Keeffe, 1918.

Jack Davison

born 1990, Essex, UK.
jackdavison.co.uk

Jack is a self-taught photographer who studied English Literature at university, an interest that influences his approach to photography. His photographs are imbued with a kind of magic and have an abstract playfulness that seems to transport you to a parallel universe or a kind of dream state. Jack describes his approach to making pictures in this way: 'You're dealing with things that are in the real world but they're things that maybe only you can focus in on or are excited by. It could be light, it could be a certain person, it could be a certain colour. It's always been about kind of being quite playful with that idea and not getting too absorbed in the theory or the technical side of it, but just the act of making pictures and finding imagery.'

You can see how Jack's interest in literature has fed into his method for making pictures. Each of his images gives you the abstract ingredients of a story. It's then up to the viewer to navigate the rest of the narrative. As Jack says, 'The most interesting interpretation of the text doesn't necessarily have to be the author's, it can be what the audience or the reader or the viewer brings to it.'

Jack's photographs make you think. Often, you're trying to work out what's going on and how he's created the image you're looking at. The image shown here, for example, is visually a lot more abstract and complex than most portraits. We can tell that the image is a portrait of a person, but we aren't given much more information than that. The purposeful lack of detail in the background leaves the subject's face almost floating in the ether. Jack's techniques with the camera, or otherwise, force us to interpret the image for ourselves. His use of layering and abstraction within the image leaves us with more questions than answers; they leave us questioning who this person is and how this image came to be.

Of his technical process, Jack says: 'Some pictures are made in the moment and it's all done in camera, so shooting through surfaces or catching reflections. Sometimes I like to work [on the images], and I find those [abstractions] in the post-production, but that's me printing and then rephotographing or shooting screens through a glass. It's a lot to me about adding layers and it's always done physically.'

Think of how you can take inspiration from Jack's approach to making pictures. How can you use layers, perspective, texture and light to create abstract images? Experiment at all points of the photographic process and be critical of your images, but most importantly break the rules and have fun! **COS**

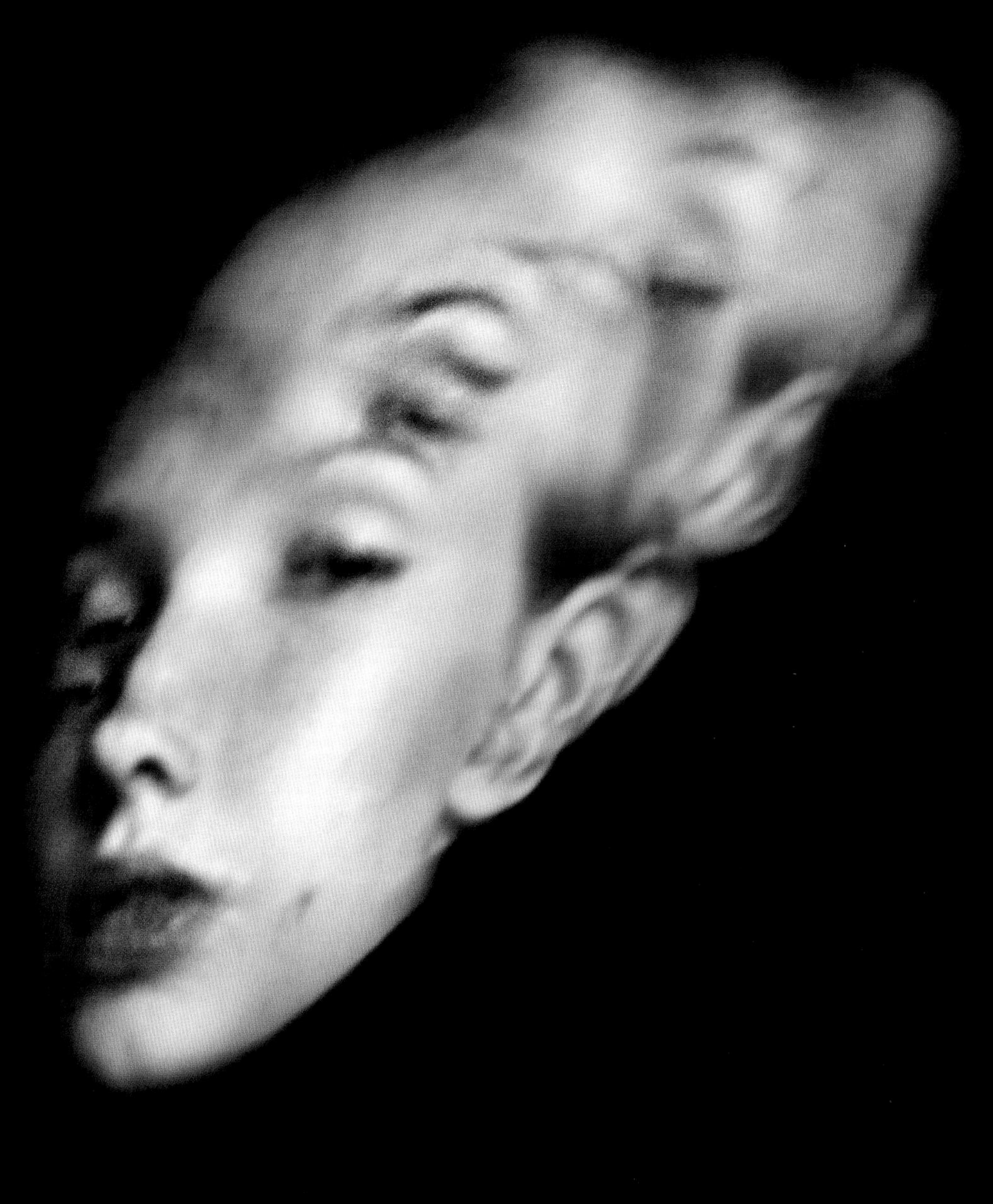

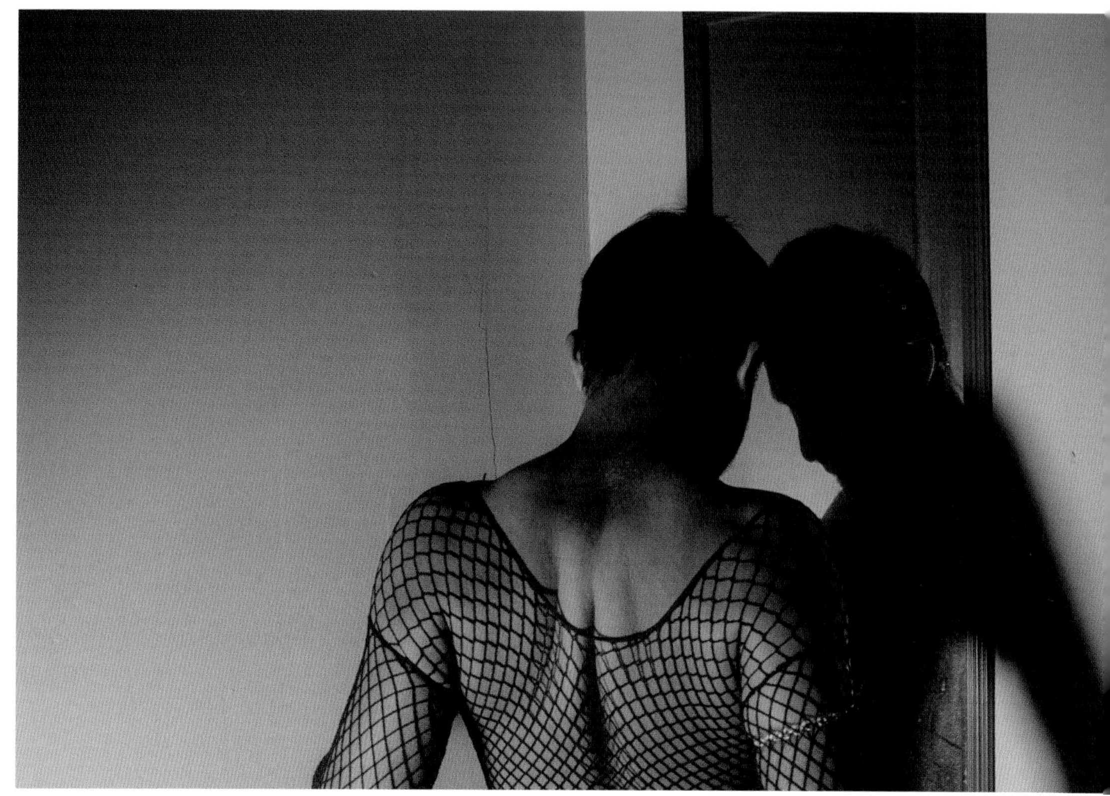

Debmalya Ray Choudhuri

born Kolkata, 1991, India.
rayd.space

At first, Debmalya Ray Choudhuri's photographs seem situated between a dreamworld and reality, as is the case with the photograph opposite. Here, a figure is caught by Choudhuri mid-movement behind a white veil embroidered with stars – perhaps this represents the veil of sleep or a world between the living and dead. On further investigation, it seems our first impressions are incorrect. Indeed, Choudhuri describes his practice as dealing 'with the "queerness" of desire, love, body, and space through personal narratives'. This adds an interesting dimension to the veil – it symbolizes a barrier between two bodies, both real and fragile, just like our own desires.

Choudhuri also makes beautiful colour photographs. The natural lighting gives some images an ethereal feel, as with the images here, while others use harsher flash lighting to create vibrant colour images. His work is a great example of why mixing black and white with colour should not be avoided

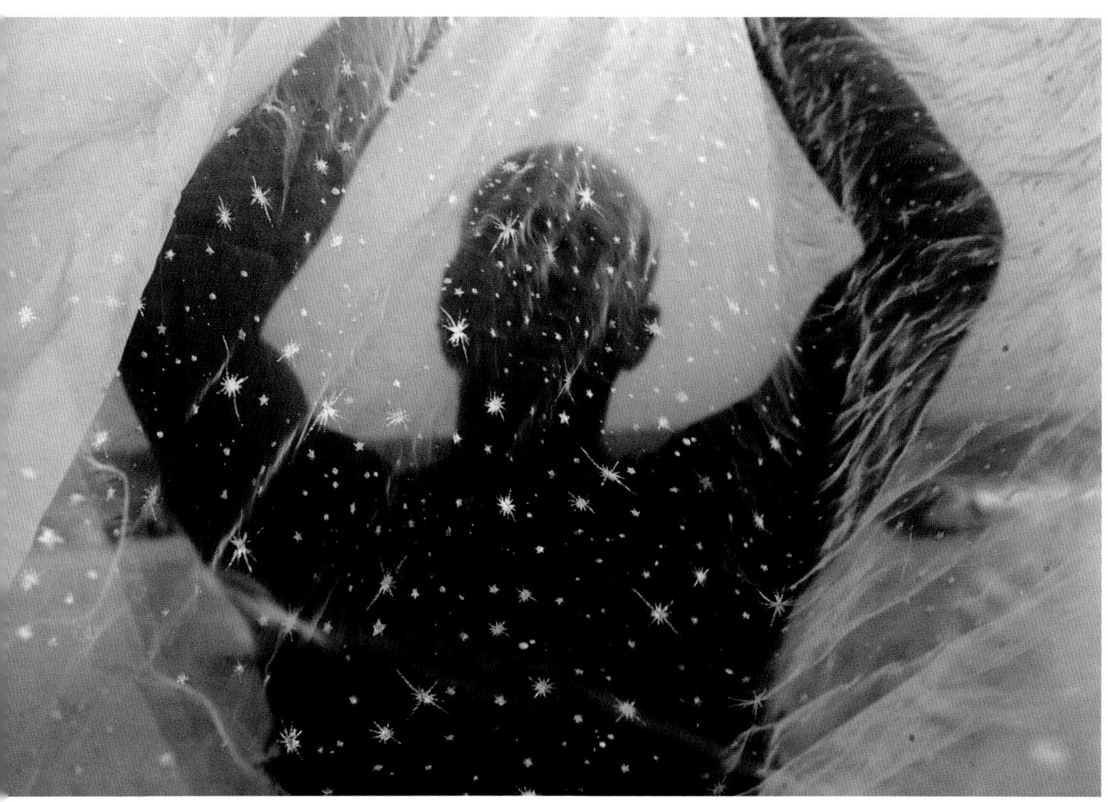

(see Bending the Rules on page 146 for more on flouting the conventions of photography). But here we decided to include two of Choudhuri's black-and-white images (both are included in 'Introduction – A Factless Autobiography') since they show some similarities and differences that are worth further discussion. Both images feature figures from the chest up. The arms of the two figures are also both cut off by the edge of the frame (another 'rule' of photography wonderfully broken) and both subjects are positioned in the centre of the image – facing away from us, they remain anonymous. In one photograph, we can see straight through the sheer fabric. This can create technical difficulties for a photographer, but Choudhuri uses these limitations to create a distorted portrait. In the image opposite, a person is facing their own reflection – this creates a dynamic image. A double portrait such as this can feel fractured, showing two different personalities, but here they are bought together where their heads meet.

Despite the similarities between the two portraits, their moods are quite different. I find the image with the starry veil euphoric – perhaps it captures a moment of ecstatic pleasure. In contrast, the man in the other image is facing the wall and touching heads with his own shadow, as if he is in dialogue with himself. It reveals a tender personal moment, but it seems to be more about solitude than joy. **MF**

Bending
the Rules

*There are various rules for taking
good photographs, some of which
are included in this book and on
formal photography courses,
but do they really make images
any 'better'?*

Photographic tips and tricks to 'improve' images can be helpful and make the photography process sound both easier and more approachable. However, although it is important to be aware of these rules, there are often occasions when bending them can make a photograph stronger and more effective. Let's consider some of the most common rules you might come across:

- Keep backgrounds clean
- Don't crop limbs
- Remember the rule of thirds
- Focus on the subject's eyes
- Keep horizons straight
- Don't mix colour and black-and-white photographs

Firstly, I'd like to remove the last of these rules immediately – there's simply no reason why you cannot mix the cameras or film stock you use, or alter what you do in post-production. So, while these suggestions can be helpful for honing your portrait-making skills, they are best treated as educational tools rather than rules that should be followed slavishly. At best, if every photographer follows them, the result is portraits that all look the same. At worst, these rules can stifle your creativity. If you like a photograph that breaks a rule, please don't discard it. Keep the photograph and think about what it is you like about it – and make more images along the same lines.

We can use the photograph opposite from a series by Gordon Parks (1912–2006) as an example. It's one of several photographs shot by Parks inside the home of Ella Watson, a cleaner in a government building, in Washington DC (see page 151). I love this series of images, which can be viewed on the Library of Congress archives website. The photograph is unusual

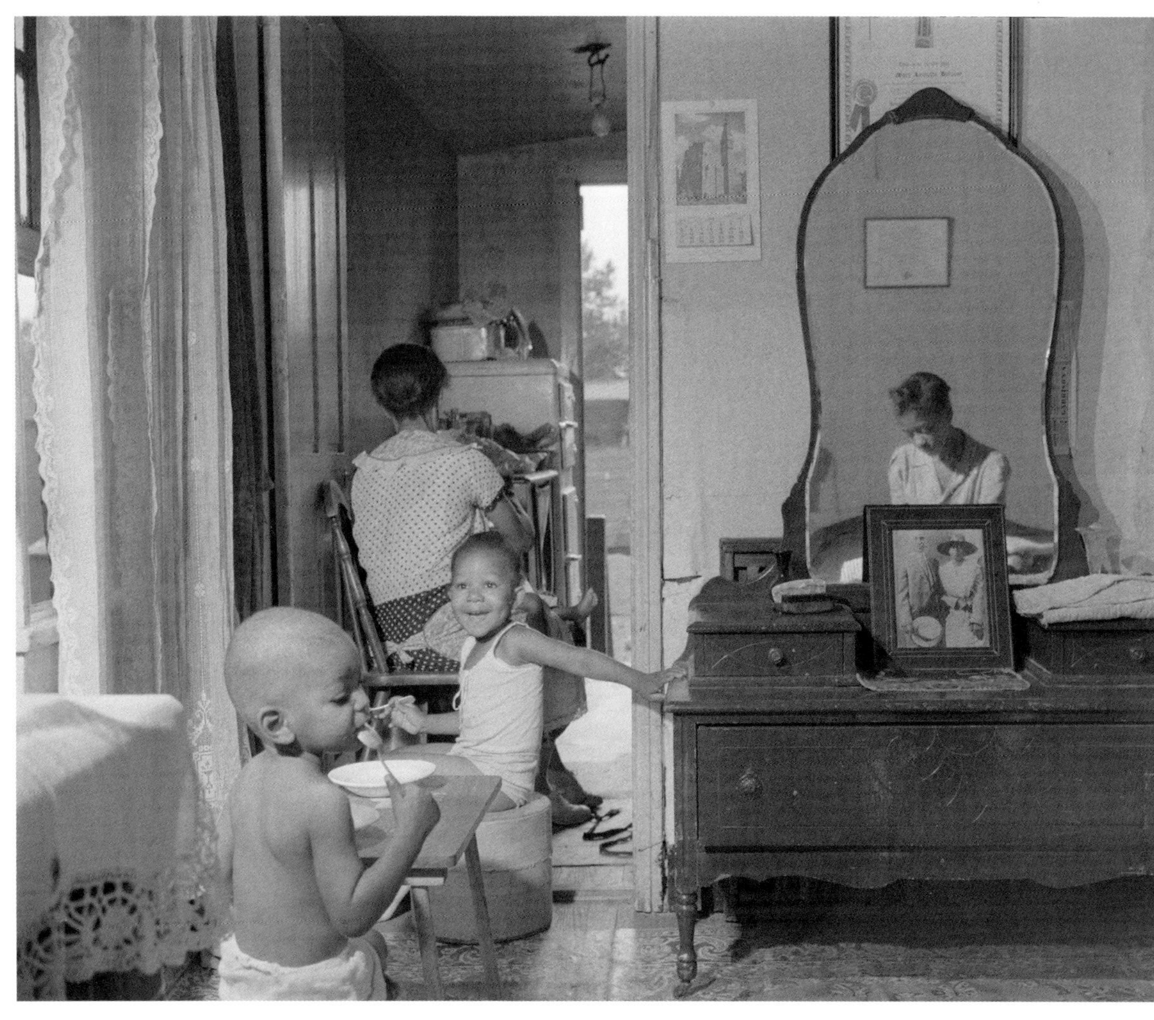

because it has no natural point of focus. Your eyes are drawn to several things: the two young children, the woman in the mirror, and the woman with her back to us in the doorway. Perhaps the natural point of focus is through that doorway to the second open door, which breaks the rule of thirds because it is more or less in the centre of the image. But people always become the main focus of a photograph. It's hard to say which person is the main subject. There is a chaos in the composition which somehow works. Also notice that the only people in the image who are posing are

Gordon Parks. Ella Watson, a government charwoman with her grandchildren, Washington DC, 1942.

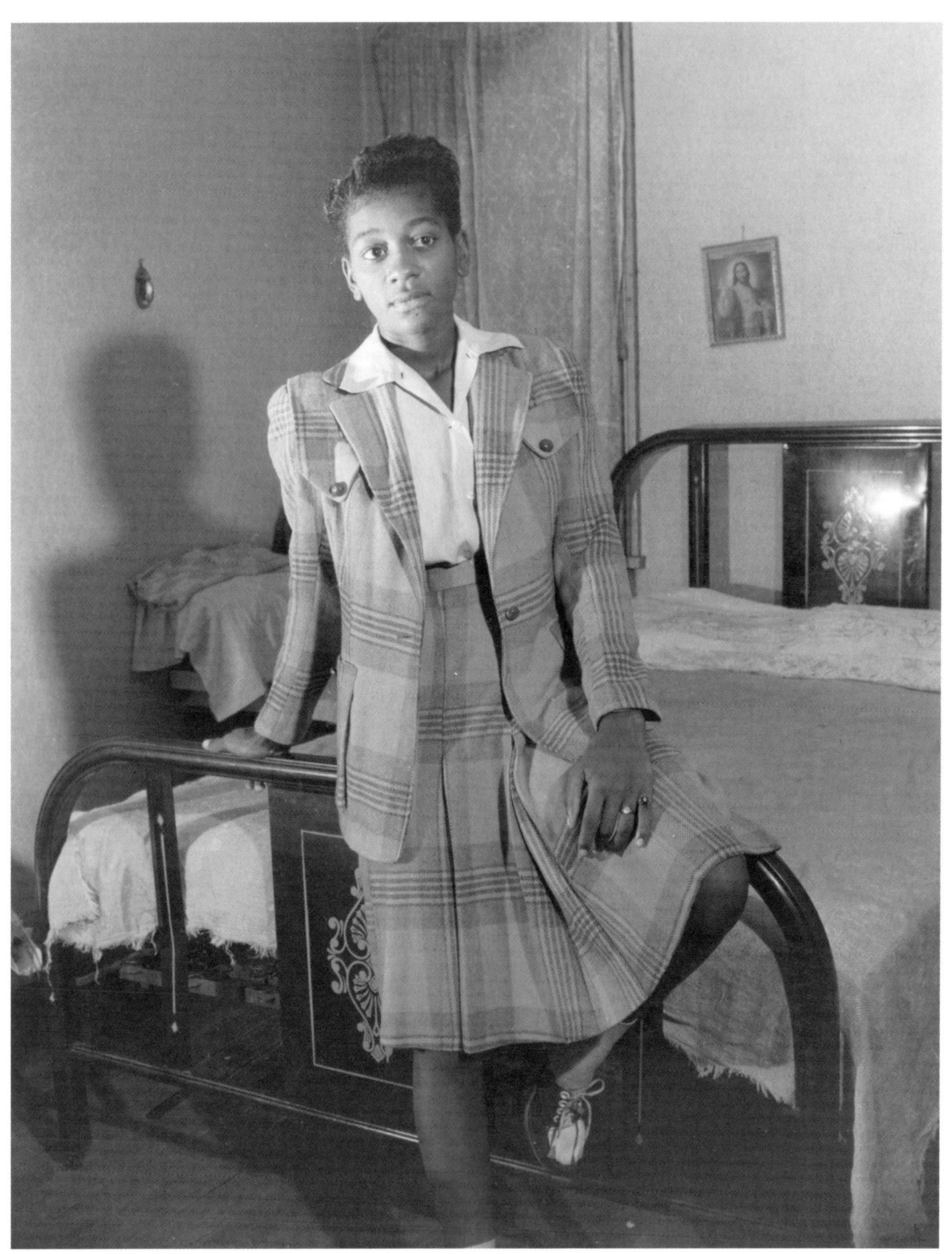

the man and woman in the framed portrait in front of the dressing table mirror. Lines of sight could be drawn from every subject, and they would criss-cross the frame randomly. This photograph always feels very modern, despite being made in 1942 during the Second World War. I think the feeling of modernity is due to the complexity of the composition and the fact that it doesn't seem to adhere to any of the rules of photography.

There is another photograph in this series that breaks a rule I have encountered so many times. It's the one that even the most anarchic of photographers finds difficult to break. And that is chopping off the subject's feet in the portrait. I have come across this frequently as a photo editor, with many photographs being rejected because the feet have been chopped off, and this often frustrates me. But before you leap in and bend this rule, it is advisable to think carefully about the reason you are taking the photograph in the first place. You may need to include the subject's feet in an advert for shoes, for example, and so it is helpful to understand the rules of photography in these situations. However, in other contexts, being able to see the shoes someone is wearing is not necessarily the mark of a good photograph.

This photograph of Ella Watson's adopted daughter is wonderful. There is so much to concentrate on within the frame, from the shadow on the left wall to the small picture of Jesus on the other wall, which is beautifully slanted. The flash, which we can see

◀ Gordon Parks. The adopted daughter of Ella Watson, a government charwoman, Washington DC, 1942.

illuminating the headboard, is given away by the young woman's shadow, but brings a hint of the informal and everyday to the image – a feeling emphasized by the fact that her right foot has been cropped off. The portrait is not too formal and not too composed. So, it is a good photograph, not in spite of the crop but in part because of it. **MF**

Task

Rules are useful in photography, but we need to ask ourselves why other people should set them for us? We are creatives after all. This task is designed to help you think beyond the rules and to bend them. So, write a set of rules for yourself as a photographer – a manifesto for your own creative practice, if you will. Consider rules that are about processes and creativity rather than aesthetics. One of your rules might be that you will always ask permission before taking a photograph or perhaps you want to shoot a roll of film each week. Or maybe you wish to set yourself a challenge always to push your research further. Write these rules in a sketchbook or stick them on the wall to provide you with a constant reminder. Then update your personal photographic rules whenever you feel this is necessary.

Conclusion

• There is no magic formula to making good photographs.
• While rules can be useful for learning the basics of photography, break them early and break them often.
• Build your style of photography based on the photographs you like and things you're interested in.
• If you like rules – make your own.

Gordon Parks

born 1912, Fort Scott, Kansas, USA.
gordonparksfoundation.org

Gordon Parks (1912–2006) was, in my opinion, one of the most important photographers of the 20th century. Born in the segregated south of the United States, Parks was a self-taught photographer who became interested in photography at a young age and spent the rest of his life using photography and art in general as a tool to fight for social justice. As he once said: 'I saw that the camera could be a weapon against poverty, against racism, against all sorts of social wrongs. I knew at that point I had to have a camera.'

Parks's experiences as a young man were clearly formative in shaping his subject matter. Growing up poor in the segregated south where racism was rampant must have had a profound effect on his motivations as an image maker. When a young Gordon Parks first visited Washington DC to work for the FSA (see page 130), he was advised by the director to start by exploring Washington without a camera. He was racially abused everywhere he went and returned to the FSA feeling deflated. Parks was encouraged to start closer to home, which is how he met Ella Watson, a cleaner in the FSA offices. This encounter led to Parks documenting Ella Watson's life for four months.

The photograph shown here, titled 'American Gothic' in reference to a portrait of the same name by the 20th-century painter Grant Wood, shows Ella Watson posing with a broom. In the background we can see the American flag and to her right is a mop. The American flag contextualizes the image and the broom and mop highlight the overlooked contributions of Black women to society and government – in this case, as a cleaner who keeps the offices of the FSA functioning. The subject matter is unusual for this period when it was rare to see pictures of Black women who were not celebrities. In this image, Parks is highlighting Ella because she is part of the glue that holds the fabric of an unequal society together, but also as a means of giving a 'voice' to the voiceless.

To quote Parks once more: 'I'm an objective reporter with a subjective heart. I can't help but have a certain kind of empathy…. It's more or less expressing things for people who can't speak for themselves…the underdogs…in that way I speak for myself.' **COS**

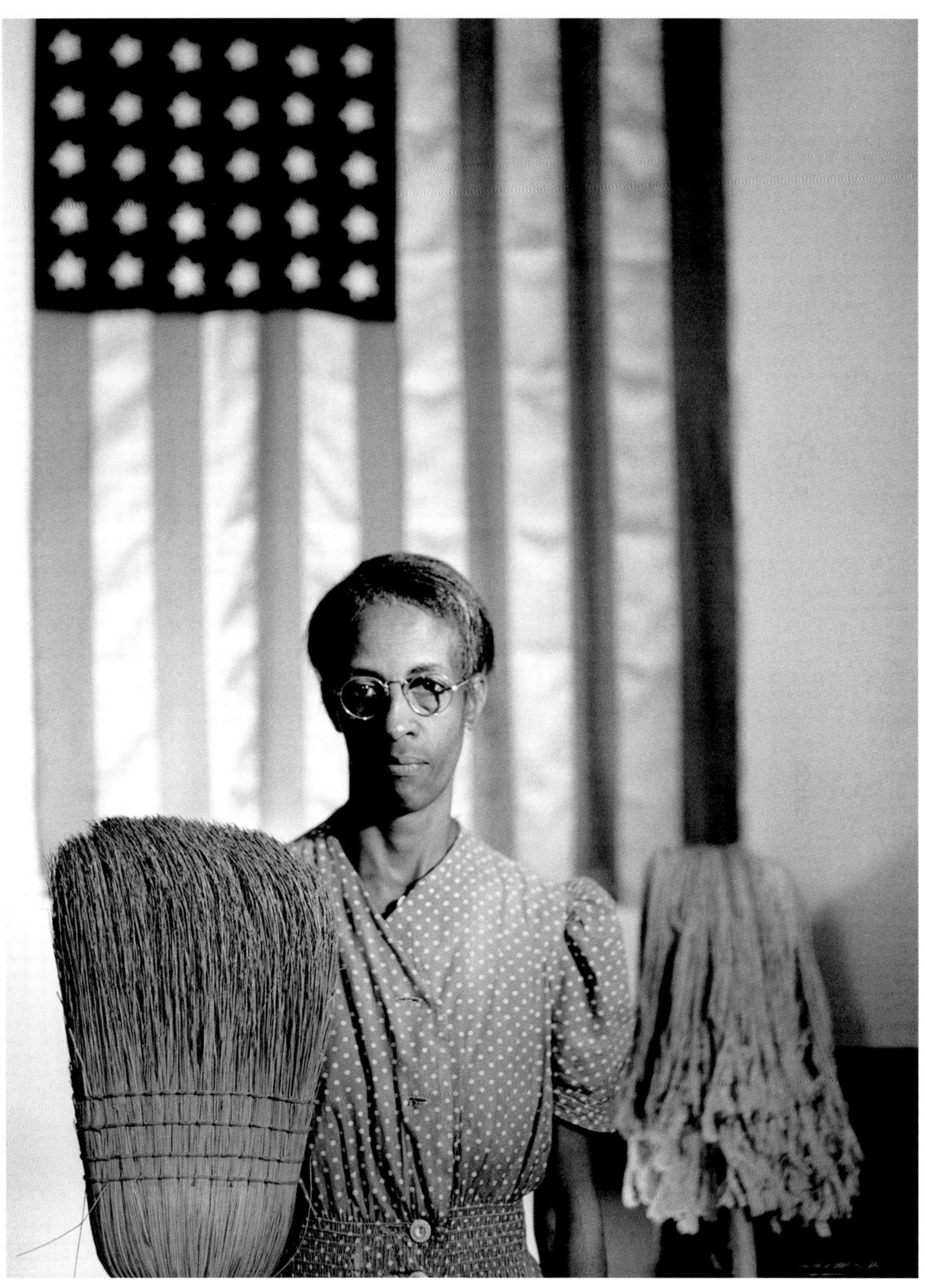

Sequencing Photographs

All photographers have a different approach to sequencing photographs. It's a deeply subjective part of the image-making process, but also a hugely important one, and it impacts how photographs are read and understood.

A single picture has its own individual meaning, but when you have a set of images or a whole project, then the order in which they are sequenced affects every other picture and can completely transform the meaning of each image. Some photographers mainly like to work on single images and may not be interested in creating larger bodies of work related to one subject matter. However, all photographers eventually have to sequence their work for a project, portfolio, exhibition or book of some kind. The approach you take to different presentations of your work may vary, but there are some similarities across the board and also some useful techniques that apply to most of them.

The first stage when sequencing a series of photographs is part of the actual process of making images. Taking stock every now and then to look at the images in your project allows you to see where there are any gaps and to create images to fill these. This can also be done by printing out the images from your series and putting them on the wall. Looking at and reviewing the project regularly in this way will keep you thinking about the overall sequence.

In my opinion, the second stage comes from working out your intention. What are you trying to say with the sequence of images and what is your end goal? For a portfolio you will generally be aiming to showcase your best work, but this can be tailored according to what you're trying to achieve. Photographers with a varied archive of work will sequence different images depending on whether they are showcasing their personal projects or trying to impress commissioning clients like editorial magazines and advertising agencies. For a project, the images you create are dictated by the particular subject you are focusing on, so your starting point is more obvious.

Regardless of your end goal, your starting point should always be to begin collating images and potentially text to represent your intention. I have found the best approach to this for a project is to print all your images as small prints. If you are short on cash, you can often find deals online that allow you to print a large number of small prints and only pay for the postage. If you're printing for a portfolio, you should only print the images you feel are your best ones. Alternatively, you can lay out all the images on a computer in a long, horizontal document and sequence them digitally. My preference is to work with physical prints wherever possible.

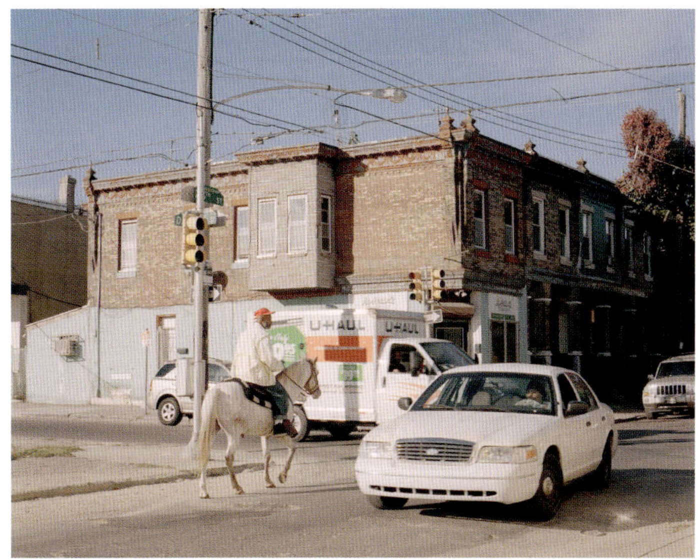

Cian Oba-Smith. Lonnie and Mont approaching the junction between Dauphin St and 26th St, Philadelphia, USA. From the series 'Concrete Horsemen', 2016.

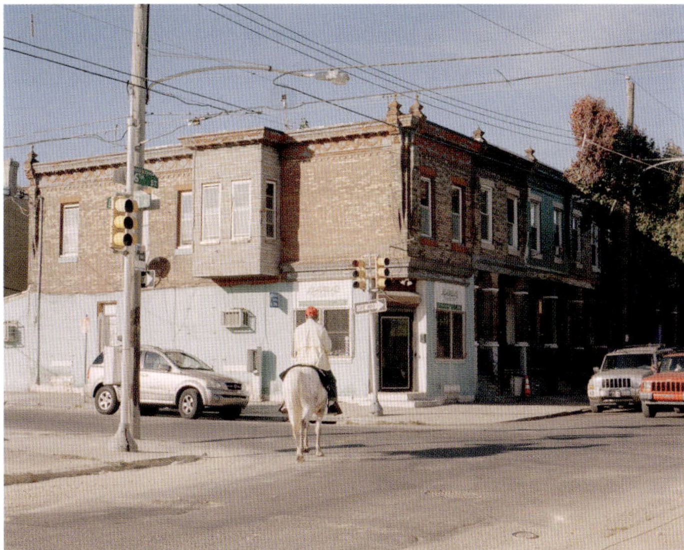

Cian Oba-Smith. Lonnie and Mont cross Dauphin St and 26th St, Philadelphia, USA. From the series 'Concrete Horsemen', 2016.

Once you have your prints, it is easier to edit out the weaker images. Start by flicking through the prints, looking for any images with technical flaws, such as out of focus or poorly exposed images. Then you should look for portraits that are similar in nature. For instance, perhaps you shot a series of portraits of the same subject and have multiple full-length portraits. In this case, you need to narrow these down to the strongest full-length portrait. From here, you should lay out your selection of images and begin sequencing them. This part of the process is really intuitive, so trust your gut and go with what feels right. Look for patterns and links between your images, whether this is the lighting, colours, themes or even the time of day that they were

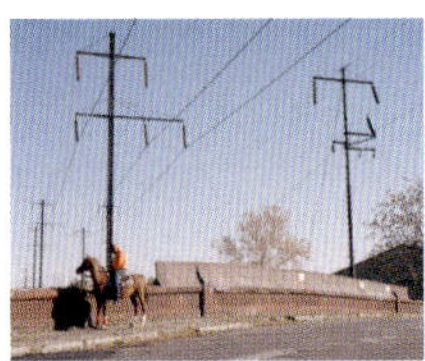 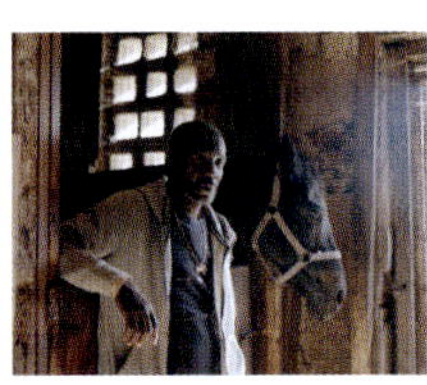 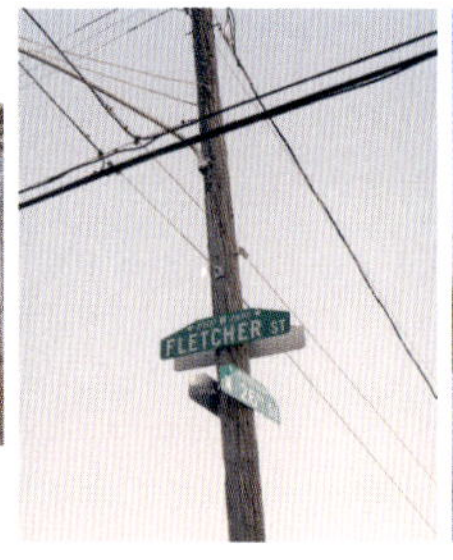 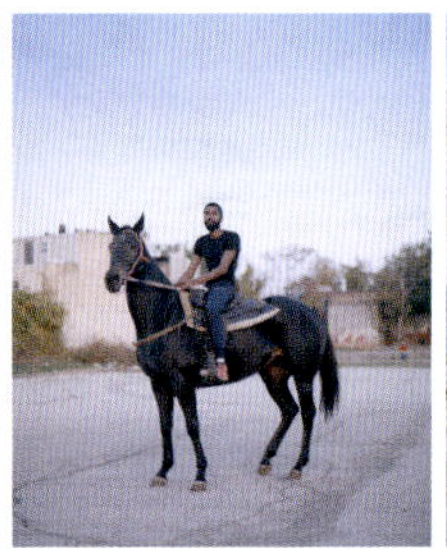 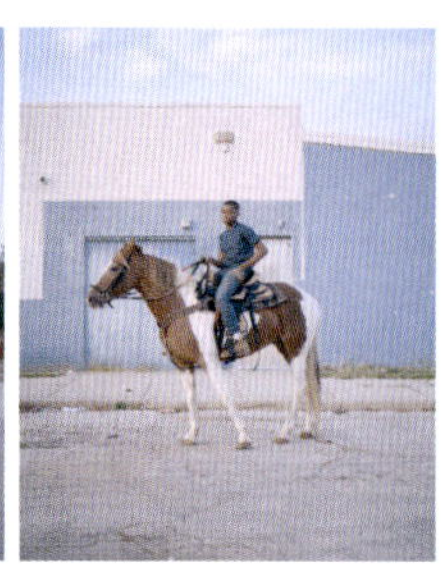

Here we have ten images from my 2016 series 'Concrete Horsemen'. This is an example of a good sequence. The first image provides a strong context, showing what the project is about: Black horsemen in the city of Philadelphia. But it doesn't spoon-feed us with too much information. The initial image also gives the viewer a good flavour of what the project is like aesthetically. We are next drawn into a closer portrait, then the following image shows us that we're on

EXAMPLE OF A BAD SEQUENCE

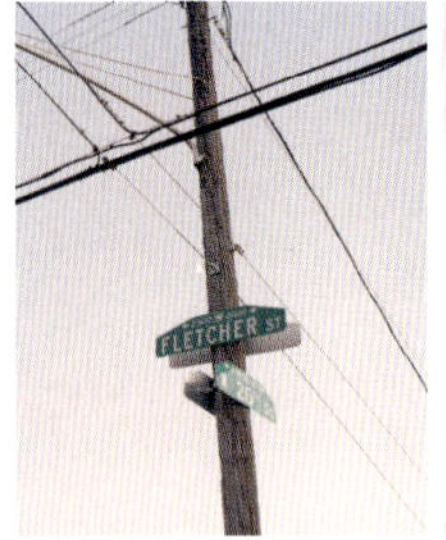 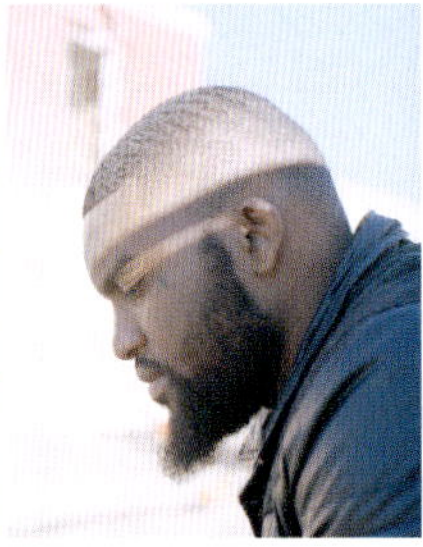 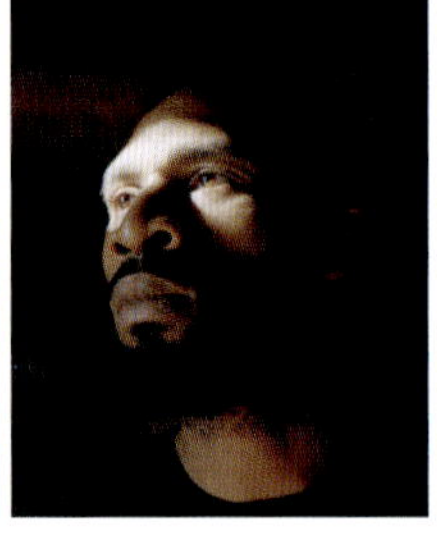 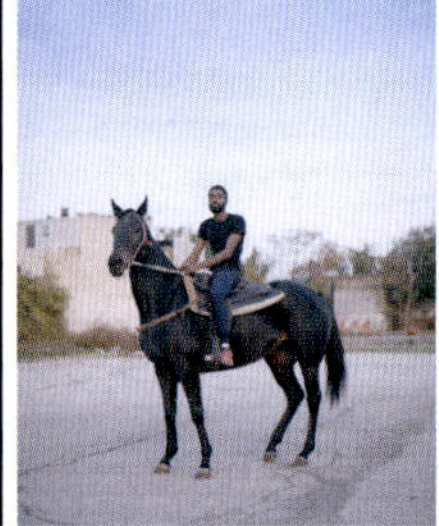 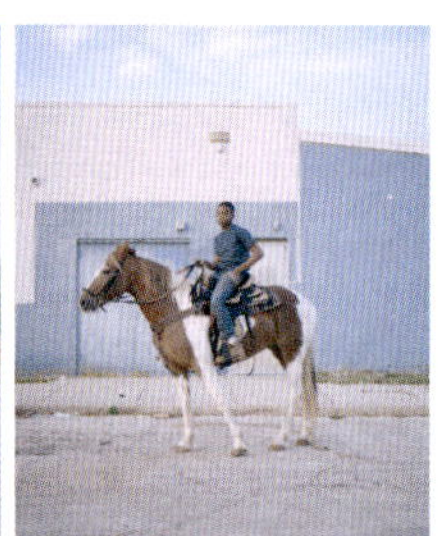

This is an example of a bad sequence. It doesn't provide any context at the start and shows only a signpost. This is more of a supporting image than one you would lead with. We jump next to a portrait of a person, but this doesn't tell us who they are or anything about the project's broader subject matter. Then we move on to another portrait with no context, before jumping to a portrait of Kassan on a horse, which finally reveals what the project is about. Next, there is a portrait of Kareem. These images of the horsemen are in the same order as the first sequence and work

taken. Anything that creates an overarching story within the series of images is a good place to start.

Once your sequence has taken shape, it's helpful to ask for the opinion of people you trust, such as family, friends and other photographers. Where possible, you should also get feedback from people with more expertise in this area, such as picture editors, publishing companies and curators.

Finally, remember that sequencing photographs is a lengthy process and it is important to allow the time you need to reach a point where you are satisfied with the final layout. Give yourself some breathing space away from your images if you feel this is necessary. A break from the work and returning with a fresh pair of eyes can breathe new life into the project. **COS**

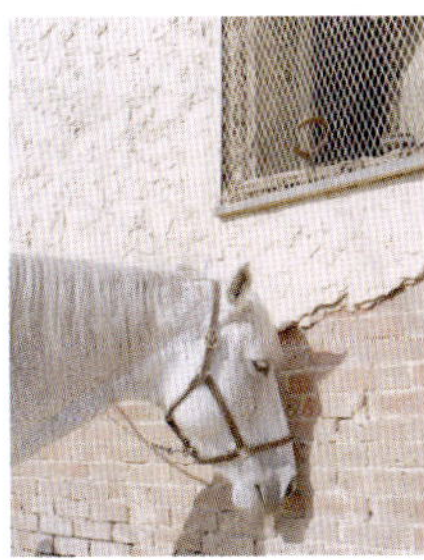 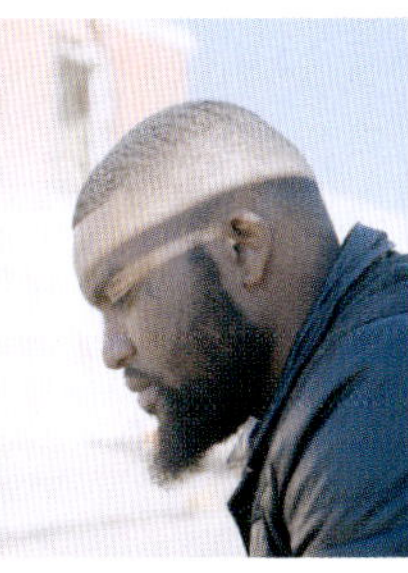 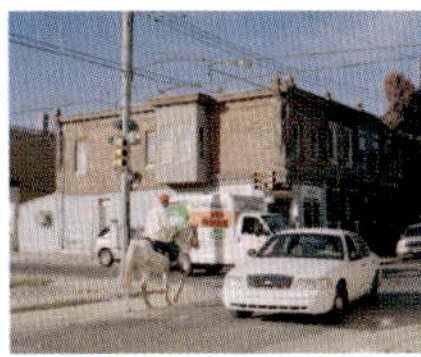 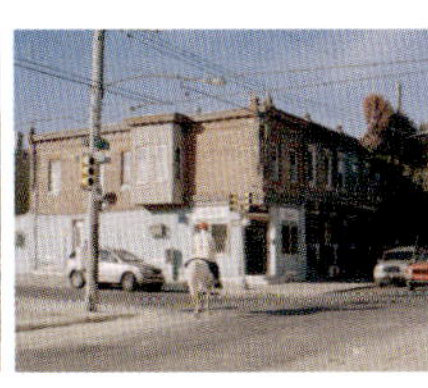 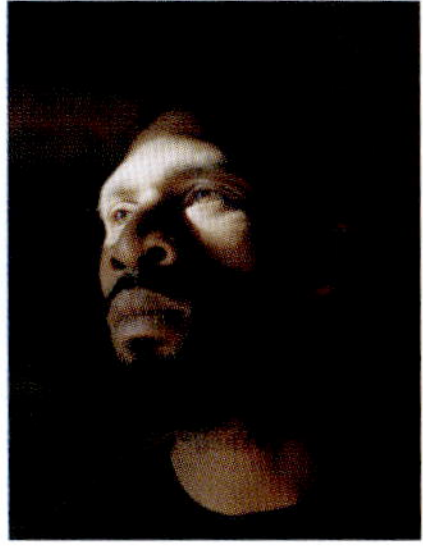

Fletcher Street. The following two images are more traditional portraits with similar colour palettes. Then we move on to a closeup of one of the horses, which guides us to a portrait of Ike in a similar pose, but facing the other way. This leads to two environmental portraits that help to create a bit of movement in the sequence, before we finish with a portrait that brings a note of optimism to the narrative.

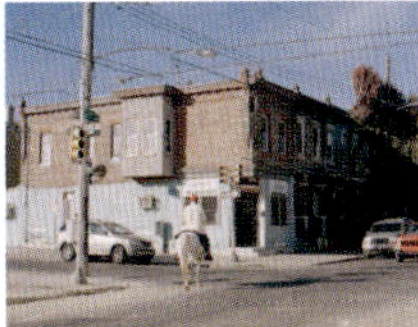 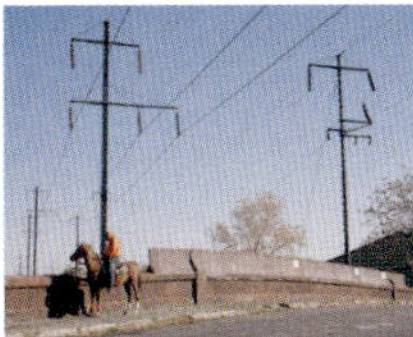 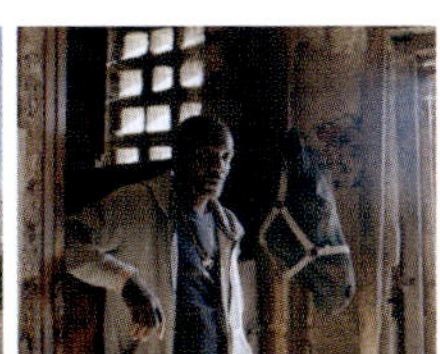 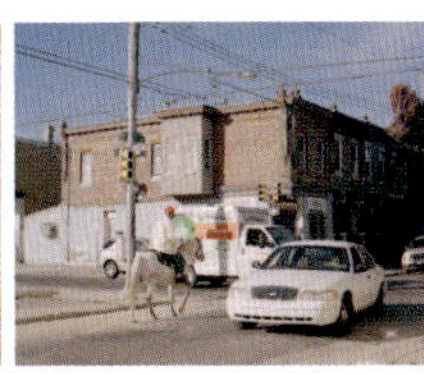 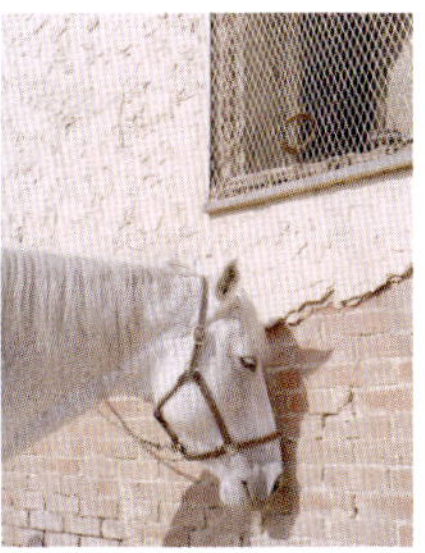

well together. There is then an environmental portrait of Lonnie, but this is on its own here, so we lose the motion of the first sequence. Next, there is another environmental portrait, then a closer one, before we return to Lonnie and Mont and finish with a portrait of a horse. The images in both sequences are the same, but are read differently due to how they are ordered, with the second sequence being the weaker of the two. This demonstrates the importance of thoughtful sequencing.

Conclusion

Sequencing photographs can be a challenging part of the image-making process, as your portraits will usually exist alongside other types of images. Try to think about the ways you can create a flow between your pictures, whether that's through colour, composition or some other kind of visual similarity. Most importantly, keep your pictures somewhere visible and make sure you continue to look at them, allowing the photographs to sequence themselves.

Amak Mahmoodian

born 1980, Shiraz, Iran.
amakmahmoodian.com

King Naser al-Din Shah Qajar (1831–1896) was, as Amak Mahmoodian says, the first 'modern monarch of Iran'. A reformist, he was fascinated by painting, poetry and photography – and was famously given a camera by Queen Victoria. In her 2019 book, *Zanjir* (which is Iranian for 'chain'), Iranian photographer Amak Mahmoodian imagines a conversation between herself and Naser al-Din's daughter, the Persian princess and memoirist Zahra Khanom Tadj es-Saltaneh (1884–1936). The project started in 2004 when Mahmoodian was studying for a bachelor's degree in Iran. While there, she spent time engrossed in the 19th-century photography collections held in the Golestan Palace archives in Tehran.

Naser al-Din photographed the women in the royal palace, of which there were approximately eight hundred. Speaking about these photographs, which sit alongside her own photographs and poems in *Zanjir*, Mahmoodian says that in a way Naser al-Din was 'the first family photographer in Iran'. These archives, made by a king of his vast family, became the 'cornerstone' of Mahmoodian's project – which she used to 'tell her story through the lives of others who came before'.

Scanning the original photographs, Mahmoodian created a series of masks. Consider the photograph here. We see portraits of five women, from the collections in the Golestan Palace, attached to a washing line with clothes pegs. The one on the far left is cut off, which gives the impression that there are more portraits we cannot see beyond the frame. On the other side of the image, a woman is clipping a blank sheet of paper to the clothesline. The fact that the person Mahmoodian photographed in 'real time' is the only woman whose face we cannot see is intriguing. Can we identify the person adding themselves to the row of women from Golestan Palace who have all long since died? Is it the photographer, someone else or even yourself? **MF**

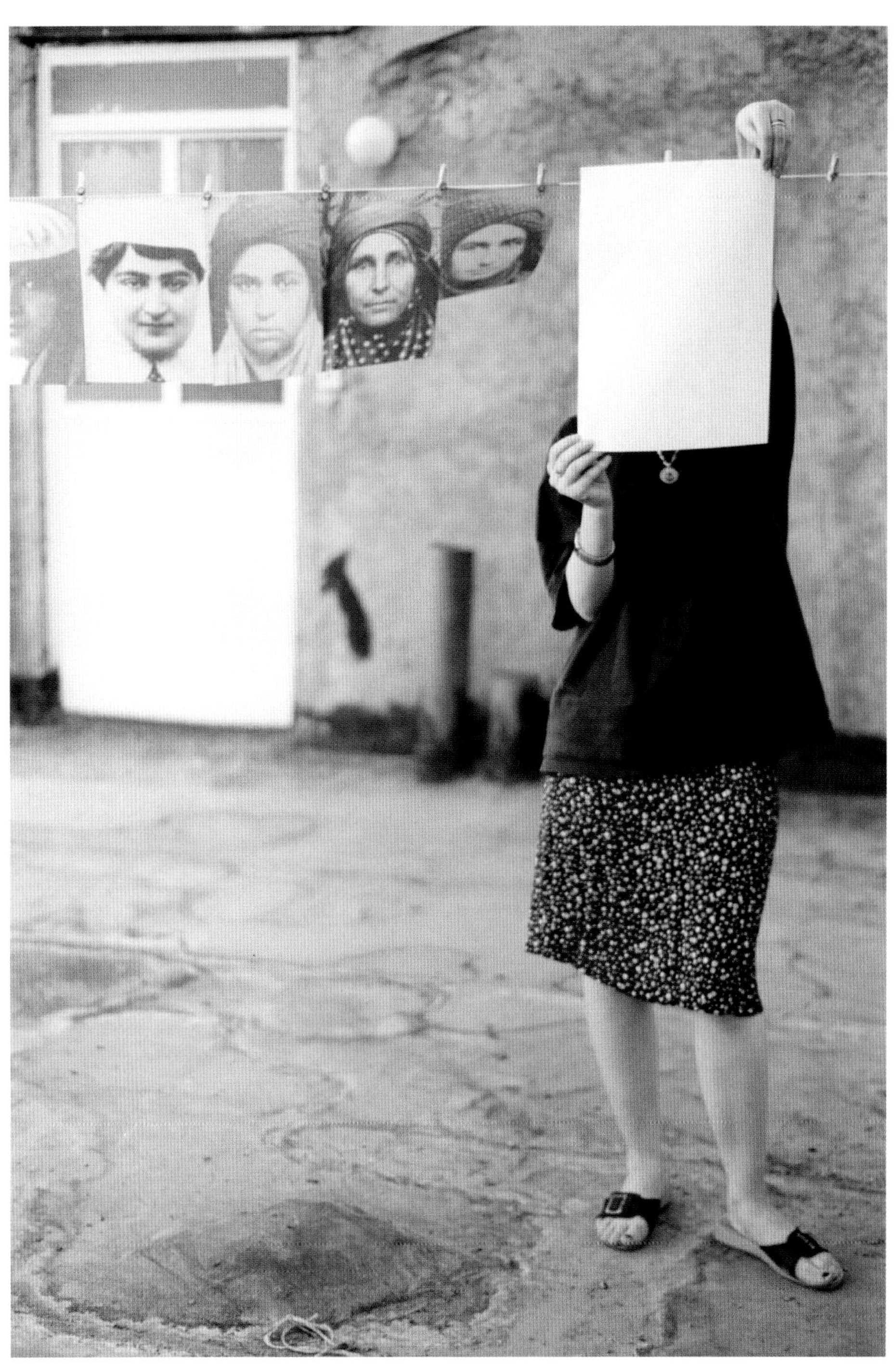

CHAPTER 6

Making a Career

You've fallen in love with photography, so the next question is how do you make a living from it? This chapter teaches you how to lay the foundations of a successful photographic career.

Projects

A photographer's first creative impetus comes from a place of passion for the art of making pictures. It is extremely rare for a photographer to become interested in photography purely because of the industry itself. More usually, the art always comes first, with the career being a secondary thought. Making art should be your priority, but without money to fund your projects, you can't create the work in the first place.

Money is seldom mentioned when discussing a career in photography, but it is an essential part of working out how to sustain a photographic practice. When I was a student at university, I had this romanticized idea based on the history of photography that I would graduate and then sustain my personal practice in documentary photography by working as an editorial photographer. In reality, this is very difficult to do and only a small group of photographers can earn a living like this. Most editorial magazines pay £200–300 per day (plus expenses), which sounds good, but when you factor in the number of commissions a month and the lack of certainty regarding how often these will come in, you realize how difficult it can be to pay rent and afford the costs involved when living in a major city. The draw of these jobs is that you are given creative freedom and often access to people or places you wouldn't otherwise have. For example, the commission opposite to photograph Popcaan for *Crack Magazine* or the one for the London bikelife scene for *The Face*,

▶ Cian Oba-Smith. Popcaan for *Crack Magazine*, 2016.

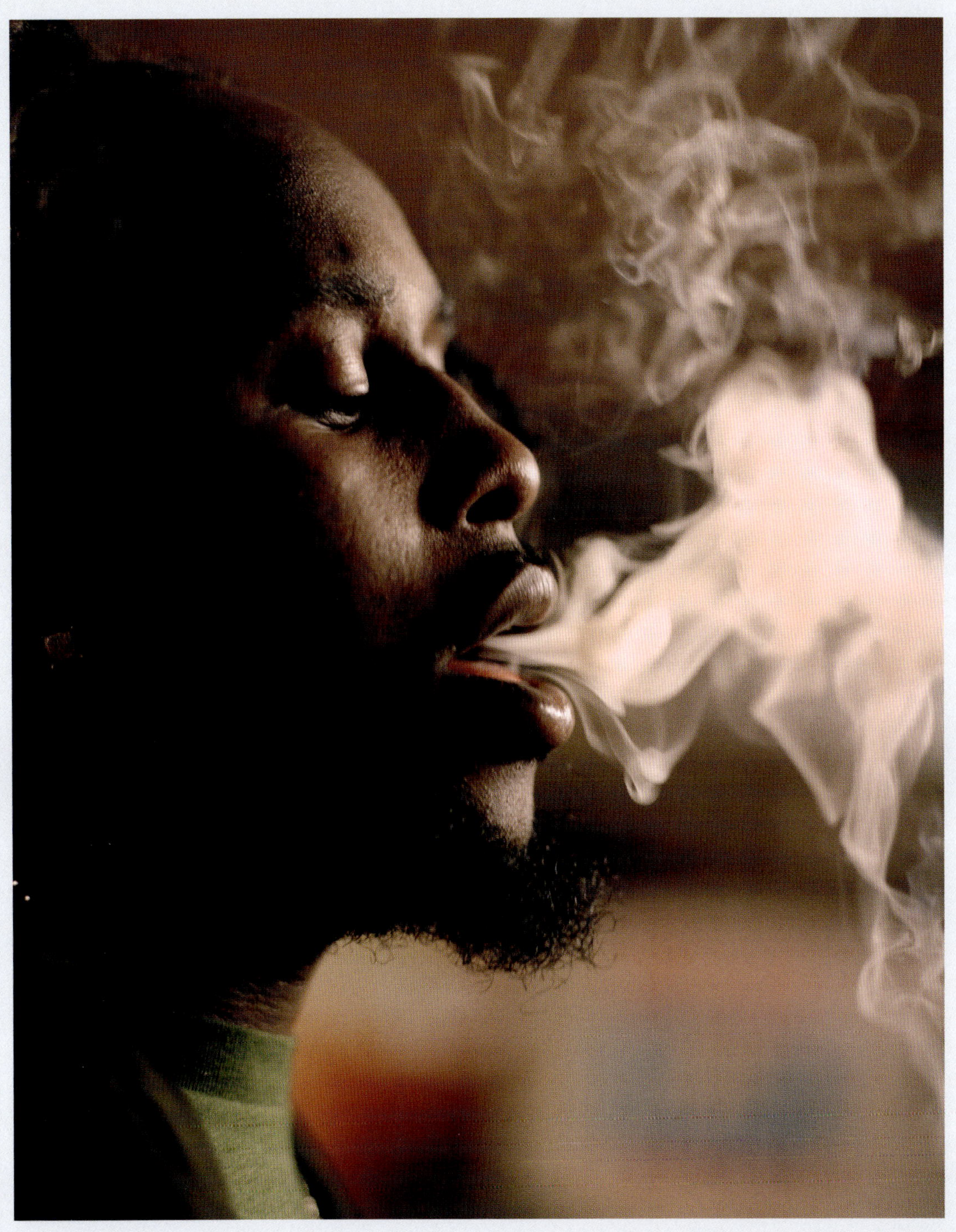

shown opposite, both allowed me to create the type of work I want to make anyway while also providing me with funding and a bigger platform.

Having a successful career in photography calls for an equal blend of talent, networking and luck. It is also one of the hardest things to teach. Each photographer's career path is unique, which makes it difficult to come up with an approach that fits all as this does not really exist. There are similarities, however, in how most photographers approach forging a career in photography. Personally, I was privileged in this respect because I grew up in London, which meant I could move back home to live with my mum when I graduated. She believed in my career as a photographer and was kind enough not to charge me or my brother any rent, meaning my main outgoings were food and camera film. Although three people living in a two-bed flat was cramped, I was lucky to have this option and wouldn't be where I am today without it (thanks mum).

Initially, when I moved back home, I was on benefits. This kept me afloat for about six months until I was able to get a job assisting Zed Nelson, a renowned documentary photographer. The work I did for Zed, along with the occasional commission, funded my day-to-day expenses as well as my personal work. Life went on in this way for a while until I was signed by my advertising agent Wyatt Clarke + Jones. I was then more able to stand on my own two feet and earn a better living from my commissioned work.

All photographers have different journeys when they are first starting out. Some are lucky and have parents who will happily bankroll their projects and living costs, while others do not have a support network and are forced to take jobs outside of the industry to fund their work. One of my friends worked in a bar for years to fund his photographic practice. Since then, he has won many awards, published books and currently lectures in photography.

The common theme I have found among photographers is that almost no one earns a full-time living from their art practice and they generally have some sort of additional income stream. Max, for example, is a photographer, but he has also forged a successful career as a lecturer and as a picture editor for various magazines. I make my own personal work, but I also earn a living from magazine commissions and advertising. Many photographers work in some sort of teaching capacity or have a role in another area of the photography industry, perhaps as an assistant, lighting tech, digi-op, curator or producer.

This chapter will hopefully give you an understanding of how the industry works in general, including the commissioning process and – looking at the commission from the other side – how picture editors and art buyers choose photographers. It also lays out the basics of networking and building an online presence through social media and a website. Photography can be a tough and isolating industry, but it is also incredibly rewarding to earn a living doing what you are most passionate about. **COS**

▶ Cian Oba-Smith. London bikelife for *The Face*, 2020.

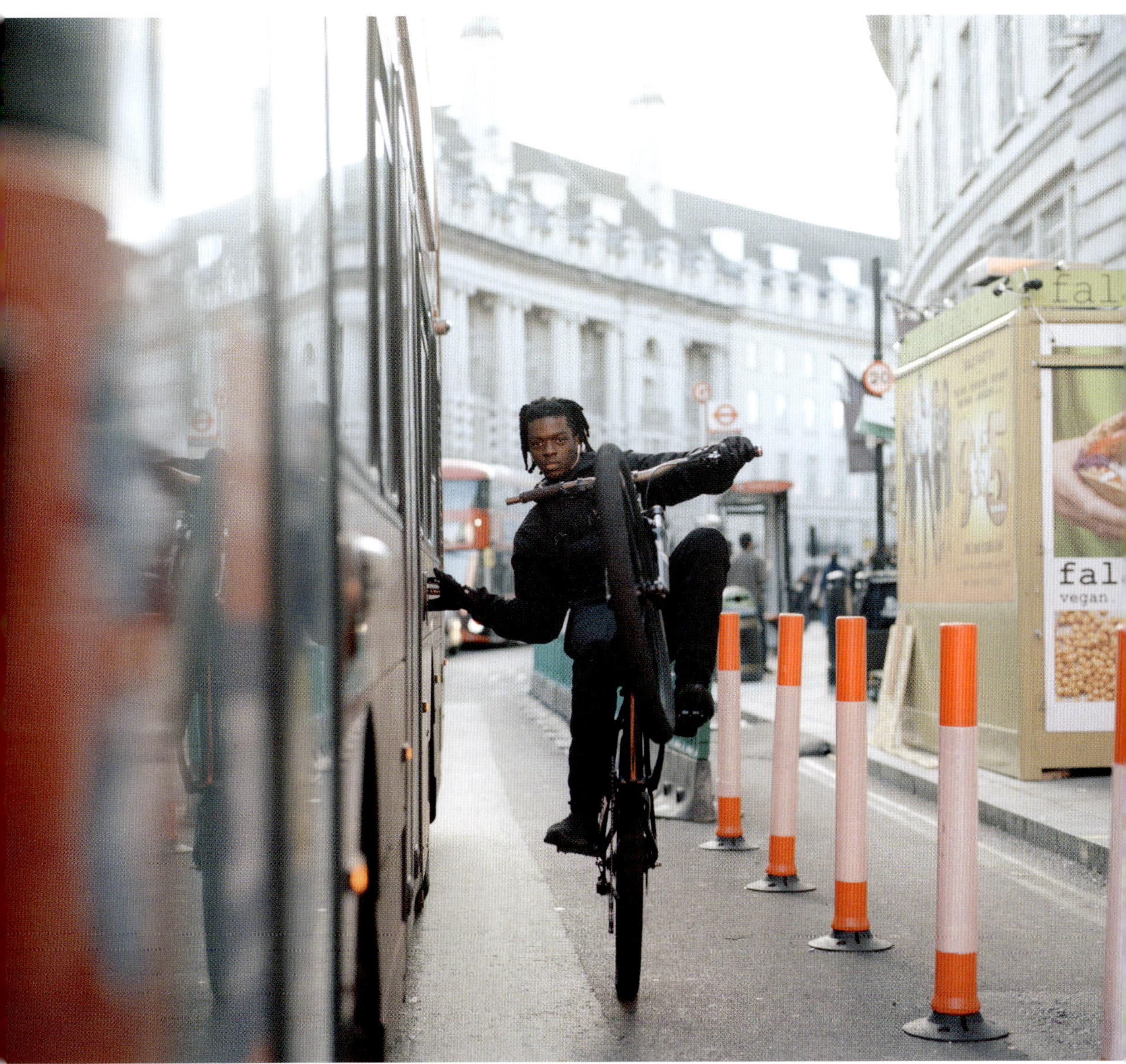

fal
vegan

Kalpesh Lathigra

born 1971, London, UK.
kalpeshlathigra.com

For Kalpesh Lathigra photography has several functions. When he first started out in the 1990s, he was a staff photojournalist for *The Independent* newspaper. He's photographed several conflicts, including a period of being embedded with the British Army on a tour of Afghanistan. Lathigra publishes his own books and in these the photographs are closer to art. He shoots regularly on commission for magazines, meeting people and taking their portraits. Sometimes he makes fashion images too, which blur the line between commercial, editorial and his art practice. At other times, Lathigra works on what he (only half-jokingly) calls 'flash-for-cash' assignments, where he uses his technical skills in portraiture and lighting to pay the bills. This sounds like a lot! But this dynamic way of working in photography is not uncommon in an industry where consistent work is hard to find. Being a photographic polymath has allowed Lathigra to thrive in a cutthroat industry for decades.

The image featured here is a good example of how Lathigra manages to slip between fashion and art – the gaze of the two subjects is borderline confrontational, creating a tension that intrigues us. The photograph is taken from his latest photobook *Memoire Temporelle* (2022), which brings together these strands to create a beautifully sequenced publication. The photographs for the book were shot over eight trips to Mumbai between 2016 and 2019 and even include some images that Lathigra made on a fashion commission shot in Mumbai for *Port Magazine*. Drawn to India due to the allure created around the country by growing up experiencing the culture secondhand in the UK, Lathigra says: 'The weekends growing up would be Indian cinema played on pirated videos and listening to the songs from the films *Abihimaan*, *Sholay* or *Khabi Khabie*.' After three years of shooting, Lathigra spent another three years editing, sequencing and designing the book – it's easy to forget how long photographers can spend working on a project.

When on commission for a magazine, Lathigra usually tries to photograph the subject on an old Polaroid passport camera (as well as his usual kit). These images sometimes make it into the magazine, but they often join those of the other celebrities, politicians, artists, actors and sportspeople he's photographed and become a new archive. This approach is indicative of Lathigra as a photographer – even when working on commissions for magazines he finds a way to conceptualize them. A good example of this approach is the Mumbai shoot for *Port Magazine* – there are always some extra images that might be useful later down the line. **MF**

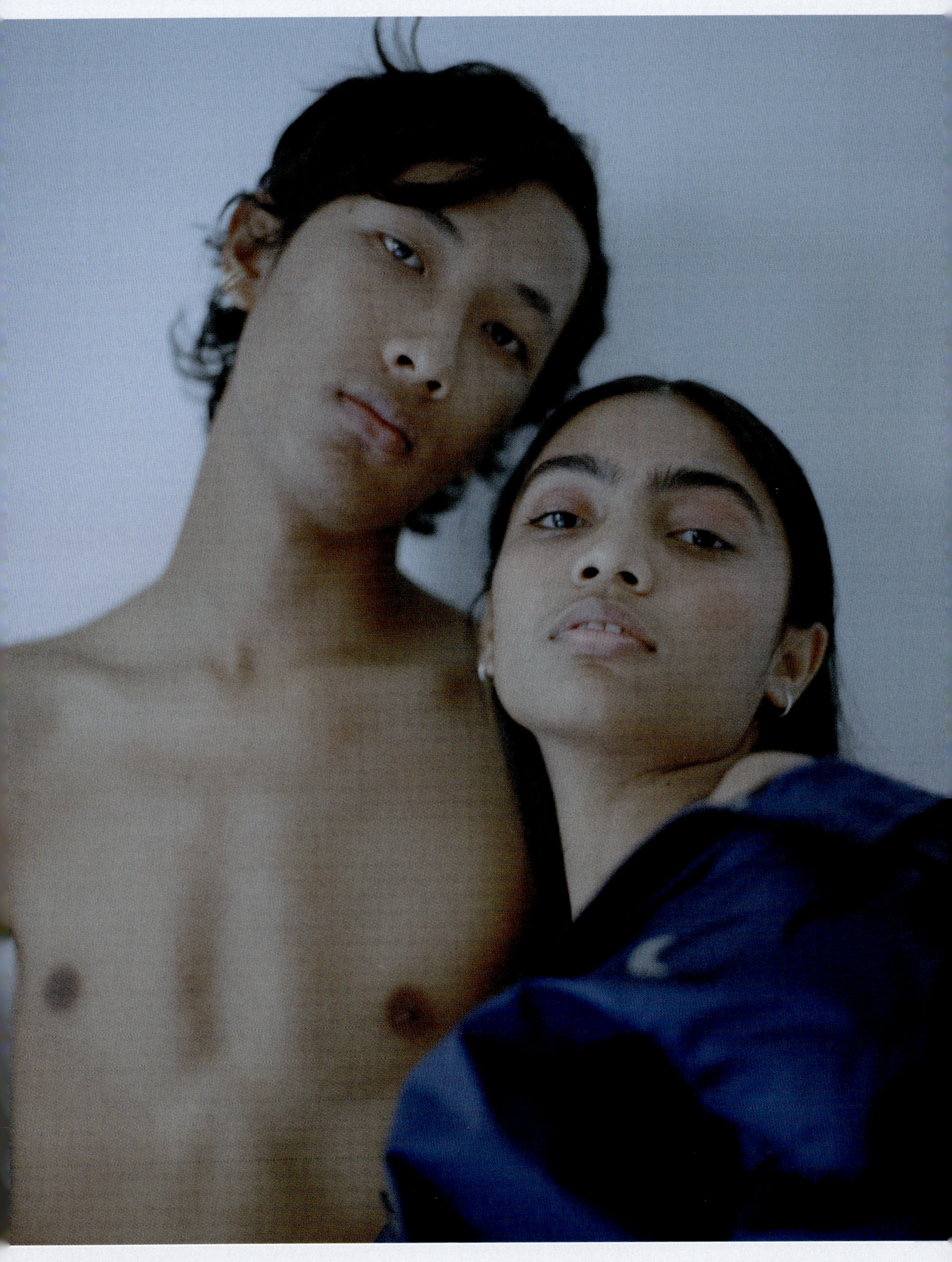

PROJECT 17

Cian and Max's *Port Magazine* Commission

You may hear photographers say they are shooting commissions (or working on an assignment) – what they mean by this is that they are on a paid job.

Photographers are usually hired for two types of commissions: editorial and commercial. Most photographic jobs are editorial, which means shooting for magazines and newspapers either for print or online. Commercial jobs are much better paid and are usually for the advertising sector. Since most people's first years as a photographer will be spent working editorially, this case study looks at a commission for *Port Magazine* (issue no. 23) that Cian and I worked on together. I was the photo director and I commissioned Cian to make a series of images for the magazine.

Cian and I have worked together many times on various commissions, but we thought this was a good one to discuss because it covers several bases. We needed a photographer to shoot portraits as well as some environmental and action shots of horses being ridden at the annual showjumping event, Saut Hermès, which takes place at the Grand Palais in Paris (Cian had worked extensively photographing horsemen in Philadelphia, so we knew he could photograph horses, but he also had an interest in them). Shoots such as this can be quite difficult. Photographers are taken around by the press team and there are always limits as to where they can go and who they can take portraits of. Cian was given a four-day itinerary, starting and finishing with being picked up and dropped off at home. Since the days were so regimented, I gave Cian a very loose brief – to make a series of images that looked like his personal work. I was worried any more control would stifle his creativity further. This is always a dream way to work with a photographer, but there needs to be trust between both photographer and editor for it to work well.

Cian submitted an edit of around one hundred photographs for the commission. This is a lot, especially when shooting on film, but it was also a large commission running over five double-page spreads in the magazine. Once Cian had submitted his wide edit, I made an initial edit of my favourite images before sharing them with the rest of the team. Then, working with designers, we whittled the edit down further to the final fourteen images we printed for the feature. The portrait of the woman standing against the wall is a fine example of a classical editorial portrait. This type of photograph balances the environment around the subject and its visual simplicity makes it great for

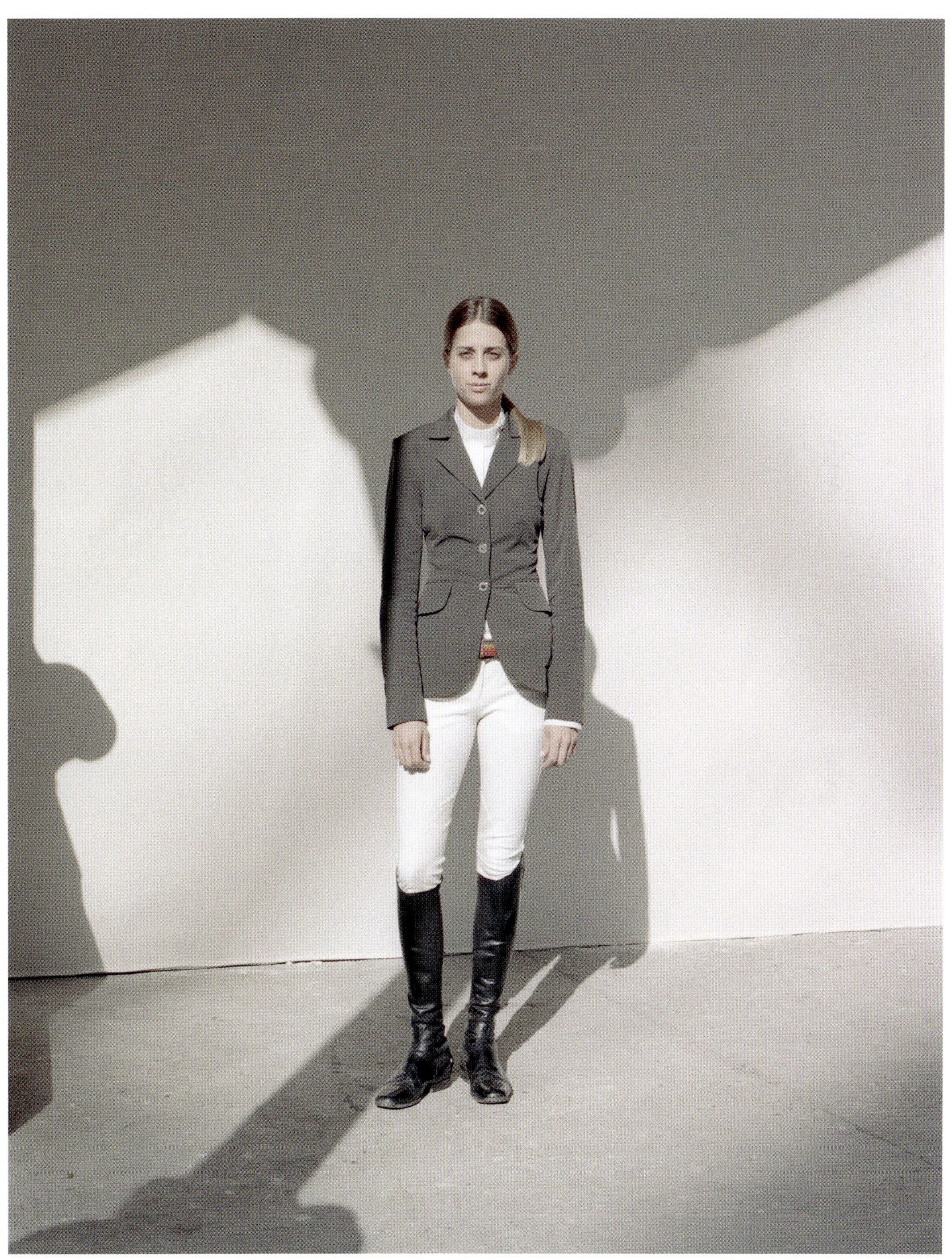

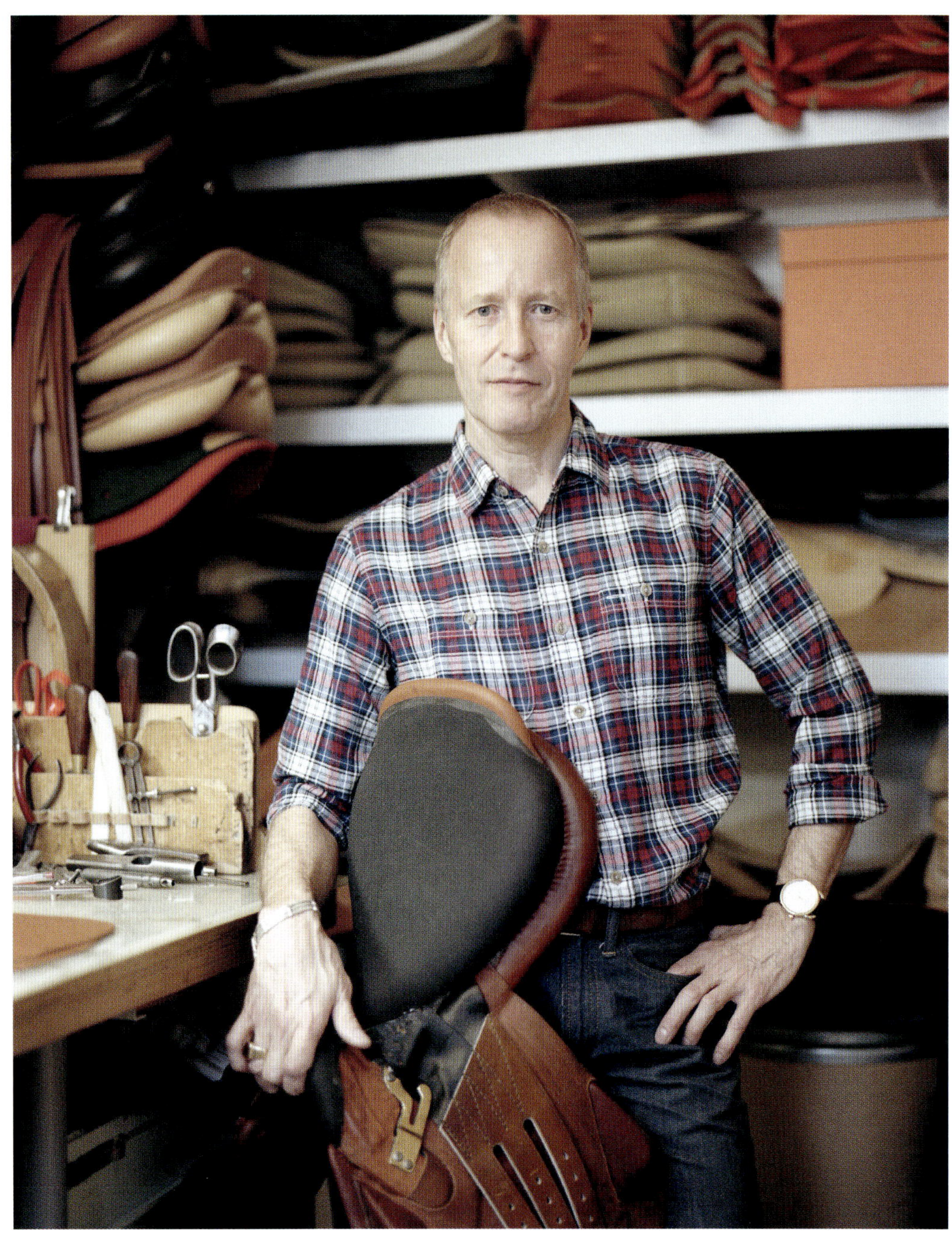

Cian Oba-Smith. Master saddler Laurent Goblet
from Cian's commission for *Port Magazine,* Issue 23.

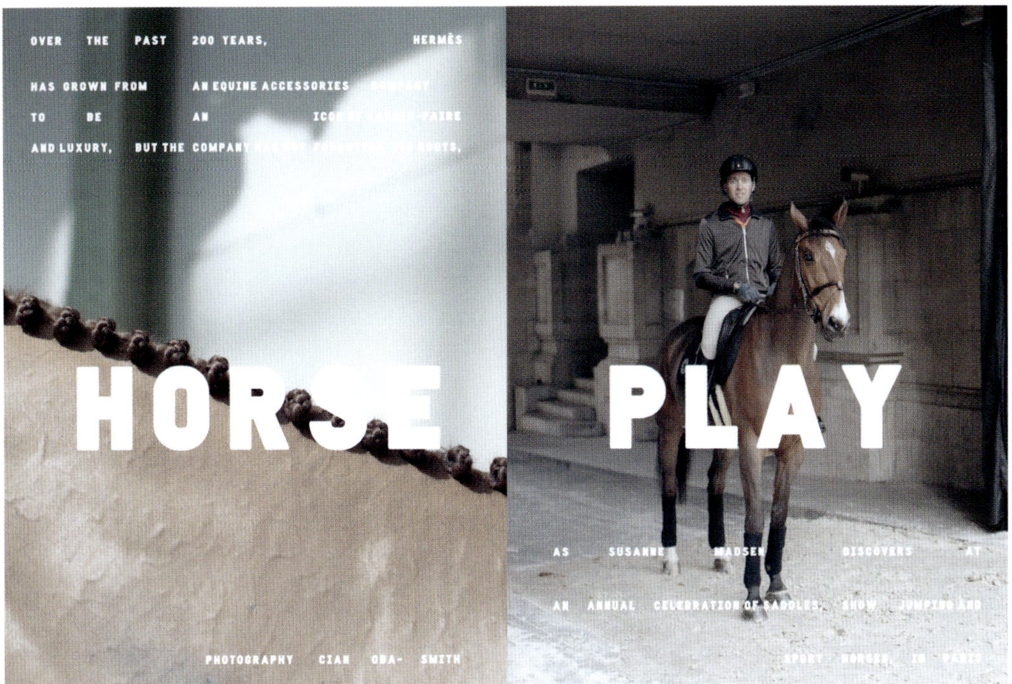

Cian Oba-Smith. Opening spread from Cian's commission for *Port Magazine*, Issue 23. Commissioned by Max.

magazine layouts. The shadows created by the lighting make the image more interesting than if it had been shot against a plain wall, while the bend in the subject's right knee makes the image slightly asymmetrical.

When you are commissioned by a photo editor, it's good to have an idea of what they want from you. Asking questions is normal but something photographers often don't do when starting out. What type of images does the client want? Are there different deadlines for low-res and high-res images (there usually are)? Is there an additional budget for travel, film expenses or an assistant (there usually isn't, but it is worth asking)? If in doubt, it's sensible to submit a tight selection of the best images rather than hundreds (although some magazines want to see everything). If it's a portrait, include a close crop of the head and shoulders, something from the waist up, and a full body option as well. That way, the client should have everything they need. Look at the opening spread layout shown above to see how details can also be useful. The designers have used two completely different types of photographs to contrast with each other, but the article title 'Horse Play' across the spread links the two images. **MF**

Conclusion

• Commissions form a vital part of the incomes of many photographers. Sometimes they may also become part of your portfolio.
• Notice how similar the images for this commission look to many of Cian's projects.
• Think carefully about how you will approach a commission if you've not worked on one before.

Cian's Approach to Commissions

To work successfully on assignments takes flexibility, a variety of approaches and intuition. In this project, I will talk you through my approach to commissions.

Portraiture takes on many forms in the world of professional commissioned photography. For example, you may be commissioned by someone independently to make a personal portrait or to take photographs for a wedding. However, you will most likely be commissioned by an organization or business client. The expectations and creative direction from each client will vary depending on who has commissioned you. A magazine or newspaper, for instance, will explain why you are photographing the subject because the images you take are intended to support and illustrate the written piece. But you will still have a large degree of creative freedom in terms of how you approach making the portrait stylistically.

The difference between this type of commission and one for an advertising client is that, for the most part, here you will get a much more restrictive brief. You can still be creative, but the approach to making the images and also the subject matter and contents of the photographs are usually decided in advance. The subjects are already cast and the styling and location both discussed in great detail prior to the photoshoot. In contrast, with a more casual editorial shoot, you mostly turn up and work within the space and around the subject.

The photographs featured here of singer/songwriter Raye were made for *The Fader*, an American music magazine. As usual, for an editorial job such as this, you are generally given a lot more creative control and artistic freedom. For this shoot I scouted out and chose the location, while the styling, hair and makeup were done by Raye's team. This is usual for photoshoots where there is a fashion element or you are photographing a celebrity. People who spend a lot of time in the public eye tend to have a more curated image, so they're more image conscious in comparison to your average person, who normally wears their own clothes and does their own makeup, and so on.

Every photographer has a different approach when working on a commission. Some photographers are meticulous in the way they work. They will plan every detail of how the images are going to look, even going as far as sketching them out beforehand. Personally, I prefer to take a looser approach, although I'll think in advance what images I need to ensure I capture what is required to tell the story. To do this, I usually write

▶ Cian Oba-Smith. Raye for *The Fader*, London, 2017.

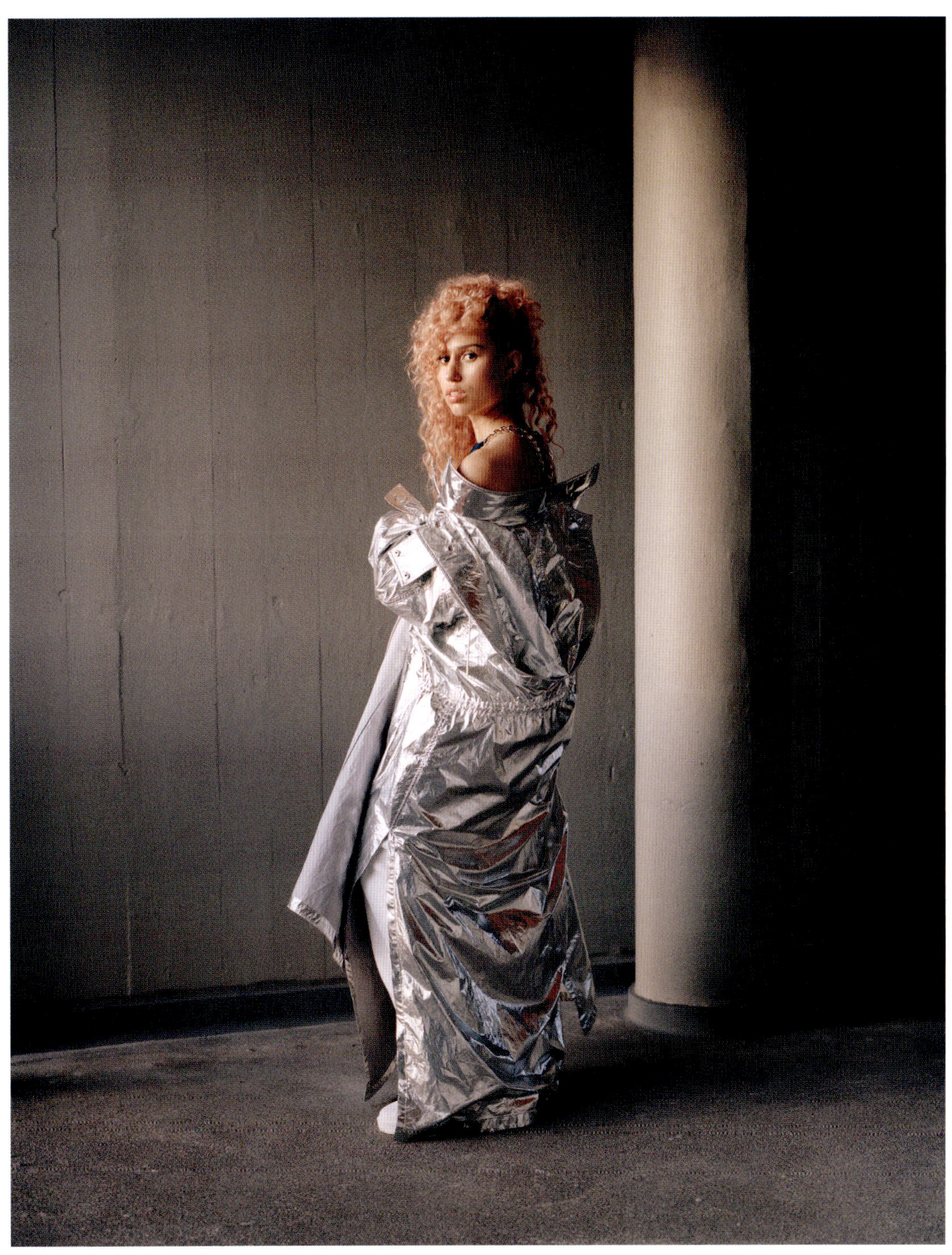

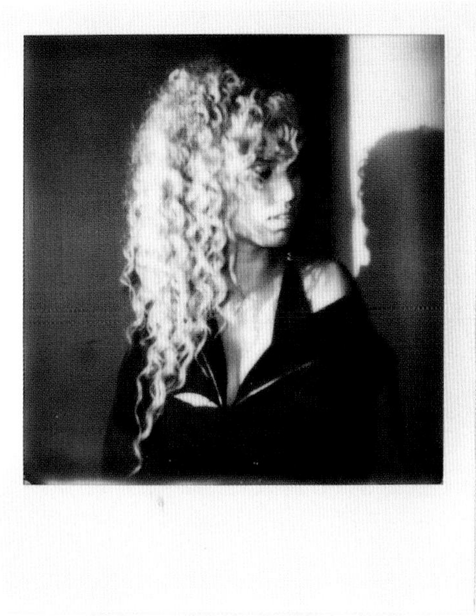

Cian Oba-Smith. Raye for *The Fader*,
London, 2017.

a list of the shots I need – for example, a full-length portrait, a head-and-shoulders portrait, one from the waist up, and then a variety of poses. I do this to get my mind thinking about how I will approach the shoot and to put me into the appropriate creative headspace.

For the commissioned shoot featured here, I decided to work with a few different cameras and formats, so that I could create a different feeling with each set of images. Medium-format film tends to work well for more formal portraits, whereas 35mm is a little more personal and candid. Polaroids have a nostalgic quality and are 'lo-fi' by nature due to the technology used in the cameras.

The full-length portrait of Raye by a pillar (see page 169) was shot on my medium-format Mamiya RZ67 camera. Here, there is one main natural light source on the subject's left-hand side. The sky is acting as a diffuser for the sun, which creates the soft light you can see in the portrait. I positioned Raye with the front of her body towards the sky and her back facing

towards the shadows. This created a nice falling away of the light because there is no significant light source on her right-hand side.

To make the portrait of Raye near a staircase (opposite), I used a cheap Canon point-and-shoot camera that I bought years ago in a charity shop for £5. I mainly use this camera for nights out with friends when I don't want to damage my more expensive cameras. There are two light sources in this image. The main source from the camera's built-in flash provides nearly all the light. The second source is the natural light from outside, which does little for the interior, but illuminates the barely glimpsed exterior and affects how the image is read. On camera, flash creates the flat look that you can see here. There are barely any shadows, apart from on the curve at the bottom of the balcony.

The portrait of Raye (left) was made with a Polaroid Sun 600 camera in black-and-white Impossible Polaroid project film. The choice to use black-and-white film was largely for technical reasons, as I prefer the way it renders images in comparison to colour film. The image was shot using the same light source as the portrait on the Mamiya, but this time I chose to overexpose the film slightly and directed Raye to look to her left, which meant that more of her face was lit by the sun. **COS**

Conclusion

Working on a commission is a very different experience to creating your own work. Be sure to plan ahead, but still leave room for experimentation and creativity. Consider the different approaches you can take to making portraits of the subject that you've been commissioned to photograph. Make sure you capture the basics first, then have fun with it.

▶ Cian Oba-Smith. Raye for *The Fader*,
London, 2017.

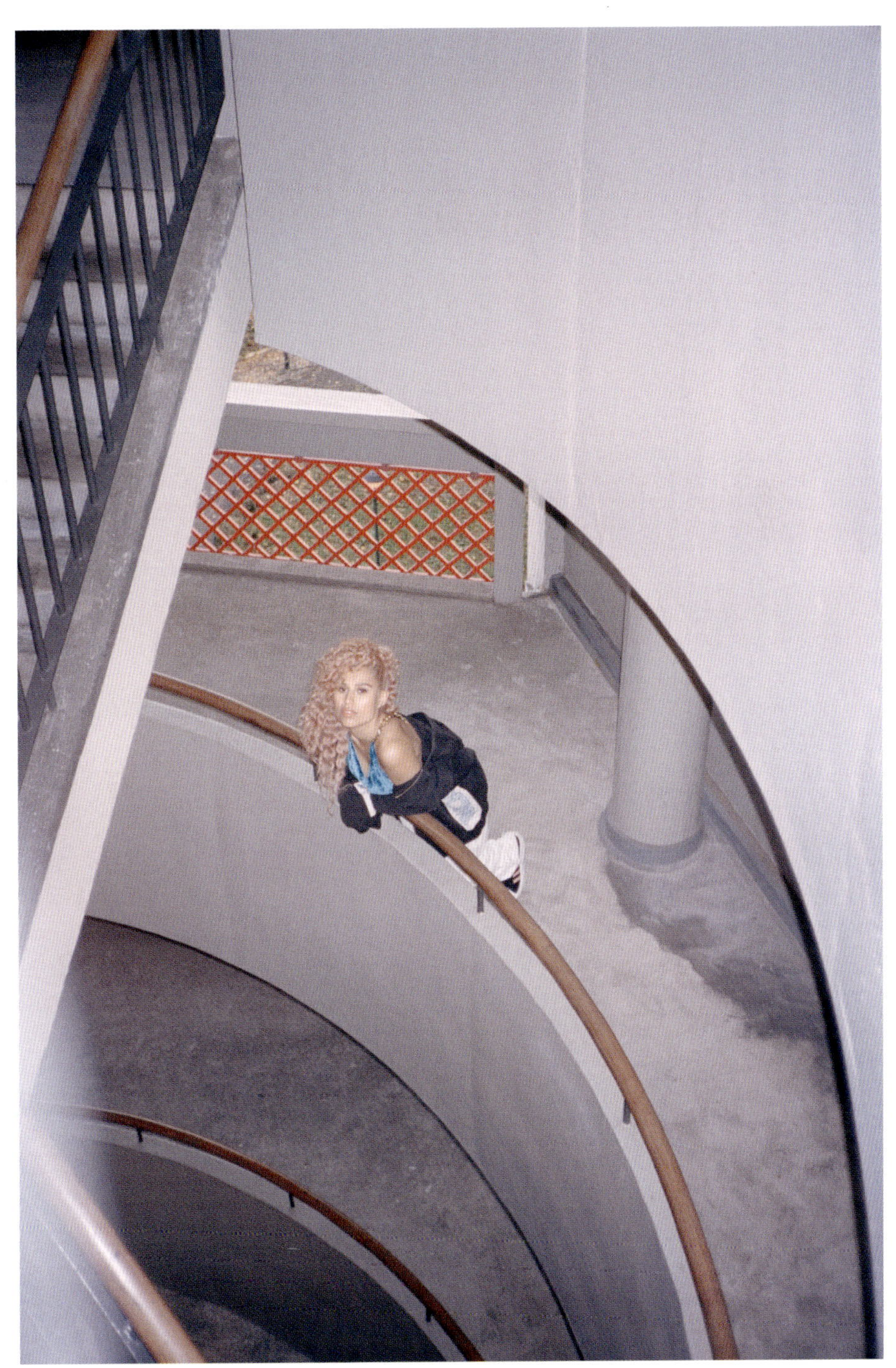

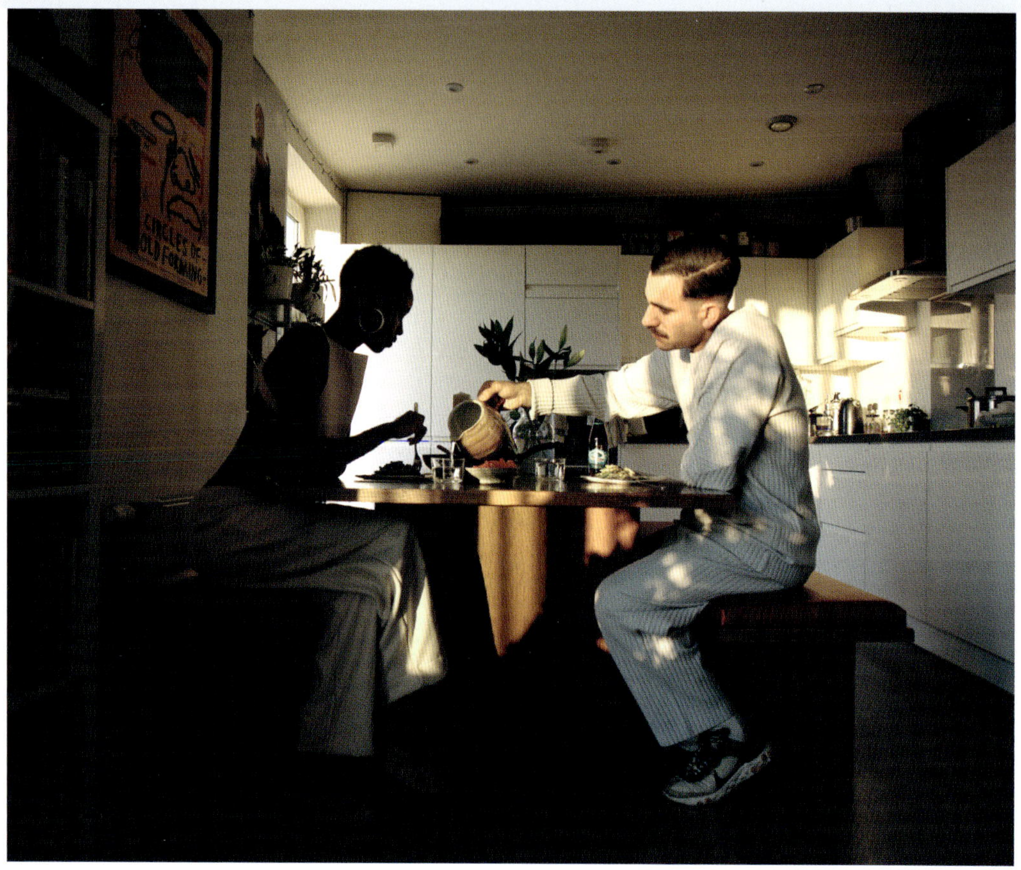

Ronan Mckenzie

born 1994, London, UK.
ronanmckenzie.co.uk

Ronan Mckenzie, like many young creatives, has a creative practice that goes beyond taking photographs. As a photographer, Mckenzie works on personal projects and commercial campaigns, but she is also a fashion designer with her own clothing brand, SELASI, and runs a multifunctional creative space called HOME, in which she curates photography exhibitions, among other areas. These elements of her portfolio may sound disparate, but they fit both stylistically and ethically and are all linked by her creative vision.

The two photographs we have chosen here have interesting similarities and differences. They both show two people sitting at a kitchen table, sharing a meal. Although we all often eat in public, there is something deeply personal about seeing people eat within their own homes. What I love about viewing these two images – which are, in fact, from different bodies of work – is how you start to notice the gestures of the subjects. The fact that the above photograph is a self-portrait of Mckenzie just adds further intrigue and also suggests that it was staged to some extent. Yet despite knowing that Mckenzie is both the photographer and one of the subjects, I find it difficult to believe that this is not a moment observed by someone else. The man in the photograph is pouring

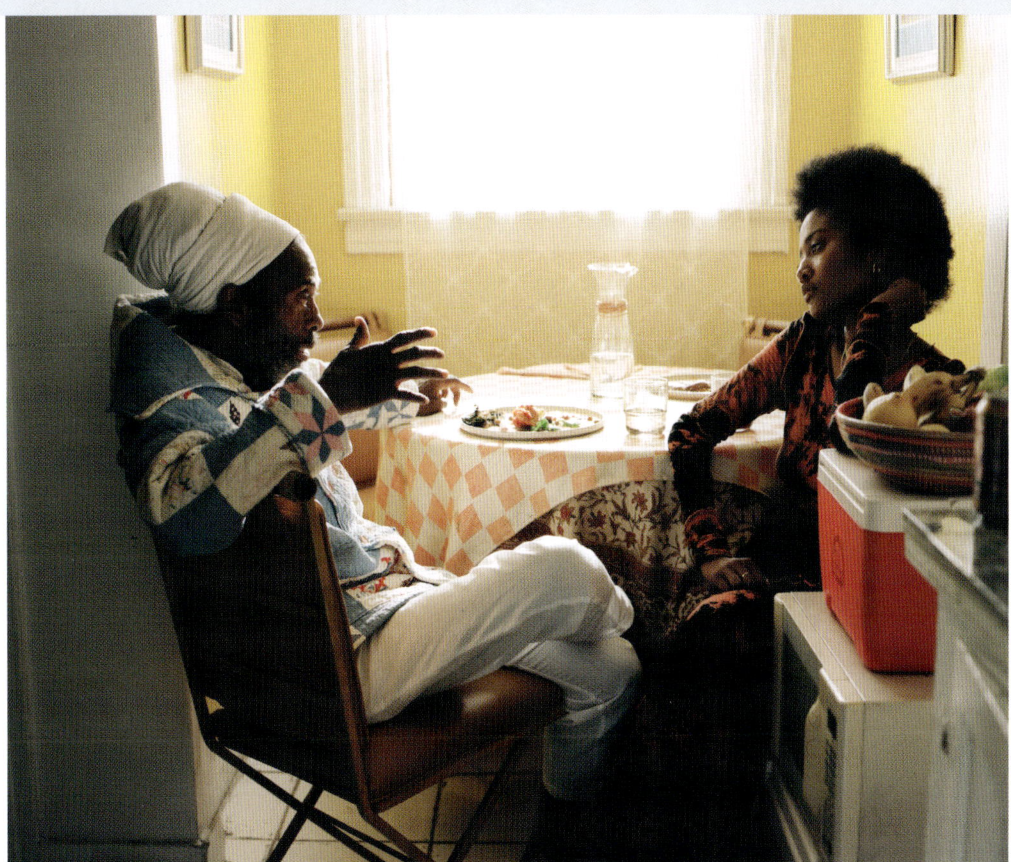

something for Mckenzie out of a jug. Although this is clearly a small gesture, it further adds to the sense of intimacy. The other image features two people in mid-conversation. Their bodies may be angled away from us, but they are opened up just enough for us to feel a part of the scene. Their hand gestures show us who is talking and who is listening. Small details such as the mostly empty places at the table recall convivial family meals.

The lighting too is interesting in these photographs. Although both images were taken indoors, the lighting appears to be coming from natural light sources and from behind the subjects. This backlighting serves to isolate the people in the scenes. In the first photograph, we notice in particular that Mckenzie herself is in silhouette because she is not sitting in the light falling on her partner. The warmth of the natural sunlight also contributes to the intimacy that Mckenzie likes to create in her photographs.

We can also see this in the photograph above of the Shabaka family sitting at their table. Notice that the main light source is the window behind them. The table is illuminated, bringing it into the photograph as an extra focal point. The two subjects also sit in this light. It's a wonderful photograph that reminds me of a film still. Perhaps this is what Mckenzie is best at – crafting casual moments that feel much more profound. **MF**

Curating Social Media Portfolios

Social media platforms are a great way to get your work noticed by more people, but how do you make the most of your online presence?

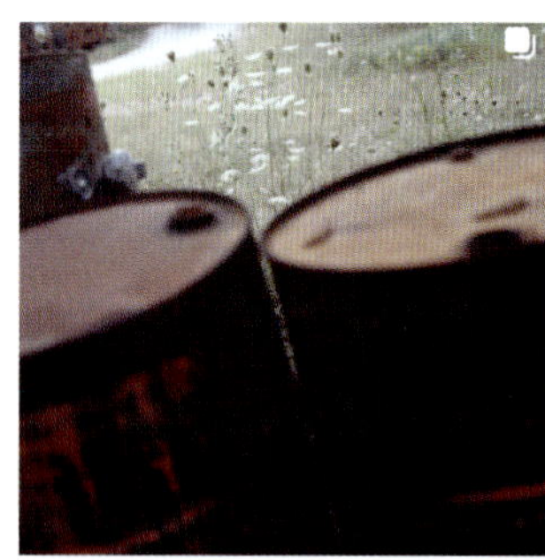
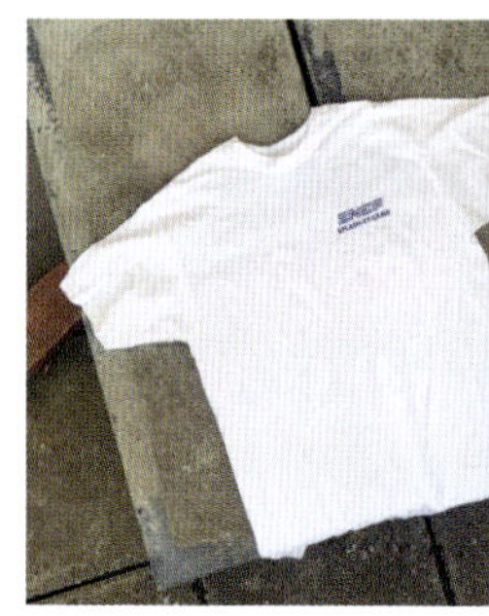
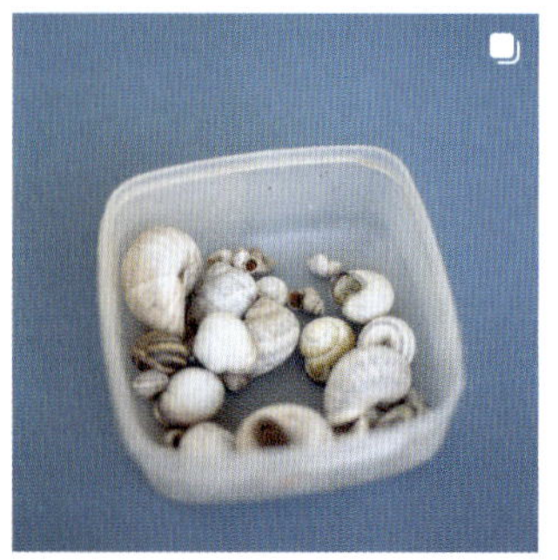
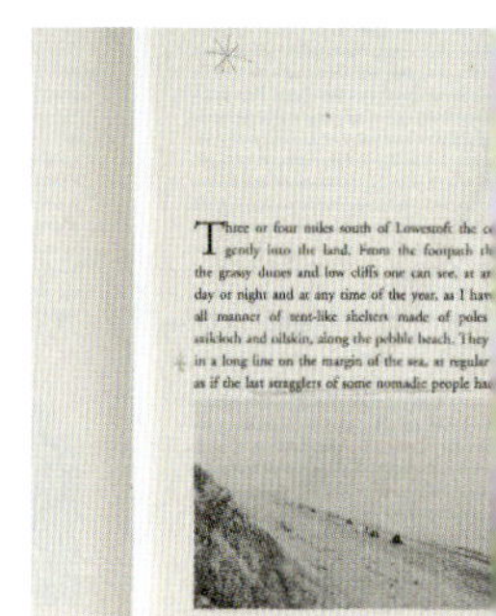
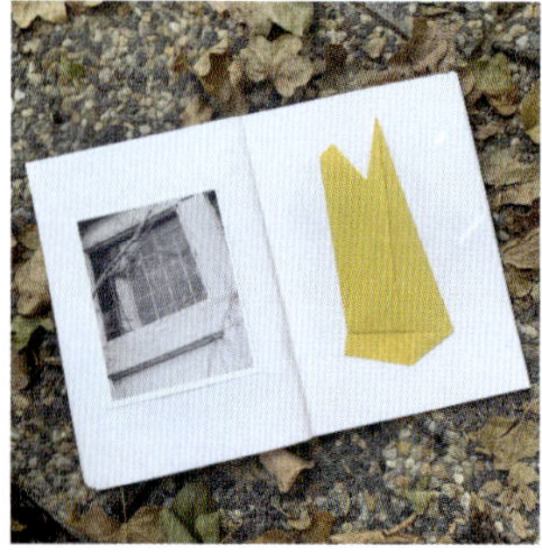
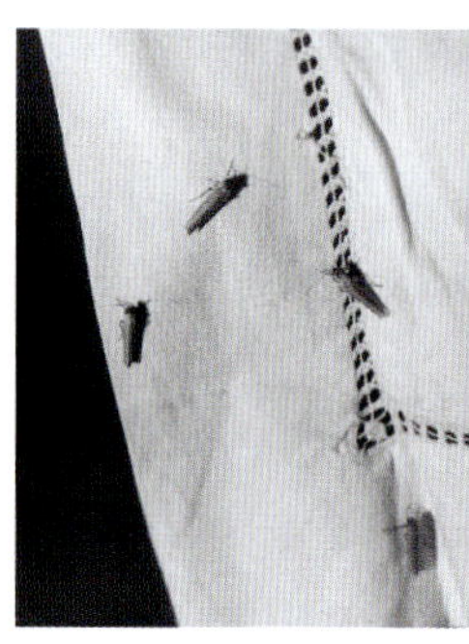

Max Ferguson. Screenshot of Max's Instagram profile, showing how he uses different types of content as part of his online portfolio.

In business circles, they say that it's crucial to diversify and the same is true when you are promoting yourself as a freelance photographer. We've already looked at Instagram and other social media platforms, and the benefits they can have for you as a photographer (see Photography and Social Media, page 64). But it's important to note here that Facebook, which owns Instagram, is making it more and more difficult for photographers to promote their work on the platform. This is because they prioritize paid content and reels, which rely on quick content and moving images rather than still photographs and artworks.

If you look at other platforms that have been used by photographers over the years – first it was Flickr, then Tumblr, briefly Facebook and finally Instagram – they have all had a finite existence and users have left them en masse for another platform. And I'm sure we will see the same happen with Instagram in the near future unless they start listening to the concerns of the artists and creators who rely on the platform and feel that the push to monetize everything means it is no longer a conducive place for sharing art and photography. Therefore, it is helpful to diversify your approach when trying to gain attention on social media. By all means, use Instagram while it still serves a useful promotional purpose, but ensure you have a presence on multiple platforms and avoid relying on any one platform to showcase your work. Try to keep abreast of the ever-changing world of social media and be prepared to leave a platform if and when it collapses. Of course, it's important to build a network beyond the Internet too.

Whichever platform or platforms you decide to use, your profile will probably be the first place many people encounter your photographs. This makes it a useful tool and one that should be considered carefully. The point of using social media as a creative is twofold: to build your networks and showcase your work. Building a network is easier, as you simply comment, message and build connections with people. Promoting your work on social media is more complicated because none of the current platforms work particularly well for displaying photographs. You can, however, use them to direct people to where they can view your images in the best light – your website. **MF**

Conclusion

- Social media apps are tools you can use and can be helpful if you are trying to widen your audience.
- Developing a presence on multiple apps enables you to reach the maximum audience.
- Social media changes fast, which means you have to be light on your feet and ready to move quickly if the platform you are using stops working for you.

Marketing Yourself Online

Marketing yourself is a key part of working as a photographer. Although meeting people in real life may create longer-lasting relationships, there is no reason why you cannot network successfully online.

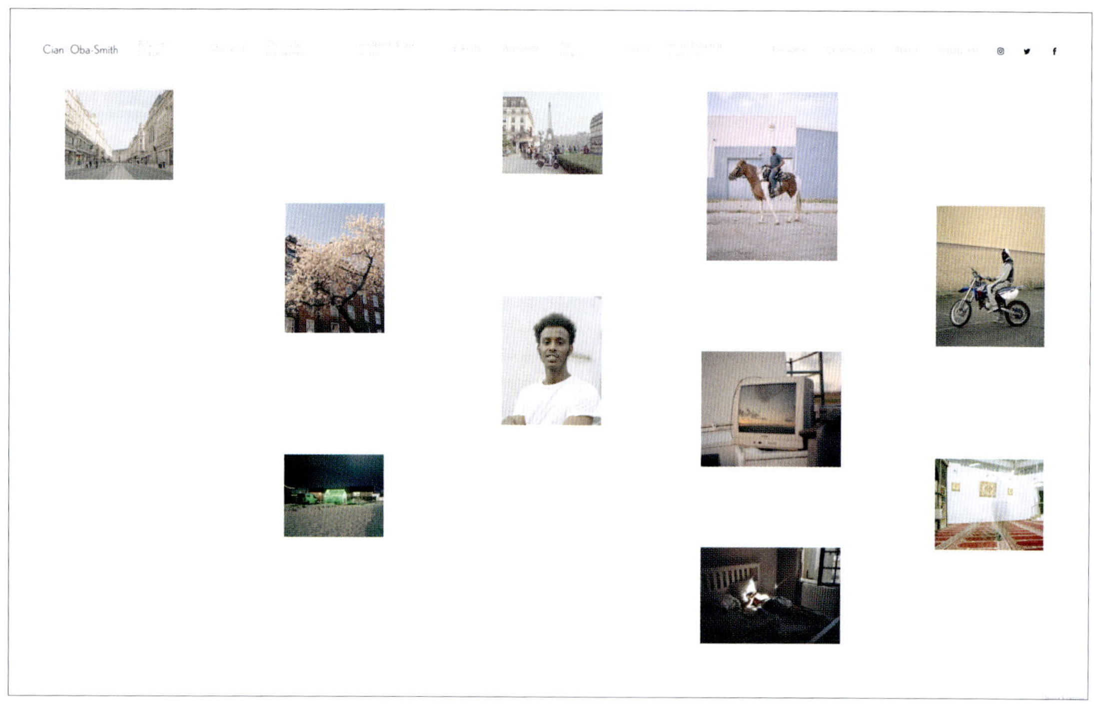

The self-marketing process should be built around creating a solid portfolio online, usually in the form of a website. Spend as much time as you can thinking about the edit and the sequence of photographs you want to show. A mistake that photographers often make is putting too many photographs on their websites. Ask other people to test the website to see how it works on a computer and a mobile phone. Remember to put the feature you want people to look at the most first on any menu (or, better still, make it the landing page). Include an 'About' section with your contact details and – this is very important – your location. And please don't have a contact box, as commissioning editors hate those.

It's important that any portfolio gives a good over-view of what you do as a photographer. Website design is difficult but platforms like Cargo Collective or Squarespace make the process much easier. You can usually purchase a custom domain name for around £10–20. In my opinion, this is a must, as it never looks professional to have your site as a subdomain of the website builder you chose.

Although there is no golden answer for how many images you should include on a website, I would limit yourself to two or three pages, each featuring no more than ten images. This might seem as if you're not showing much of your work, and that's rather the point. The user experience is as important as the choice of pictures. And keep refining the website as you develop as a photographer – it's astonishing how many photographers have outdated websites.

If your website is strong, you can use it as a base around which you revolve the rest of your online marketing. Social media can be used to divert traffic to the website and when emailing industry people, such as commissioning editors, other photographers, curators or producers, you can link them directly to it rather than attaching a large PDF. **MF**

Conclusion

- It's never been easier to reach the people who can help your career in photography.
- Think about adopting a holistic approach to your online presence.
- Emails are usually the best way to contact people about your work.

◀ Cian Oba-Smith. Screenshot of Cian's website, showing the home page which features thumbnails of his projects.

Donavon Smallwood

born 1994, New York, USA.
donavonsmallwood.com

The project that put Donavon Smallwood on the photography map was 'Languor'. I can't think of many photographers who have risen so quickly because of a single body of work. Perhaps it is because he studied literature, rather than photography, that he was able to enter the industry from a sideways direction. The images in his 'Languor' collection, which are now published in a monograph by Trespasser Books (run by photographer Bryan Schutmaat, see page 62) are a mixture of portraits of Black people and photographs of nature made in New York's Central Park. Speaking to me from New York, Smallwood described the project as being 'both a love letter and a note of disillusionment'. This internal conflict comes from his enjoyment of Central Park as a space and what he has learned about Seneca Village. Seneca Village was founded in 1825 by free Black Americans, but it was dispersed in 1857 so that Central Park could be built.

When I asked Smallwood about the photograph of the woman featured here, he commented that it is interesting because he had wanted to photograph someone by the water in the park before he found the subject. As he explained: 'I saw the water and the reflection of the tree-line and then I went around looking for someone I could photograph in front of it. I was interested in the water with tree-line reflections because I was directly inspired by Doris Ulmann's *Baptism, South Carolina* image.' It's fascinating that a portrait could be led by its out-of-focus background.

Due to the strength of his personal work, I commissioned Smallwood to shoot the cover of the rapper, writer and activist Akala for *Port Magazine* while I was photo director there. The portrait accompanied a piece of Akala's fictional writing. I love the fact that the portraits he made for the commission, which are very much fashion images styled with luxurious clothes, feel as if they could easily fit into his personal body of work. I believe his photographs have a quietness that disrupts the vibe of traditional fashion photography. **MF**

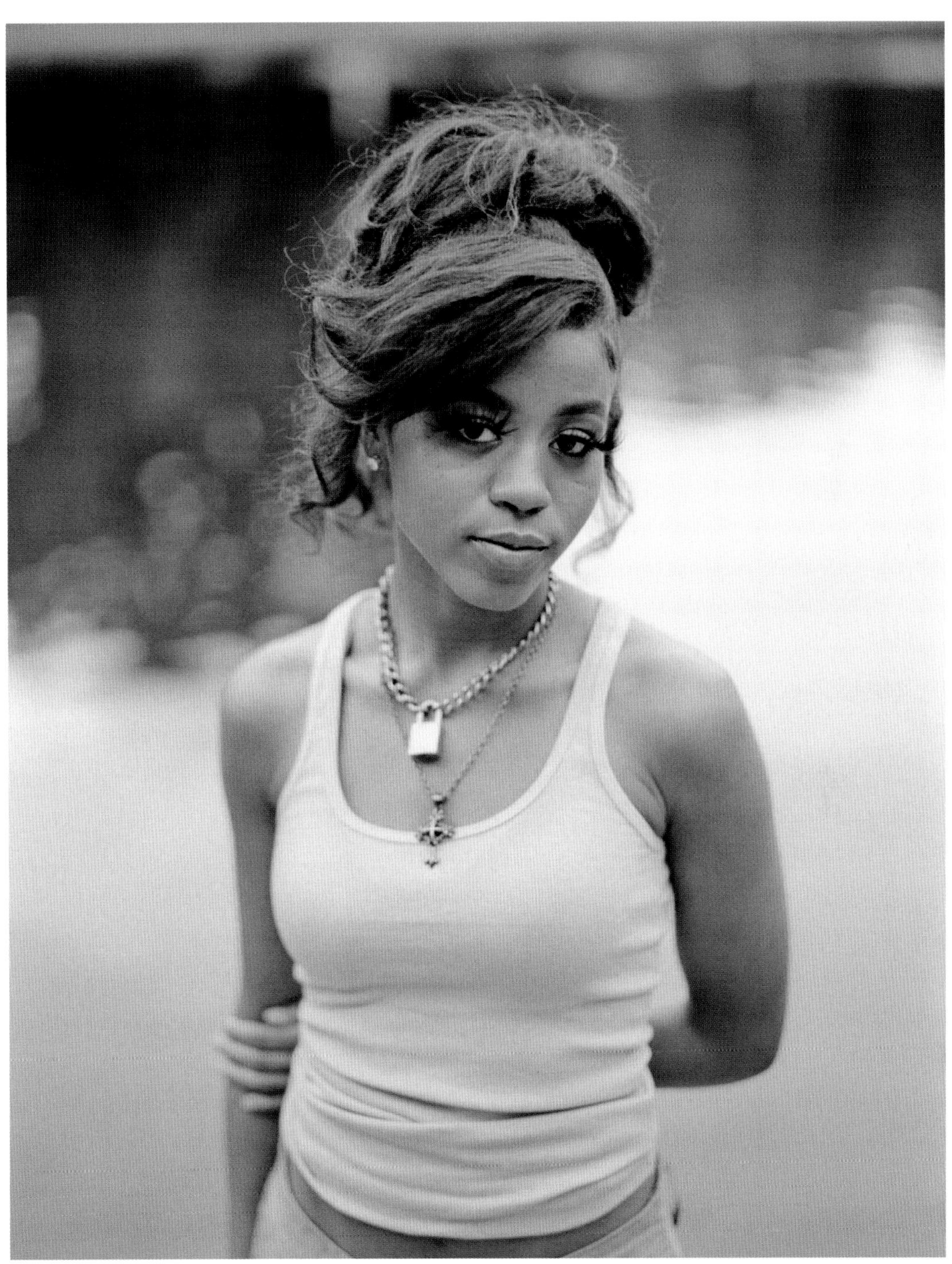

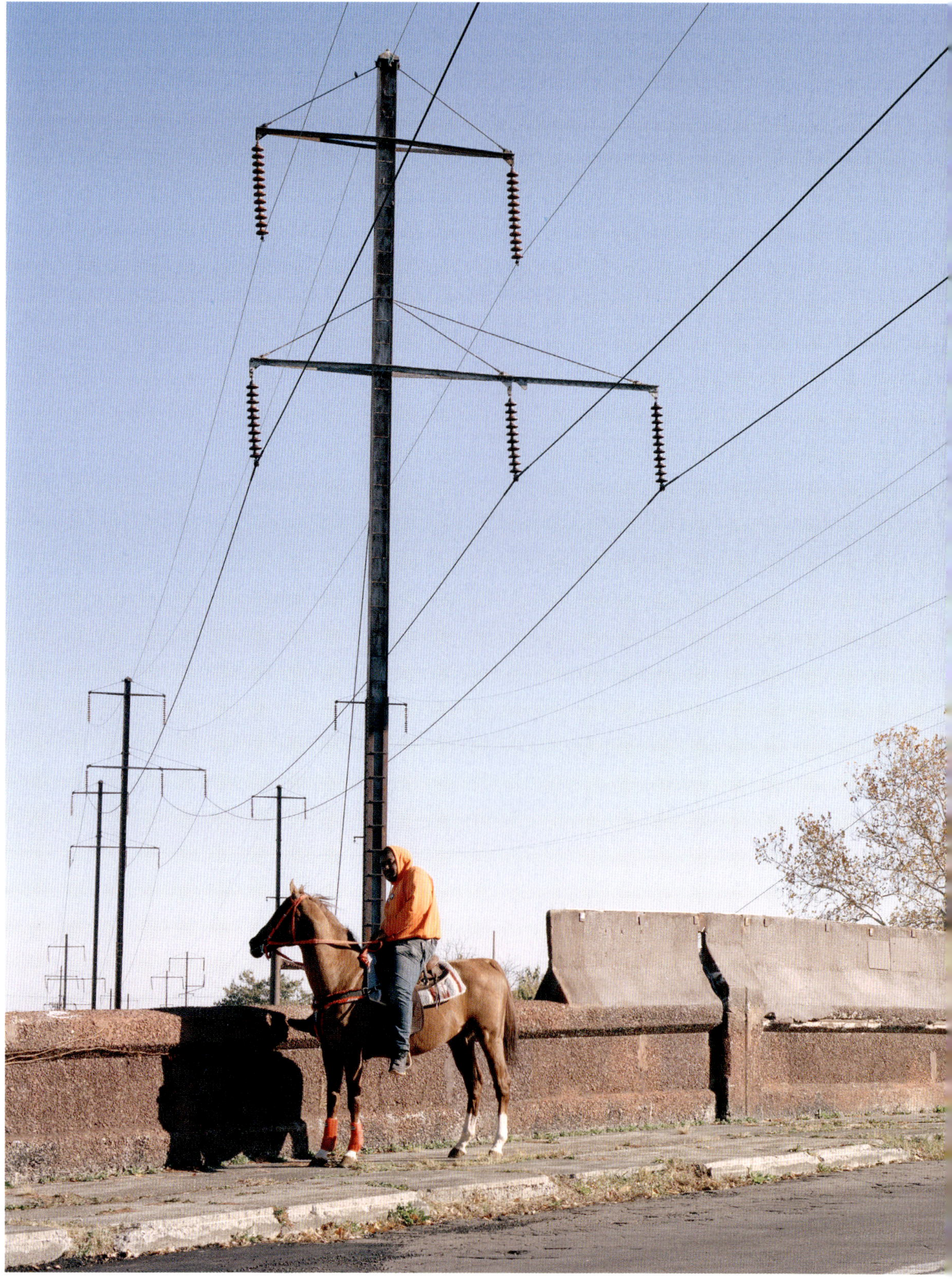

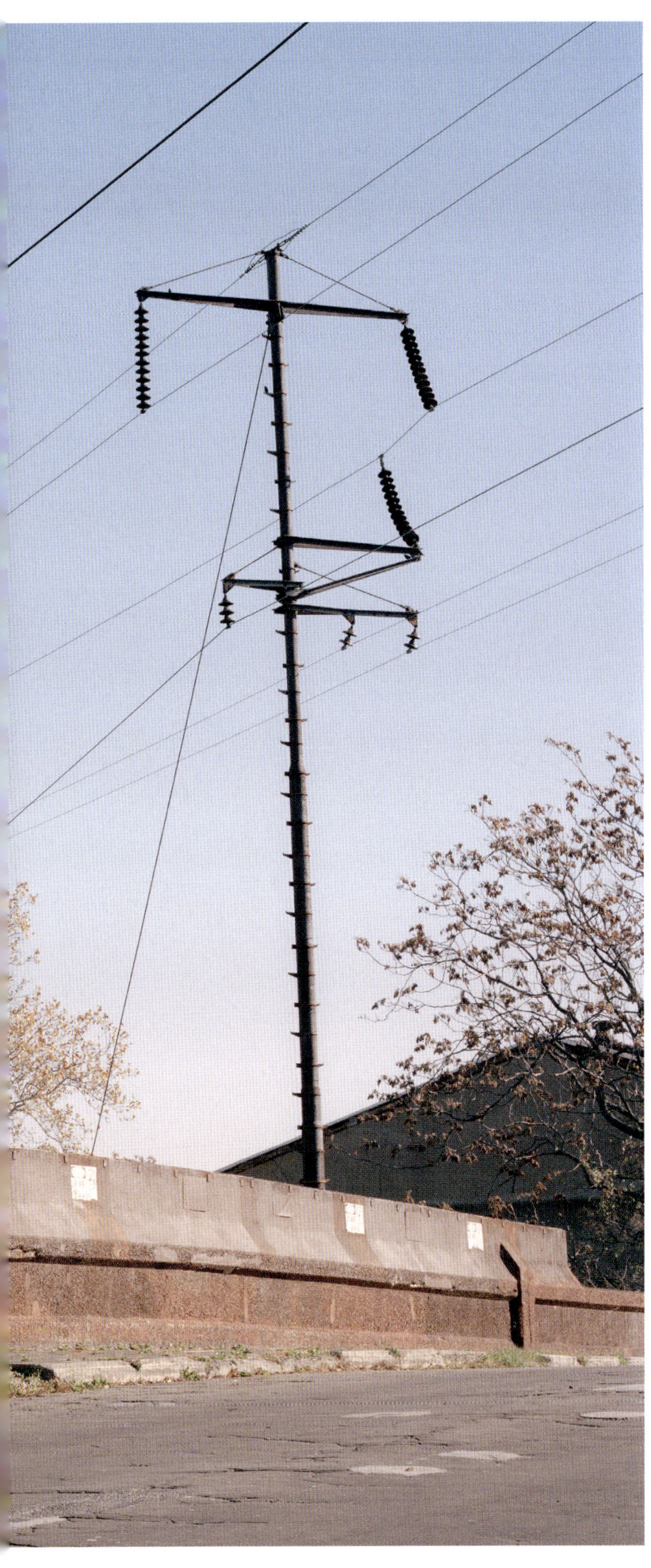

Cian Oba-Smith. Milan and Dusty,
Philadelphia, USA. From the series
'Concrete Horsemen', 2016.

Conclusion

Having come to the end of the book, hopefully feeling inspired by some of the photographers and concepts that most excite us in portrait photography, it's now up to you to continue thinking, learning and pushing yourself photographically. This book is really a series of starting points and any one of them could become the beginning of your next project, area of research or set of photographs. It should also have helped to lay the foundations of your understanding of portrait photography, as well as to fill in any gaps if you're more experienced.

At its best, photography can bring people closer together, help us understand each other and make the world a kinder place. However, like all tools, it can also make matters worse. Questioning why you take photographs shouldn't act as a barrier to making work, but it should open up new avenues for you. This book is intended to be a provocation to make work, take photographs, be inquisitive and take risks. Follow strands of your interests down the deepest rabbit holes and then, when you can't go any further, branch off into another area.

For some of you, photography may become a tool of activism, as it is for LaToya Ruby Frazier (see page 134). Perhaps it will become a way for you to investigate issues that run deeply through our societies or a means of building your career in an area of the industry in which you'd like to work (see Chapter 6, Making a Career). Only you can say which photographs you will make and build into projects or bodies of work. Some of these projects might be short-lived, linking a few photographs that mean something together – perhaps you shot several rolls of film in a single day. They might also last longer if, for example, you shoot the same person every week for a year. At other times, they will be more complex and multilayered, taking years to finish and eventually being published in books or displayed at exhibitions. Every project, no matter what its duration, is viable and everything you are interested in is a reason to take photographs.

Photography is a journey in which self-reflection is key. Take away some of the ideas that have been discussed throughout the book and put them into practice. See how you feel about the portraits you're producing and come back to the book as a point of reference. In particular, think about implementing some of the ideas around community that we have talked about and aim to build a network of people who can help you to reflect and be critical of the work you're producing.

Just as we have while writing this book, enjoy the process and embrace your mistakes. **COS+MF**

Bibliography

PHOTOGRAPHIC THEORY

Azoulay, Ariella, *The Civil Contract of Photography*, Zone Books, 2008.

Berger, John, *Ways of Seeing*, Penguin Modern Classics, London, 2008.

Broomberg, Adam, and Chanarin, Oliver, *Ghetto*, Trolley Books, 2003.

Campt, Tina M., *Listening to Images*, Duke University Press, 2017.

Clark, Tim, series ed., *Curator Conversations*, 1000 Words Photography, 2021.

Clark, Tim, series ed., *Writer Conversations*, 1000 Words Photography, 2022.

Cole, Teju, *Known and Strange Things: Essays*, Random House, 2016.

Lewis, Emma, *Photography – A Feminist History*, Tate Publishing, 2021.

Sargent, Antwaun, *The New Black Vanguard: Photography Between Art and Fashion*, Aperture, 2019.

Sealey, Mark, *Decolonising the Camera: Photography in Racial Time*, Lawrence & Wishart, 2019.

Sng, Paul, *Invisible Britain: Portraits of Hope and Resilience*, Policy Press, 2018.

Sontag, Susan, *On Photography*, Farrar, Straus and Giroux, 1977.

Sontag, Susan, *Regarding the Pain of Others*, Penguin Books, 2003.

Tagg, John, *The Burden of Representation: Essays on Photographies and Histories*, University of Massachusetts Press, 1988.

Wilson, Laura, *Avedon At Work: In the American West*, University of Texas Press, 2003.

BOOKS BY CONTRIBUTORS

Davey, Sian, *Looking For Alice*, Trolley Books, 2015.

Davey, Sian, *Martha*, Trolley Books, 2018.

Davison, Jack, *Photographs*, Loose Joints, 2019.

Frazier, LaToya Ruby, *Flint is Family in Three Acts*, Steidl, 2022.

Ijewere, Nadine, *Our Own Selves*, Prestel, 2021.

Keïta, Seydou, *Photographs, Bamako, Mali 1948–1963*, Steidl, 2011.

Lathigra, Kalpesh, *Memoire Temporelle*, 2022.

Liao, Pixy, *Experimental Relationship*, Jiazazhi, 2018.

Mahmoodian, Amak, *Zanjir*, RRB Photobooks, 2019.

Muholi, Zanele, *Somnyama Ngonyama: Hail the Dark Lioness*, Aperture 2018.

Parks, Gordon, *I Am You: Selected Works 1934–1978*, Steidl, 2016.

Schutmaat, Bryan, *Good Goddamn*, Trespasser, 2017.

Schutmaat, Bryan, *Grays the Mountain Sends*, Silas Finch, 2014.

Smallwood, Donavon, *Languor*, Trespasser, 2021.

Starkey, Hannah, *Photographs 1997–2017*, Mack, 2018.

OTHER RESOURCES

1000wordsmag.com

granta.com

ovalpress.co.uk

1854.photography

port-magazine.com

bensmithphoto.com/asmallvoice

magichourphoto.org/interviews

nearesttruth.com/browse

Contributors

AMAK MAHMOODIAN

Born in Iran, but now resident in the UK, Mahmoodian's work questions notions of identity and home, bridging the space between the personal and political. She explores the effects of exile and distance on memory, dreams and daily life. In 2015, Mahmoodian completed a practice-based doctorate in photography at the University of South Wales, having previously studied at Tehran's University of Art. Working with images, poems and archives, she looks for the lyrical realities that are framed in photographs. Amak has exhibited her work extensively and won numerous awards.

BRYAN SCHUTMAAT

Bryan Schutmaat is a photographer based in Austin, Texas, whose work has been widely exhibited and published. He has won numerous awards, including a John Simon Guggenheim Memorial Fellowship, the Aperture Portfolio Prize and an Aaron Siskind Fellowship. Bryan's prints are held in many collections, including at the Baltimore Museum of Art, Museum of Fine Arts Boston, Pier 24 Photography, Amsterdam's Rijks Museum and the San Francisco Museum of Modern Art. He cofounded the publishing imprint, Trespasser.

DEBMALYA RAY CHOUDHURI

Originally from Kolkata, in India, but now based in New York City, Choudhuri's interdisciplinary practice uses photography, performance and text to confront personal trauma and grief. He also addresses societal questions on the 'queerness' of identity in contemporary society. Through collaborations with both friends and strangers, he raises issues around gender, identity and mental health. The lines between the subject and the photographer are fluid in his work. These dual conversations reveal new perspectives on the relationship between the self and the other.

DONAVON SMALLWOOD

After receiving his BA from Hunter College, New York City, in 2016, Smallwood's work has been exhibited nationally and internationally at numerous institutions. His photographs have been displayed at the Philadelphia Museum of Art and the Art Museum of West Virginia University. He is the recipient of numerous awards, including the 2021 Aperture Portfolio Prize. Periodical features and editorial clients include *The Atlantic*, *The New York Times*, *The New Yorker* and *The Guardian*. His first monograph, Langour, was released by Trespasser in winter 2021.

GORDON PARKS

The late Gordon Parks was deeply committed to social justice, using his work to record American life from the early 1940s to the 2000s and shining a light on racism and other social and economic issues. Parks was self-taught, but on winning the Julius Rosenwald Fellowship in 1942, he began working for the photography section of the Farm Security Administration (FSA) and later the Office of War Information (OWI). His personal style earned him worldwide acclaim for images that focus on the impact of racism and poverty.

HANNAH STARKEY

Exploring the physical and psychological connections between the individual and their everyday urban surroundings, Starkey predominantly works with women and uses stark architectural backdrops and strong associations of colour and imagery. In 2019, she was awarded an Honorary Fellowship by The Royal Photographic Society and one of her many solo exhibitions, 'Celebrating City Women', was held at London's Guildhall in 2020. A recent monograph, *Photographs 1997–2017*, was published in 2018. She will present her first major exhibition at The Hepworth Wakefield in 2022.

JACK DAVISON

London-based photographer Jack Davison studied english literature at the University of Warwick, but spent most of his time there experimenting with cameras. Since the age of fourteen, he has photographed those around him. He works for numerous publications, including *The New York Times Magazine*, *M le magazine du monde*, *Luncheon* magazine, *Double* magazine and *British Vogue*. His first monograph, *Photographs*, was published in 2019 by Loose Joints. He then released *Song Flowers* in collaboration with Loose Joints and the Italian fashion house Marni in 2020.

JUNO CALYPSO

A London-based artist working in photography, film and installation, Calypso began taking pictures of herself as a character named 'Joyce' while studying at the London College of Communication. In 2015, she took Joyce to a romantic-themed hotel in America. Posing as a travel writer, she staged a series of self-portraits in different rooms. Studying solitude, desire and femininity through a dark comedic lens, 'The Honeymoon' was awarded an international prize by the British Journal of Photography. For 'What To Do With A Million Years', Calypso staged photographs in an underground Las Vegas mansion built as a nuclear shelter in the 1970s.

KALPESH LATHIGRA

After studying photography at the London College of Printing, Lathigra worked for *The Independent* before freelancing for other national newspapers. In 2000, he began working on long-term projects and magazine and commercial assignments. After a 2003 project covering the lives of widows in India, he moved away from photojournalism. His first book, *Lost in the Wilderness* (2015), explores the effects of colonialism on the community at the Pine Ridge Indian Reservation in South Dakota. For his recent work, *Memoire Temporelle* (2022), he collaborated with Emmanuelle Peri. He has been a visiting lecturer at Syracuse University, in the US, and at the London College of Communication.

LATOYA RUBY FRAZIER

Frazier's practice spans a range of media, including photography, video, performance, installation art and books, to examine social justice, cultural change and the American experience. She uses collaborative storytelling with the people in her work to address issues such as Rust Belt revitalization, access to healthcare and clean water, family and communal history. This builds on her commitment to the legacy of 1930s social documentary and the conceptual photography of the 1960s and 1970s, which addressed social and political issues. She is associate professor of photography at the School of the Art Institute of Chicago.

NADINE IJEWERE

Ijewere's work focuses on identity and diversity and is informed by her Nigerian/Jamaican background. She is drawn to non-traditional faces with the aim of showcasing a new standard of beauty and giving life to the uniqueness of disparate cultures. She studied photography at the London College of Fashion, and credits social media for helping her to build her reputation as a photographer. Her January 2019 cover for *Vogue*, featuring Dua Lipa, Binx Walton and Letitia Wright, was the first by a woman of colour in the magazine's history.

PIXY LIAO

Chinese artist Pixy Liao currently lives in Brooklyn, New York. She has taken part in international exhibitions and performances at Fotografiska, The Rencontres d'Arles, in France, and the National Gallery of Australia, among others. Winner of multiple awards, including the LensCulture Exposure Awards and The Santo Foundation Individual Artist Awards, she has also had residencies at Light Work and the University of Arts in London. Liao has an MFA in photography from the University of Memphis, in Tennessee.

RONAN MCKENZIE

After dropping out of a BA in fashion communication at London's Central Saint Martins in 2014, Mckenzie has since managed to put on a solo show, create her own publication and shoot for *i-D* magazine, *Wonderland* magazine and *Vogue Paris* in the space of just four years. She also counts Nike, Stella McCartney and Adidas among her clients. Her work offers a frank and intimate celebration of the female body and soul.

SEYDOU KEÏTA

The photographs of the late Malian studio photographer Seydou Keïta reveal Bamako society as it transitioned from a French colony to an independent city in West Africa. Keïta's photographic career began at a young age when he was given a Kodak Brownie Flash by his uncle in 1935. After learning the technicalities of shooting and printing, he purchased a large-format camera and eventually opened a highly successful studio in Bamako in 1948. In the early 1960s, the studio closed, but his work has since been recognized worldwide.

SIAN DAVEY

Following a fifteen-year period as a psychotherapist, in 2014 British photographer Sian Davey launched a career in photography, drawing on her professional and maternal experiences to inform her practice. Her images investigate the psychological landscapes of both herself and those around her, with her family and community being central to her work. Davey studied fine art (Bath Academy of Fine Art, 1985), social policy (University of Brighton, 1990), humanistic psychotherapy (Karuna Institute, 1995) and, more recently, photography (namely, an MA in 2014 and MFA in 2016 at Plymouth University).

TEREZA ČERVEŇOVÁ

With work characterized by the juxtaposition of delicate imagery and soft light with political and personal references, Červeňová often photographs people who play an important role in her life, since she is drawn to the connections that exist between herself, the sitters and society at large. Portraiture is at the heart of her artistic practice and she likes to blur the line between her personal and commissioned work. Originally from Slovakia, she now lives and works in London.

TOM JOHNSON

The work of London-based photographer Tom Johnson exists at the crossover between fashion, documentary and portraiture, creating authentic environments in which people's unique stories can be told through imagery. He began his career shooting music gigs and eventually opened Box Studio in East London. He has since shot editorials for both *Dazed* and *AnOther* magazines, as well as campaigns for Burberry and Opening Ceremony. When not shooting editorials or ads, Johnson can be found capturing striking images of life on society's fringes.

YUSHI LI

Chinese artist Li was chosen as one of the Foam Talents in 2022 and the Royal Photographic Society's 'Hundred Heroines' in 2019. Her work has been showcased in various countries, including in solo exhibitions in Malmö, Oslo and London, as well as in group exhibitions at RIBA and Fotografiska. It has also appeared in several international publications, such as *The Guardian* and *Libération*. Li's work mainly engages with the question of the gaze, using photography to explore gendered power relationships in the Internet age.

ZANELE MUHOLI

An acclaimed photographer and activist, Muholi's work has been exhibited internationally. From the early 2000s, Muholi photographed South Africa's Black lesbian, gay, trans, queer and intersex communities and the series 'Only Half the Picture' captures the prejudice endured by members of South Africa's LGBTQIA+ community. In 'Faces and Phases' sitters boldly hold the viewer's gaze. Such series contribute to today's archive portraying people courageously facing discrimination. A series of self-portraits appears in 'Somnyama Ngonyama', which examines ideas around racism and sexual politics.

ZORA J. MURFF

Currently assistant professor of art at the University of Arkansas and co-curator of Strange Fire Collective, Murff studied for an MFA at the University of Nebraska-Lincoln and holds a BS in Psychology from Iowa State University. Drawing on these studies, his photographs highlight the convergence between art and social systems. Murff's monograph, *At No Point In Between* (2019), won the Independently Published category at the Lucie Foundation Photo Book Awards and the 2020 Next Step Award by Aperture and Baxter St at the Camera Club of New York. His latest book, *True Colors (or, Affirmations in a Crisis)*, was published in 2022.

Glossary

35mm camera A camera that uses 35mm rolls of film.

Aperture A hole (diaphragm) in a camera lens that can be controlled to allow more or less light to reach the film or sensor (in a digital camera). The aperture is measured in f stops. The wider the aperture (for example, f/2.0), the more light is let in; the smaller the aperture (for example, f/22), the less light is let in. The aperture also has an effect on depth of field.

Assignment A paid commission from a client; a term more typically used in editorial and photojournalistic photography.

Burn A traditional darkroom technique used to darken parts of an image. Photo-editing software usually has an equivalent tool.

C-41 processing A colour film developing process for C-41 film types, typically colour negatives.

CMYK A four-colour model used to create different hues; the letters stand for cyan, magenta, yellow and key (which indicates black).

Colour temperature A measurement of the warmth or coolness of light. Measured in kelvins, a lower number equates to warmer light and a higher number to cooler light.

Commercial A type of photography used to advertise a product or place.

Contrast The ratio between tones in an image, typically the brightest and darkest points.

Curves An image-editing tool that allows you to adjust the brightness and contrast of the shadows, midtones and highlights individually.

Daguerreotype A traditional photographic process that uses an iodine-sensitized silvered plate and mercury vapour to take a picture.

Depth of field DOF affects the shallowness of the focus point in an image. The easiest way to see this is to hold your finger close to your face, then slowly move it further away. The closer your finger is to your face, the shallower the depth of field. A wider aperture creates a shallower depth of field and vice versa.

Dodge A traditional darkroom technique used to lighten parts of an image. Photo-editing software usually has an equivalent tool.

DSLR A digital single lens reflex camera (the digital equivalent of an SLR); see SLR.

Dynamic range The ratio between the brightest and darkest parts of an image.

E-6 processing A colour film developing process for E-6 film types, typically slide film.

Editorial Photography that traditionally accompanies an article, although it can also be a standalone piece. Usually found in a magazine or newspaper.

Environmental portrait A portrait in which the subject sits within an environment; the person is typically smaller in the frame than in a traditional portrait.

Exposure The amount of light reaching a camera's film or sensor over a period of time.

Grain/noise Grain is the random texture of silver particles or dye clouds that make up the film's emulsion. Noise is the random variation of colour or brightness information in an image. Grain is an artistic preference, whereas noise is generally avoided.

ISO A camera sensor or film's sensitivity to light; a lower ISO (for example, ISO 100) corresponds to less sensitivity to light, meaning you need more exposure to light than at a higher ISO (for example, ISO 1600). The higher the ISO, the more grain or noise in the image.

JPEG A file format that compresses the image to reduce the file size. Convenient for small files but avoid as the main format you use. Stands for Joint Photographic Experts Group.

Large format A camera that uses 4 × 5 inch film or larger.

Latitude The amount by which you can overexpose or underexpose and still produce an acceptable result.

LED A type of continuous lighting (LED stands for light-emitting diode); LED lights are compact and relatively cheap but lack power.

Medium format A camera that uses film or a digital sensor bigger than the 35mm film size, but smaller than the 4 × 5 inch film size.

Mirrorless camera A digital camera without a mirror; instead, the camera uses an electronic viewfinder to display what the lens sees.

Prime lens A lens with a fixed focal length. Prime lenses tend to have wider maximum apertures than zoom lenses, allowing more light into the camera and providing a shallower depth of field if needed.

Pushing and pulling film To deliberately underexpose or overexpose film and then make up for this when developing. Pushing is the practice of underexposing the film, then keeping it in the developer for longer. Pulling is the practice of overexposing the film, then removing it from the developer sooner. Pulling reduces contrast and pushing adds more contrast and grain.

Rangefinder camera A film camera without a mirror that uses a separate viewfinder and focusing system (the rangefinder) to frame and take the image. Rangefinder cameras tend to be more compact and quieter than SLRs.

RAW A RAW file is the equivalent of a digital negative; it retains all the information from when the photograph was taken.

RGB A three-colour model used to create different hues; the letters stand for red, green and blue.

Rise/fall The upward and downward movement that controls the vertical placement of an image on the ground glass; typically used with large-format cameras.

Saturation The depth of intensity of colour in an image; higher saturation means 'punchy' colours, whereas low saturation results in more delicate colours.

Sequence The order in which a series of photographs is displayed.

Sharpening A tool used to reduce blur and softness in an image to create a sharper-looking image.

Shutter speed The length of time that a camera shutter opens and closes, exposing the film or sensor to light.

SLR A single lens reflex camera uses a mirror and prism system that allows you to look through the viewfinder and see directly through the lens.

Tilt/shift The backwards/forwards (tilt) and side-to-side (shift) movement of the lens in relation to the film or sensor in order to alter the depth of field and focus of an image.

Tungsten A type of artificial continuous lighting that produces a warm colour. This can be balanced by using gels to create a more neutral colour temperature.

White balance Used to adjust the colour temperature of an image, usually to make it appear more neutral.

Zoom lens A lens that allows you to get closer and further away without moving.

Index

Credits

Picture Credits

p7: © Cian Oba-Smith; p9: © Rahim Fortune; p10–11: © Cian Oba-Smith; p14: © Cian Oba-Smith; p17: © Cian Oba-Smith; p18: © Cian Oba-Smith; p21: © Cian Oba-Smith; p22: Max Ferguson; p25: © Cian Oba-Smith; p29: © Cian Oba-Smith; p30: © Cian Oba-Smith; p33: © Cian Oba-Smith; p34: © Cian Oba-Smith; p36: © Cian Oba-Smith; p37: © Cian Oba-Smith; p39: © Cian Oba-Smith; p49: © Cian Oba-Smith; p50: © Cian Oba-Smith; p52: © Cian Oba-Smith; p53: © Cian Oba-Smith; p54: © Cian Oba-Smith; p57: © Cian Oba-Smith; p58: © Cian Oba-Smith; p59: © Cian Oba-Smith

p13, 43, 45, 46, 69: Wikimedia Commons, Wikimedia.org

Hannah Starkey p60: Untitled, May 1997, 1997 framed c-type print 122 x 162 cm © Hannah Starkey, courtesy Maureen Paley, London, and Tanya Bonakdar, New York / Los Angeles; p61: Untitled, October 1998, 1998 framed c-type print 122 x 152 cm © Hannah Starkey, courtesy Maureen Paley, London, and Tanya Bonakdar, New York / Los Angeles

Bryan Schutmaat p63: © Bryan Schutmaat

p66: © Cian Oba-Smith; p71: © Kaitlin Maxwell; p73: © Library of Congress Prints and Photographs Division

Juno Calypso p74: Slendertone I, 2015 © Juno Calypso. From the series 'Joyce'; p76: A Dream In Green, 2015 © Juno Calypso. From the series 'The Honeymoon'; p77: Sensory Deprivation, 2016 © Juno Calypso. From the series 'The Honeymoon'

p79: Self-portrait by Mario, Rene Vallejo Psychiatric Hospital, Cuba, courtesy of The Goodman Gallery and the late estate of Broomberg & Chanarin. C-type print, 16 × 20 inches, 2003; p80l: Self-portrait by Anais, Rene Vallejo Psychiatric Hospital, Cuba, courtesy of The Goodman Gallery and the late estate of Broomberg & Chanarin. C-type print, 16 × 20 inches, 2003; p80r: Self-portrait by Celia, Rene Vallejo Psychiatric Hospital, Cuba, courtesy of The Goodman Gallery and the late estate of Broomberg & Chanarin. C-type print, 16 × 20 inches, 2003; p81: © Cian Oba-Smith; p83: © Cian Oba-Smith; p85: © Cian Oba-Smith; p86: © Cian Oba-Smith

Yushi Li p89: The Nightmare, 2019 © Yushi Li; p91: © Cian Oba-Smith; p92: © Cian Oba-Smith

Nadine Ijewere p95: © Nadine Ijewere / Trunk Archive

p97: © Cian Oba-Smith; p99: © Laura Wilson, Richard Avedon talking with a cowboy in Augusta, Montana, from 'Avedon at Work', 1983

Tom Johnson p2: © Tom Johnson; p65: © Tom Johnson; p101: © Tom Johnson; p103 © Tom Johnson; p104 © Tom Johnson; p105 © Tom Johnson

Zanele Muholi p107: © Zanele Muholi, courtesy of Stevenson, Amsterdam/Cape Town/Johannesburg, and Yancey Richardson, New York

p109: © Cian Oba-Smith; p110: © Cian Oba-Smith; p111: © Cian Oba-Smith

Seydou Keïta p113: © Seydou Keïta/SKPEAC, courtesy of The Jean Pigozzi African Art Collection

p115: © Cian Oba-Smith; p116: © Cian Oba-Smith

Tereza Červeňová p119: Tomky, Borský Svätý Jur, Slovakia, August 2016 © Tereza Červeňová

p121: © Cian Oba-Smith; p122: © Cian Oba-Smith; p123: © Cian Oba-Smith

Sian Davey p26: Sian Davey; p125: © Sian Davey

p127: © Cian Oba-Smith

Pixy Liao p128: Things We Talk About, 2013 © Pixy Liao; p129: Moro in Sunset, 2018 © Pixy Liao

p131: Library of Congress, Prints & Photographs Division, FSA/OWI Collection; p132: Library of Congress, Prints & Photographs Division, FSA/OWI Collection

LaToya Ruby Frazier p135: Shea Cobb with Her Mother Ms. Reneé and Her Daughter Zion at Nephratiti's Wedding Reception, Standing Outside the Social Network Banquet Hall, Flint, Michigan, 2016–2017 © LaToya Ruby Frazier. Used by permission. Courtesy of the artist and Gladstone Gallery

Zora J. Murff p137: Zora J. Murff, Jerrod and Junior (Talking about Fatherhood), 2019, courtesy of Zora J. Murff/Webber Gallery

Jack Davison p143: Untitled, 2014 © Jack Davison

Debmalya Ray Choudhuri p144: © Debmalya Ray Choudhuri; p145: © Debmalya Ray Choudhuri

Gordon Parks p147: © Gordon Parks/Library of Congress Prints and Photographs Division; p148: © Gordon Parks/Library of Congress Prints and Photographs Division; p151: American Gothic, Washington, D.C., 1942 © Gordon Parks/Library of Congress Prints and Photographs Division

p153: © Cian Oba-Smith; p154–155: © Cian Oba-Smith

Amak Mahmoodian p157: One image from 'Neghab' project. This image presents a woman holding a blank mask/photograph in front of her face to conceal it and next to her there is a line of archive photographs. © Amak Mahmoodian

p159: © Cian Oba-Smith; p161: © Cian Oba-Smith

Kalpesh Lathigra p163: © Kalpesh Lathigra

p165: © Cian Oba-Smith; p166: © Cian Oba-Smith; p167: © Cian Oba-Smith; p169: © Cian Oba-Smith; p170: © Cian Oba-Smith; p171: © Cian Oba-Smith

Ronan Mckenzie p172: Lockdown Luncheon, 2020 © Ronan Mckenzie; p173: Our Place, 2019 © Ronan Mckenzie

p174: © Max Ferguson; p176: © Cian Oba-Smith

Donavon Smallwood p179: © Donavon Smallwood

p180–181: © Cian Oba-Smith

Author Credits

Thanks

We would like to thank our partners, Aurore and Hannah, for their love and support. Our family and friends for always having our backs. Our teachers, past and present, Emma Bowkett, Zed Nelson, Chris Scott, Clare Hewitt, the whole team at Wyatt-Clarke + Jones, Jim Campbell and everyone at UWE for their guidance. All the photographers who have contributed their incredible work to this book. Lastly, we would like to thank all the people featured in these portraits, who have allowed us a window into their lives and shared a piece of themselves with us.